SHRINKING VIOLETS

The Secret Life of Shyness

JOE MORAN

P
PROFILE BOOKS

This paperback edition published in 2017

First published in Great Britain in 2016 by
PROFILE BOOKS LTD
3 Holford Yard
Bevin Way
London WC1X 9HD
www.profilebooks.com

1 3 5 7 9 10 8 6 4 2

Typeset in Sabon by MacGuru Ltd

Printed and bound in Great Britain by
CPI Group (UK) Ltd, Croydon CR0 4YY

A CIP catalogue record for this book is available from the British Library.

ISBN 978 1 78125 264 2
eISBN 978 1 78283 067 2

In memory of my grandmother
Ellen Evaskitas, *née* Roberts (1917–1958)

CONTENTS

A TENTATIVE HISTORY

It was October 1939, the start of Michaelmas term. Oxford was at war. College buildings were being commandeered as ARP centres, hospitals and maternity homes for pregnant women evacuated from London. Painted white lines now ran through the archways, quadrangles and courtyards so people could see in the black-out. Air raid shelters made of sandbags and canvas had been hastily raised on college greens.

But a young South African and freshman at Oriel College, David Wright, was barely thinking about the war at all. He was suffering from a shyness so intense that it colonised his waking thoughts and threatened to turn him into a total recluse. Whole days went by without him speaking to anyone. The all-male dining rooms and common rooms now had to be shared with female students turfed out of the women's colleges. Introduced to one, Wright would, he wrote later, 'shake hands, say nothing whatsoever, slowly but remarkably assume a sunset tinge, and stand there thinking furiously, until such time as the girl's nerve broke and she fled'.

Wright was lucky. Eventually his boredom got the better of his bashfulness. He resolved to tackle the problem head-on by striking up conversations on trains – at a time when carriages were divided into small, closed compartments where it was hard to escape if a stranger trapped you in talk. This high-stakes game led to moments of deep awkwardness, when he imagined the hands of these captive strangers straying towards the emergency cord. No matter: he had begun a lifelong effort to inure himself to social unease. He was resourceful, and joined the college boat club because, although he considered rowing a futile activity, it served as a conduit for social contact. For the same reason he took up bridge, thinking it equally pointless but rightly surmising that the conversation would be easy to join in with because it would always be about bridge.

On graduating in 1942, an aspiring poet, he continued his education in the University of Soho. His tutors were the musicians, artists, writers and Montparnasse exiles who met in the pubs of Dean Street, Old Compton Street and Rathbone Place. This society, united by an interest in art, words and drink, met nightly, fast-tracking acquaintance into intimacy. Wright discovered, like countless timid souls before him, that the symptoms of shyness were relieved by a liquid first concocted about ten thousand years earlier, perhaps for this very purpose: beer.

Wright never shook off his shyness, but he worked round it ingeniously. He became a Soho stalwart and liver-on-his-wits, forever rolling cigarettes assembled from the stubs left in pub ashtrays and startling those in earshot with the odd klaxon blast of laughter. A 6-foot-2 hulk of a man with an unkempt thatch of near-white hair, he even acquired a certain charisma. As poet-in-residence at Leeds University in the mid-1960s, his impromptu seminars in the Fenton pub near the campus attracted hordes of students.

His poetry – wry, conversational, urbane, all the things he longed to be but never was in person – produced the usual half-shelf of slim volumes but was too modest and well mannered to become widely known. Unlike the great majority of bolder writers, though, he did manage to write something that changed people's lives: a guide to the Algarve, co-written with the Irish artist Patrick Swift, which introduced middle-class Britons to that region and started the craze for buying second homes there. Wright and Swift were often found together in Soho pubs, silently mouthing words, waving hands and nodding animatedly at each other, oblivious to the baffled looks coming from other pub-goers.

For Wright's shyness was compounded by a much more serious problem. An attack of scarlet fever at the age of seven had left him profoundly deaf. He never worked out whether his deafness caused his shyness or just aggravated it, but he knew that both felt like being marooned from the world. And since he could only lip-read, he had to talk on an un-nuanced level that did not allow for casual interjections or throwaway asides. It made him seem heedless to social niceties: all his time at Oxford he persevered with the strange idea that male undergraduates addressed each other as 'sir'. One aspect of his deafness that he found especially distressing was that it made other shy people embarrassed, for they had to mouth their words exaggeratedly and still risk being misunderstood, adding an extra layer of jeopardy to any encounter.

Deafness prevented him not just from hearing but from over-hearing, so he could not judge the mood of a gathering but had to focus on one speaker at a time, manoeuvring for a seat with his back to the light so he could see their faces. Those punctuation marks of normal conversation – that nod, eyebrow lift or assenting murmur that shows we are cued in emotionally to our interlocutor – were beyond him. The spoken word could never serve for Wright as convivial noise, only as the vehicle for blandly literal meaning.

※

I am not quite so self-regarding that I imagine my shyness to be a misfortune on a par with deafness. But I do think Wright's predicament suggests, in extreme form, something fundamental about this thing I want to write about, which is that it is about much more than just timidity or fearfulness. Shyness also arises from a kind of social deafness, a tin ear for non-verbal cues, a sense that you have failed to grasp some invisible thread that holds communal life together. It feels like coming late to a party when everyone else is about three beers in and entering that state that allows them to have fluent exchanges that settle on some pre-agreed theme as if by magic.

All my life I have been trying, as Wright did, to make algorithmic what other people seem to find natural. I still cannot dial a new phone number without having written down, like a call centre worker with a corporate script, what I am going to say when the person I am ringing picks up. (It should be a liberation for a shy person to be invisibilised by the telephone receiver, like the Wizard of Oz throwing his voice from behind a screen, but somehow it isn't.) I keep a notebook of things to say to people in case I run out of small talk – and however full the notebook gets, it never seems to stop me running out. At parties I no longer look intently at bookshelves or fridge magnets as I used to, but have cultivated a cryptic smile which, I hope, suggests I am benignly amused by the human comedy unfolding before me and unfazed about not being part of it.

The real problem comes with informality, when conversations are meant to form artlessly through casual encounters, as if out of thin air. At work this happens at places like the photocopier, that office-life equivalent of the parish pump, where gossip is exchanged and alliances cemented, or in corridors, which are officially meant for direct access to somewhere else but are unofficially meant for chance meetings and lingerings. It is in these liminal spaces that I come unstuck, never knowing if I am supposed to stop and say hello or for how long. I might pass two colleagues deep in conversation, stop and greet them and, while they carry on talking, wonder when to interject. Eventually, having simply smiled and nodded, I slope off and leave them to it.

The evolutionary anthropologist Robin Dunbar once worked out that there is a natural limit of four on the size of conversational groups. If the group gets any bigger, no one can retain the attention of all its members and it splits into smaller units. I have found the Dunbar rule to be pretty infallible over the years, but knowing about the problem never makes it easier to solve. When a conversational group subdivides, I attempt to join one of the sub-groups but hear the other one in my head, unable to tune out. I end up joining neither and become stranded between two sets of people oblivious to each other and to me. I am often in a circle of people that closes up suddenly like a scrum and leaves me standing outside it, as its constituent parts forget I am there and absent-mindedly nudge me out of the loop.

Coming up with the right words, or at least good enough words in some semblance of order, is hard enough. But words, as David Wright discovered, are not even the first language of *homo sapiens*. We have more discrete facial muscles than any other animal: even when our palates and larynxes were not developed enough for us to do more than grunt, squeal and whimper like other apes, we could move our lips, cheeks and brows to convey what we were thinking to others. We came to recognise the crow's feet wrinkles that form at the sides of the eyes when we smile as a sign of pleasure and appeasement. We learned to dispense laughter, that placating music that no other animal makes and which the shy find it so hard to fake.

Alongside this wordless language of gesture, expression and vocal grunt, humans have evolved a complex and ever-evolving etiquette of tactility. I have watched on nervously as, over the course of my adult life, hugging has been transformed from a marginal pursuit into a constant of social life, with the proliferation of variants such as French cheek-kissing and that 'bro hug' where the shaken hand becomes a vertical handclasp pulled forward until you bump shoulders. Hugging has always felt to me like an odd mix of the natural and artful: natural because bodily contact is the first, endorphin-releasing language we learn as babies and share with other apes, and artful because it has to be silently synchronised with the other person – unlike a handshake, which can be offered and accepted asynchronously.

For the truly socially inept, even a handshake can be fiddly. As a young man I used to botch them all the time, offering the wrong hand (being left-handed didn't help) or grabbing the other person's fingers instead of their palm. And then, just as I had completed my long internship in the art of the handshake, I realised it was losing currency and I had to hastily re-skill in hugging, or at least allow myself to be hugged while I managed a sort of bear-claw hold with my arms hanging limply down my huggee's back. Hugging me is like trying to cuddle a scarecrow.

The sociologist Susie Scott suggests that the shy are conducting 'an unintentional breaching experiment'. A breaching experiment is an ethnographic exercise which examines people's reactions to the breaking of social norms that we normally take for granted. The researcher might, for example, cut ahead in a queue without explanation or, on a crowded train, approach random strangers and ask them to give up their seats for no reason. (On the whole, it is better if this researcher does not suffer from shyness.) The behaviour of shy people, Scott argues, can be similarly jarring. Their body language shouts discomfort. Their silence unnerves. They lack the split-second timing that allows those deep in discussion to perform like riffing musicians; instead, while mentally scrolling through all the different ways in which the conversation might fail, they miss the beat and the discussion moves on. So their interventions are rare and erratic, and their words carry too much weight or disrupt the dialogic rhythm. Shy people unsettle others because they unsettle the tacit conventions of social life.

It must have been my bafflement at these conventions that stirred my scholarly and writerly interest in the taken-for-granted rituals of daily life. Shyness turns you into an onlooker, a close reader of the signs and wonders of the social world. Eventually I came to see that this was also the best way of assuaging the self-preoccupation that comes with shyness. I could convert my personal interest in this phenomenon into anthropological curiosity, and start to explore it as a participant-observer, a field biologist of the shy. I learned that shyness had many faces. People who at first seemed to be models of social deftness turned out, from other angles, to be no such thing. The most unlikely people confessed to me that they were shy. I had thought I was surrounded by virtuosos of social rules, delivering word-perfect performances while I was alone in fluffing my lines. I came to see that everyone was struggling to learn these rules that were never written down, although some of us were the class dunces, learning them more slow-wittedly and unwillingly than most.

§

Shyness is not a rare mutation that sets an unfortunate few of us off from the mass of tribal humankind. Some form of it seems to be common not just in humans but in other animals. Many creatures, when they feel threatened or fearful, adopt conserving or vegetative states that are meant to be self-protective but which may also render them defenceless. The Virginia opossum affects a sham death or 'thanatosis', the origin of the phrase 'playing possum'. Birds and rodents adopt cut-off postures such as turning the head away or feigning sleep. When toads sense danger, they do not hop away, as would be more sensible, but shrink and shut their eyes and burrow into soft ground with their hind legs, in the same way that embarrassed people cringe and curl in on themselves, in order to take up less space in the world.

Some animals seem so enigmatic that they positively invite anthropocentric ascriptions of shyness. The silent solitariness of albatrosses at sea has long made them seem mysterious to sailors, although the specific breed known as *Diomedea cauta*, or shy albatross, was named thus in 1841 by the English naturalist John Gould when he saw it off the south coast of Tasmania, on the dubious grounds that it did not follow boats, like other albatrosses, and was thus hard for him to shoot.

For the seamen who explored the colder waters of the north, the shyness of seals was proverbial. They looked so knowing and elusive, with their huge eyes and bewhiskered faces popping up teasingly out of the sea. In 1856, in her *Sketches and Tales of the*

Shetland Islands, Eliza Edmonston wrote that Shetland fishermen admired the native seals for 'their shyness, their great strength, and the singular intelligence of their aspect,' which made them seem like 'fallen spirits in metempsychosis, enduring in the form of seals a mitigated punishment'. In one version of this myth, seals were angels who sided with Satan, were cast out from heaven with him and fell into the sea. And so, while the fishermen killed the seals for their skins, they did so with misgivings, believing them to be 'powerful to injure, and malevolent to revenge'. The inscrutability of seals probably inspired the Northern Isles legend of the selkie, the seal that could shed its skin on land and take human form, but which would gaze longingly at the sea and one day return to it, without saying goodbye to its heartbroken human lover.

The Norwegian scientist and explorer Fridtjof Nansen had a more systematic explanation for seal shyness, informed by his encounter with the theories of Charles Darwin while studying zoology at the University of Oslo in the early 1880s. When making the first crossing of Greenland in 1888, he noted that the bladder-nosed seal was much shyer than when he had first joined the Norwegian seal-hunting expeditions as a student a few years earlier, when the sealers just clubbed them where they lay. Now they had to use rifles, because the seals had sussed that ships with crow's nests and swarms of boats around them spelled danger, and had taken to the water or retreated to the closely packed ice inland. Nansen was puzzled by the fact that the younger seals were as shy as the older ones, which meant either that the parents had taught their children to be shy, or that, in less than a decade, heredity had achieved the same result 'by the mere weeding out of the lazier and less cautious among the flock'.

The serious scientific study of this kind of evolved shyness in animals began with the domestic dog. One of its pioneers was Helen Mahut, a Polish Jew and Holocaust survivor who had seen her father, mother and brother burned alive by the Nazis in a village schoolhouse and watched a German soldier crush a baby's head against a wall. Having witnessed such unspeakable acts, she became interested in the immutable aspects of personality and drifted towards the behavioural sciences. In the mid-1950s, at McGill University in Canada, she began experimenting on dogs by inflating balloons and opening umbrellas in front of them and scaring them with slithering mechanical snakes and Halloween masks. The most fearful were the working dogs, such as corgis, collies and alsatians; the boldest were the boxers and terriers.

Just as Darwin saw that pigeon fanciers had created an accelerated form of evolution by breeding multiple variations from the same common rock pigeon, so Mahut thought that dog breeds showed clearly how a trait like shyness could be inherited. Over the past century and a half this has happened more systematically as the kennel clubs established in both Britain and America have imposed strict breed standards. An expert dog breeder is supposed to be able to breed out any trace of shyness along with other undesirable traits, such as a shallow ribcage or badly arched toes. An animal behaviourist, meanwhile, might do the opposite, showing the importance of heredity in personality by breeding shyness *into* dogs. In a laboratory at the University of Arkansas in the early 1960s a group of scientists, led by Roscoe Dykman and Oddist Murphree, established the Arkansas line of nervous pointers from a very shy pair. When people approached them, these nervous pointers became wide-eyed and frigid, their backs arched and their flank muscles trembled. The scientists were Pavlovians, who thought they could condition the dogs to stop being so neurotic. They failed. The pointers never got used to people, however much they were stroked and cosseted, and they developed severe, stress-related mange.

This process of artificial selection began about forty thousand years ago, when humans domesticated grey wolves to create *Canis lupus familiaris*. It seems likely that they selected the wolves that were bold enough to befriend us but timid enough to know their rightful place in the human–dog hierarchy. If you yell at a dog it cowers, not out of fear or remorse but because over thousands of years it has evolved this trick to avert our hostility. Working dogs, in particular, as Helen Mahut found, have to be compliant. Despite the myth spread by Jack London's 1903 novel *The Call of the Wild* that Arctic huskies are all alpha-male wannabe-wolves, they are, in fact, biddable and shy.

※

Once dismissed as anthropomorphic pseudo-science, the study of animal personality is now a flourishing field. One of its pioneers was Andy Sih of the University of California, Davis, who in the early 1990s began studying the behaviour of salamander larvae in streams. Some of the larval salamanders, he noted, were quite intrepid. They ate more and grew faster than their shyer counterparts, and this helped them in small streams, which might dry up in late summer before the shyer larvae had eaten enough plankton to become air-breathing grown-ups. But because they just bumbled around, the bold salamander larvae were also more likely to be gobbled up by their predators, green sunfish. In a phenomenon that evolutionary biologists call fluctuating selection, the shy and bold larvae each thrived in different situations – which may explain why natural selection prefers a range of personalities in the same species.

In the study of animal personality this became known as the 'shy–bold continuum'. At one end of the continuum animals are aggressive, adventurous and risk-taking; at the other they are fearful, unadventurous and risk-averse. The shy–bold continuum has been found in over a hundred species, and, since distantly related creatures exhibit it, it may exist in all animals, including humans. Life for most animals is a trade-off between eating or being eaten, between looking for a mate and fleeing from danger, and they manage this trade-off between success and survival in all kinds of inventive ways. Among male field crickets, for instance, louder and longer singing attracts females, but it also attracts predators – so those with the longest trills are slower to break cover, offsetting the greater risk of long singing with greater shyness.

Animal scientists have deployed ingenious research methods to measure the shy–bold continuum. If you lie low in the frozen tundra on the uninhabited Possession Island in the southern Indian Ocean and push an inflatable plastic toy cow towards a nesting albatross with a carbon-fibre pole, as the seabird ecologist Samantha Patrick has done, the bold albatrosses will clack their bills and grumble while the shy ones pretend not to have seen it. The bold albatrosses turn out to be better at foraging for food; the shy ones make more attentive parents and uxorious partners.

Just as humans can be rendered shy or bold in particular settings, so local contexts seem to shift the axis of shyness and boldness in animals. In Banff, Alberta, a tourist town in the Rocky Mountains, the elk have become abnormally bold. These elk 'townies', as locals call them, started arriving in Banff in the 1990s, probably escaping from wolves. Signs were erected all around the town warning that the elk were dangerous, especially during the rutting season, when they were known to flatten car tyres, punch holes in radiators and smash windscreens. Rob Found, a doctoral student at the University of Alberta, began measuring the shyness or boldness of the Banff elk with a basic 'flight response' measure: how quickly they ran away when he chased them for ten minutes apiece with a hockey stick with a rustling bin bag attached to it. He had cameras trained on old bicycle frames, traffic triangles and other flotsam salvaged from rubbish dumps, to see if the elk were bold enough to approach these objects, triggering the cameras and leaving behind a sample of their hair on some sticky tape. Found concluded that the elk herd did not act as one, as most people thought, but that individual elks ran along a gradient from bold to shy, and that a few bold ones could lead the shy astray.

As well as being individually shy or bold, certain animals seem, like people, to have recognisably social personalities. Only recently, with the development of tiny tagging and GPS devices, has it been possible to see how such animals behave in groups. In the mallee scrub near Morgan, north-east of Adelaide, Michael Bull of Flinders University studied the social life of sleepy lizards by strapping GPS data loggers to their backs to track their movements, and discovered that they formed a complex network.

Some were loners, while others hung around in what he called 'lizard cliques'.

In the tank room at the Marine Biological Association's laboratory in Plymouth they have measured the sociability of small-spotted cat sharks, by exploring how they chose to keep safe when they were less than a year old and at risk from bigger fish. The bold ones rested on top of one another, forming shark fraternities; the shy ones did their best to camouflage themselves, matching their skin colour to the colour of the gravel at the bottom of the tank. In the experimental pools at the Bimini Sharklab in the Bahamas, they found similar levels of clubbability in the lemon shark. Like the cat sharks, the lemon sharks had to meet a pretty low bar to be deemed sociable: they just had to follow another shark for a few seconds, and even I could manage that. But these tiny differences were of huge import. The friendlier lemon sharks were less likely to be killed but more likely to catch parasites and diseases from their shark friends. Where you sit on the shy–bold continuum is, it seems, a matter of life and death.

A hardline evolutionary biologist would insist that shyness among humans is a similarly adaptive trait, a fossil behaviour from our prehistoric past. Human shyness, the psychologist Jeffrey Kahn has argued, evolved out of the same percentages game of boldness and timidity played by our ancestors, and especially out of the need for a social ranking system that would reconcile beta males and females to being at the bottom of the tribal hierarchy, reducing the chances of conflict.

There is indeed some evidence of inherited shyness among the higher primates. As long ago as the 1970s the American animal behaviourist Stephen Suomi, working at the Poolesville Animal Center in Maryland, observed that about 15 per cent of rhesus monkeys were shy, showing an increased heart rate and rise in blood cortisol, an adrenal stress hormone, in tense situations. By blood testing, and reassigning shy infant monkeys to more outgoing mothers with no effect, Suomi showed that the shy trait was inherited. Around the same time the Harvard psychologist

Jerome Kagan was conducting experiments which suggested that the same percentage of human babies were born shy. Being fearful, they reacted to stressful events, such as balloons popping or a man dressed as a clown, with the same higher blood cortisol and quicker heartbeat.

Kagan's studies of temperament suggested that we have a fixed emotional range, that even as babies we have some basic, immovable core of a personality. Many parents know this intuitively, insisting that their children were easy-going and extrovert, or anxious and introverted, from the day they entered the world. If shyness is hereditary, then most likely it has an evolutionary gain, and some ancestral part of our brains clings to the memory of the benefit it brings.

§

And yet ... I must admit that something in me still balks at seeing my shyness as equal to that of a salamander larva or a Rocky Mountain elk that runs away when you chase it with a stick. Many scientists think animals make better subjects than humans for investigating personality because they let us deploy these neat experimental methods, which would never work with actual persons, and which allow us to identify character traits clearly before social and cultural influences arrive to muddy the picture. But isn't the muddied picture the truer one? Nature, especially human nature, is messily multifarious; humans are more than just their fears and instincts. Our shyness is unique because we are alone in being gifted, and burdened, with self-consciousness. We are meaning-making animals, compelled to reflect on and tell stories about our lives. Our shyness is intimately tied up with the ways we think and talk about it and the connotations we attach to it.

This, after all, is what makes shyness so baffling to the more literal-minded among the non-shy: it appears to make no rational sense. Thinking about your shyness can make it worse, just as being aware that you are blushing makes you blush more. Shyness is a longing for connection with others which foils that longing through the circular, self-fulfilling thoughts at which humans excel. We are the only animals to construct these self-propelling cycles of meta-thought, feelings that feed on and nourish themselves.

The seventeenth-century writer, physician and polymath Sir Thomas Browne reflected often on this irrational aspect of shyness. He suffered from what he called, variously, bashfulness or *pudor rusticus* (rustic shame). No amount of his formidable skills of scientific logic and self-dissection seemed able to dispel it. His modesty, wrote his friend John Whitefoot, rector of Heigham, near Norwich, manifested itself in 'a natural habitual blush' which had no obvious cause. Those that knew him first by 'the briskness of his writings' were astonished, according to Whitefoot, to encounter 'the gravity and sobriety of his aspect and conversation, so free from loquacity'. Although he and his wife had eleven children, Browne found the sex act absurd and belittling, and wished 'that there were any way to perpetuate the world without this triviall and vulgar way of coition'.

But Browne's shyness was, as it so often is, uneven. He had a lifelong sense of himself as melancholy and reclusive, but he deliberately sought out company to allay these tendencies, and his quiet affability and sympathetic ear seem to have made him well loved as both friend and doctor. Of the portrait of Browne made when he was given a knighthood in 1671, one contemporary observer said that it purveyed a 'most amiable sweetness of aspect, grave without Dulness, thoughtfull without sourness; and with a most engaging Blush of Modesty suffused over his Countenance'. This modesty and civility, a charming side-shoot of his shyness, infuses his writings – even *Pseudodoxia Epidemica* (1646), an exhaustive encyclopaedia of 'vulgar errors', deluded popular beliefs of his day, which he deflates with gentle reason and dry humour.

In his first published work, *Religio Medici* (1643), a declaration of his complex Christian faith intended to refute the then common accusation that doctors were atheists, Browne confesses to the potentially heretical feeling of shyness about being a corpse. 'I am naturally bashfull; nor hath conversation, age, or travell, been able to effront, or enharden me,' he writes. 'Yet I have one part of modesty, which I have seldome discovered in another ... I am not so much afraid of death, as ashamed thereof.' Death so disfigures us that our loved ones can suddenly 'stand afraid and start at us ... This very conceite hath in a tempest disposed, and left me willing to be swallowed up in the abysse of waters; wherein I had perished unseene, unpityed, without wondring eyes.'

Browne's shame at the thought of being a corpse remained a refrain in his writing. 'To be knav'd out of our graves,' he writes in *Hydriotaphia, or Urne-Buriall* (1658), 'to have our sculs made drinking-bowls, and our bones tuned into pipes, to delight and sport our enemies, are tragicall abominations, escaped in burning burials.' As Browne must have known, there is no rational reason to care what becomes of our bodies when our consciousness – or, as he would have believed, our soul – has left them. No danger can befall a dead body, nor could any social mortification be worse than mortification itself. And yet self-consciousness is such a resilient trait that we believe, quite illogically, that it will survive our transition into non-being. Perhaps some element of shyness, as our modern-day sociobiologists suggest, makes evolutionary sense. But surely its most human property is that it often makes no sense at all.

※

The historian Theodore Zeldin once proposed an intriguing thought experiment. How different might human history seem, he wondered, if you told it not through the lens of great public events, or the primal struggle for resources such as food, land and wealth, but through feelings such as love, fear, frustration or boredom, and how they made people act? 'One way of tackling it might be to write the history of shyness,' he mused. 'Nations may be unable to avoid fighting each other because of the myths and paranoias that separate them: shyness is one of the counterparts to these barriers on an individual level.'

Zeldin was, by his own account, a shy, studious boy whose

'life began in silence'. He went on to form a sub-discipline that he called intimate history, writing about ordinary people's worries and desires, their feelings of fear, happiness or loneliness. From his base at St Antony's College, Oxford, he promoted the art of conversation as a way of breaking down the estrangement of people from one another. He hosted meals in which groups of strangers came together and, with the aid of a specially designed 'conversation menu', laid aside their inhibitions and shared their ideas and feelings. His Oxford Muse project encouraged people to write detailed self-portraits which would help others to understand them more deeply and quickly.

Zeldin's life's work has been a triumphant prevailing over his own shyness and a public-spirited urging of others to do the same. But his history of shyness remains unwritten, and no wonder. Shyness is a low-intensity, mundane, chronic, nebulous and hard-to-define condition. It has none of the pathos of afflictions such as madness or melancholia, and none of the drama of major life experiences like love, loss and grief. It leaves little evidence behind in archives for historians to consult, its sufferers being disinclined to speak or write about it and tending to communicate its effects on them mutely and tangentially. Given their large numbers in real life, shy people appear quite rarely in books and films, perhaps because they are not the natural protagonists who propel narratives along. A history of shyness would have to be a suitably tentative one, assembled from shards and fragments just as a scholar of the ancient world might piece together papyrus scraps, aware of all the ellipses in the record, the words and feelings for which there is no historical trace.

'A doom of reticence is upon all our shy confraternity, and we seldom make confidences even to each other,' writes W. Compton Leith in his short work *Apologia Diffidentis* (1908), the nearest thing we have to a history of shyness. W. Compton Leith was the pseudonym of Ormonde Maddock Dalton, a curator at the British Museum. A brilliant scholar, his catalogue of early Christian antiquities and colossal *Byzantine Art and Archaeology* (1911) became standard works. But little is known about him, except that he was unmarried and prone to tortured silences in company, which, according to a colleague, he filled with equally awkward interjections such as 'Surely this mead is most pleasantly umbrageous?' In the only known photograph of him, Walter Stoneman's 1925 bromide print for the National Portrait Gallery taken when he was fifty-nine and two years off retirement, a thin-lipped, aquiline but still gentle face looks out, with a slight squint, at the world. Dalton's professional armour of dark three-piece suit with neat handkerchief corner fails to entirely dispel an impression of helplessness and vulnerability.

'In their depths are delicate fronded seaweeds and shells tinted with hues of sundawn,' Dalton writes of the shy tribe to which he belonged, 'but to see them you must bend low over the surface, which no lightest breath must furrow, or the vision is gone.' The highly strung prose has what used to be called the smell of the lamp about it, from burning the midnight oil, and reads as if its author is forever on the verge of tears. 'Man was not made to be the worm of Eden, darkly creeping in the dust, but rather its noblest creature,' he declares, 'with the light crowning his head and the winds tossing his hair.'

If you can get past the sombre blank-verse rhythms, though, Dalton has an interesting thesis: shyness is a modern invention. In ancient Greece, where body and mind were 'consentient in one grace of motion', it had no habitat in which to thrive. In ancient Rome things began slowly to change. Now closed doors and courts created a sense of secrecy, and gradations of wealth and rank introduced unease into public life. Still, Dalton claims, this did not create what we know as shyness, for Italy is a sunlit, clear-aired land that bred strong heads not compelled by 'onset of outer mists and darkness to tend a flickering light within themselves'.

Whatever Dalton may have thought, the ancient world did know something akin to shyness. 'A bashful man will make a sorry beggar,' as Penelope says in Homer's *Odyssey* of a vagrant who refuses to come and see her. A starving man cannot afford to be shy, Penelope suggests, which implies that a man who isn't starving *can* afford to be. Perhaps shyness arose not as a result of our animal fears and instincts but as a corollary of human civilisation, at the moment when our primitive fears about finding the next meal, or being someone else's meal, subsided. This gave us the time and space to be anxious about how others saw us. A pseudo-Hippocratic text translated by Robert Burton in his *Anatomy of Melancholy* (1621) describes a patient in fourth-century BCE Athens who 'through bashfulness, suspicion, and timorousness, will not be seen abroad, "loves darkness as life, and cannot endure the light" ... He dare not come in company, for fear he should be misused, disgraced, overshoot himself in gesture or speech, or be sick.'

One of history's first named shy people was the philosopher Zeno of Citium (*c.*335–263 BCE), who, according to Diogenes Laertius in his *Lives and Opinions of Eminent Philosophers*, disliked being close to others and so would always take the end seat of a couch, 'thus saving himself at any rate from one half of such inconvenience'. He surrounded himself with beggars while teaching, so as to deter crowds. His own teacher, Crates, tried to cure Zeno of shyness with an early form of aversion therapy, asking him to carry a pot of lentil soup through the Kerameikos, the potters' quarter, in Athens. When Zeno tried to hide the pot in his cloak, Crates broke it with his staff and, as Zeno hurried off with soup down his legs, called out, 'Why run away, my little Phoenician? Nothing terrible has befallen you!'

Zeno founded the school of Stoicism, a philosophy of self-reliant estrangement from the world and of equanimity in the face of the baubles of public approval such as status and fame. 'Stoicism has qualities which seem foreordained for the bracing of shy souls, as if the men who framed its austere laws had prescience of our frailty,' writes Dalton in *Apologia Diffidentis*. 'It is the philosophy of the individual standing by himself, as the shy must always stand, over against a world which he likes not but may not altogether shun.'

The ancients knew all about the nonsensicalness of shyness, the way it ebbed and flowed in peculiar ways, so that those suffering from it could at other times be confident and even courageous. Some of the most eloquent orators in the theatres and courtrooms of the ancient world were afflicted by stage fright. The great Athenian orator Demosthenes, at least according to the partial account of his rival debater Aeschines, trembled before his first meeting with Philip of Macedon in 346 BCE at Pella, and 'with all listening so intently, this creature offered an obscene prologue in a voice dead with fright, and after a brief narration of earlier events suddenly fell silent and was at a loss for words, and finally abandoned his speech'. The greatest orator of ancient Rome, Cicero, wrote to the politician Lucius Lucceius, to whom he was too shy to speak, because 'a letter has no blushes'. According to Cicero's essay 'On the Orator', his mentor, the consul Lucius Licinius Crassus, admitted to being 'shattered and fainting with fear' before a speech. The first-century Roman Stoic Seneca wrote that 'certain even very constant men, when in the public eye, break out in a sweat … I know of those whose teeth chatter, whose tongues falter, whose lips quiver.'

The idea of the cheeks as what Pliny the Elder called 'the seat of shame' was so familiar to Romans that the similar-sounding words *pudor* and *rubor*, shame and redness, were often poetically juxtaposed. 'Purple shame,' wrote Ovid in his *Amores* about a bride being gazed on by her husband, 'appeared on her guilty face.' The blush, which occurred without warning – *pudor* means 'to strike' – was an affront to the importance the Romans placed on self-mastery. But since it was involuntary and could not be insincere like an apology, the blush was also the *signum pudoris*, the mark that society imprinted on the face, suggesting that its owner was capable of shame and therefore trustworthy and sane.

The ancient philosophers, from Aristotle onwards, held this belief that shame was excellent in moderation, for a truly shameless person was capable of loathsome behaviour, but that it was always in danger of tipping over into the excessive shame of bashfulness. The first-century Greek historian Plutarch wrote an essay usually translated as 'On shyness', although in fact he used a word of his own coinage, *dusôpia*, meaning the state of being discountenanced – a sort of shamefacedness felt when we were required to put on a social face that did not marry with our private desires. Plutarch agreed with Aristotle that shyness was fine in small doses, but if left unchecked it caused an unhealthy self-obsession and the abandonment of 'noble ventures'. Thus, he wrote, 'it is the fate of bashfulness, in fleeing from the smoke of ill-repute, to throw itself into the fire of it'.

Oddly for a classical scholar, Dalton overlooks all this evidence of sophisticated reflection on shyness in the ancient world. It was in the northern Alps, he speculates, where Roman decorum met barbaric roughness, that 'the first ancestor of all the shy, this timid Adam, was born'. Shyness began to take root with the arrival of Christianity, with its prizing of modesty and monastic retreat. And it ripened with the arrival of modern systems of manners, such as the Provençal code of *courtoisie*, which created tyrannies of social expectation that overwhelmed the timid. A shy temperament, Dalton writes, is 'chilled by this everlasting urbanity ... this finished science of illusion'. The chief cause of shyness now was the intricate artifice of modern social life, and the main culprit was obvious: 'Woman, having curbed the brute man by conventional restraints of outward demeanour, has made human intercourse smooth and seemly, but imposed upon mankind the wearing of unnatural masks.'

Dalton has one final, very English explanation for the evolution of shyness: the weather. Considering what zoologists would call the area of distribution of the species, he concludes that all of southern Europe, the east and 'the savage world' has little idea of shyness and that it is mainly in northern Europe that one finds the 'haunts of the diffident'. Here the indoor lives dictated by the cold, humid air have created a culture of refinement that means ease of manner emerges only with effort, just as grapes will only grow there in greenhouses. The most hopeless cases were to be found among his own people. The Englishman, he notes, 'conceals his benevolence by a frigid aloofness of manner, or blurts out friendliness like an indiscretion'.

❧

One such Englishman was Dalton's contemporary George Macaulay Trevelyan, the most celebrated and popular British historian of the first half of the twentieth century. His Cambridge colleagues and students would never have thought him shy; in fact, he seemed wholly indifferent to how he was perceived, often neglecting to shave and, in the middle of conversations, taking out his dentures to give them a wipe. He seldom laughed, but when he did the sound was said to carry from Trinity Great Court to the nearby college quads. He cowed undergraduates and junior colleagues with the combined force of his fame, his gruff manner and his terrifying silences.

The archaeologist and television personality Glyn Daniel, who went up to St John's College in 1932, recalled how he and his fellow freshers gathered excitedly for the first time to hear Trevelyan, who had thrilled them all at school with popular books full of narrative drive and lyrical awareness of the transience of human life. In the first week of term he stood before them in the largest lecture hall in the Arts School, a tall, stooped figure, with austere, steel-rimmed glasses, a wiry thatch of white hair and drooping moustache – looking, in his fellow historian George Kitson Clark's words, like 'a very distinguished, but slightly dilapidated bird of prey'. Trevelyan began not with a welcome to the new undergraduates but with a housekeeping announcement. Next week he would be lecturing in Room B, and after that Room G. Daniel supposed this was because his audience would be snowballing in size. On the contrary, when the students saw that all he did was read out his own books in a grating monotone, his audience fell away, and by the end of term Daniel was one of the very few left. Trevelyan's response to his own inadequacy as a lecturer was both ingenious and sad: he had made sure the university's room timetabling accommodated it.

A year after Daniel's disappointing encounter with greatness in a Cambridge lecture hall, a nervous working-class grammar school boy and graduate of University College, Leicester, Jack Plumb, was summoned to an ugly Edwardian house on West Road, Cambridge, for his first meeting with Trevelyan, who had reluctantly agreed to supervise his PhD on the Convention Parliament of 1689. Trevelyan led him into an unlit study and sat himself in the corner, almost obscured, saying nothing. When the silence became unbearable, Plumb launched into a garbled, ten-minute ramble about his research. This was met by more silence, before Trevelyan finally said: 'Good. Quite good. Good.'

It would be some years before Plumb realised that his supervisor felt as ill at ease as himself, and as much of an outsider in Cambridge. Trevelyan scorned social chit-chat, never talked about himself and was too shy even to admit he was shy. Towards the end of his life this self-effacement culminated in his destroying all his personal papers and leaving instructions in his will that no biography of him be written. It was as if all his human warmth – his compassion for the ordinary men and women of the past, from medieval peasants to Tudor yeomen, now nameless and forgotten by posterity – had been burned up as fuel for his writing, leaving only this shell of a man behind. When Plumb joined the university's historical society, he saw that Trevelyan chaired its meetings with the same 'curious manner of barking shyness'.

'Barking shyness' is an inspired oxymoron which elegantly captures the self-contradictoriness of the shy. We tend to see shyness as a recoiling or withdrawing, which is why the metaphors we use to describe it often draw on molluscs and crustaceans: close as an oyster, clam-like, in one's shell. Hermit crabs have a particular reputation for being shy, scuttling to hide their fleshy, vulnerable bodies in borrowed periwinkle or whelk shells. And yet many of them are not shy at all. In fact, they are bold enough to dislodge other hermit crabs from their bigger and more desirable residences, in a brutal eviction process that involves the aggressor grabbing hold of its rival and clacking their shells together like a rutting stag. The marine biologist Mark Briffa, working in rock pools along the Devon and Cornwall coasts, found that hermit crabs were yet another example of the shy–bold continuum. He upended them and poked them until they tucked their abdomens back into their shells, and then timed how long it took them to venture out again. The crabs he caught in Devon turned out to be shyer than those caught in Cornwall, probably owing to local differences in the number of predators and the size of waves.

Nature is always messier than the human-inflected metaphors we attach to it, and human shyness is messier still. Hermit crabs do not all hide timidly in their shells, nor is this an especially good way of imagining shyness. It is true that shyness can make us retreat from others, tongue-tied, blushing and subdued. But it can also make us the opposite of these things: aloof-seeming, skilful wearers of social masks, awkwardly loud and loquacious – barking shyness indeed.

§

The poet, critic and leading light of the Romantic movement Leigh Hunt first used the term 'shrinking violet' in his magazine *The Indicator* in 1820. Long before this, though, the *viola odorata*, or sweet violet, had been synonymous with shyness because of its bent neck, its small flowers blossoming briefly in March and April, and its intense but fleeting smell, which is partly produced by a chemical, ionine, that temporarily anaesthetises the nerve endings in our noses. The romantics fastened on the violet as the diffident harbinger of spring. The Irish poet Thomas Moore, in his 1817 oriental romance *Lalla Rookh*, wrote of a maiden who 'steals timidly away, / Shrinking as violets do in summer's ray'. In an 1818 sonnet Keats called the violet 'the Queen of secrecy'. For the Quaker poet Bernard Barton, writing in 1824, violets were 'mutely eloquent ... Rejoicing in their own obscure recess'.

There is, in fact, nothing very shrinking about violets. The Edwardian plant collector Reginald Farrer, who travelled the world in search of samples and certainly knew more about violets than any Romantic poet, called them 'rampageous' because they spread so vigorously and would 'thrive anywhere and make unobtrusive masses in any cool, good soil'. The great naturalist-explorer Alexander von Humboldt, in his travels in Latin America in the early 1800s, gathered violets everywhere from the valleys of the Amazon to the slopes of the Andes. Violets grow in scrub, woodland, prairies, swamps and bogs, and in suburban gardens they are as tenacious as any weed.

Individual violets may shrink, but collectively they are eye-catching and attention-grabbing, showing up like chunks of amethyst in the undergrowth. The ancient Greek lyric poet Pindar described Athens as 'violet-crowned', a phrase that even today nicely describes the purplish tinge that Mount Hymettus assumes from a distance at sunset. Goethe used to carry violet seeds in his pockets, scattering them on his walks around Weimar as his own contribution to the beauty of the world. In Britain violets were a favourite of flower sellers, who were often heard crying 'lovely sweet violets' on street corners, and of municipal gardeners looking for a splash of colour for their park flowerbeds and traffic roundabouts.

Perhaps, then, the violet is rather a good metaphor for shyness after all – the shyness that is about much more than just shrinking away. Violets 'shrink' not as a way of retreating from the world but simply as part of nature's talent for endless variation and for sustaining life in the most varied habitats. Shyness, too, can flourish in many climates and soils, and express itself in many ways. It can, like the violet, be accompanied by a surprising resilience, even bloody-mindedness. And its effects may be inconspicuous in individuals but, when viewed *en masse*, like that violet glow on Mount Hymettus, seem to run like a vein through much human endeavour, from the sublimations of art, music and writing to the masquerades of social life.

This book tries to think about shyness in this way, as part of common human experience. It is a field guide, a collective biography and a necessarily elliptical history of the shy. While there may be the odd nugget of memoir smuggled through customs here in the lining of my luggage, it is not meant to be an *apologia* for my own *diffidentia*. Instead I want to see if I can write about my shyness obliquely, by hiding behind the human shield of people more interestingly and idiosyncratically shy than me. For one result of my shyness has been to leave me feeling somewhat adrift in our age of oversharing, distrustful of this modern fondness for filtering narrative through cathartic confession – although I can also see that holding forth on one's shyness, however indirectly, within the pages of a book might seem rather … paradoxical. But then that is what shyness so often is.

Out of the bunch of shrinking violets whose experiences and reflections make up this book, some have dealt with their shyness stoically, others creatively, others self-pityingly, others with such seamless social skill that they hardly seemed shy at all. Shyness breeds reclusives, self-obsessives, brooders, procrastinators, sceptics, non-joiners, daydreamers, deep thinkers, artists, performers, quiet heroes, defenders of the underdog and humanitarians who channel their buried sociability into public works. It is, I have come to see, a multilayered and unsummarisable condition, the persistent backbeat of life on top of which we all improvise our own unique riffs and refrains.

Even if it were in my shy nature to cheerlead, which it isn't, it would be hard to be a cheerleader for a state as awkward to pin down as shyness. But I hope I can also avoid Ormonde Maddock Dalton's monotonously melancholic perspective and provide some solace for the shy. I want to show them that our condition can sometimes allow us to see fresh angles that others might have missed, and to reroute our dormant social impulses into new and creative areas. 'Les grands timides', as the French psychiatrist Ludovic Dugas called them in a 1922 book of that name, lead lives of 'complicated dissimulation, full of subtleties and detours'. Humans are social animals by instinct and default setting, so all that shyness does is to make us social in peculiar and circuitous ways. It is less a shrinking away from the world than a displacement or redirection of our energies. It can offer us accidental compensations, prodding us into doing what we might not have done if we had found our everyday encounters more congenial. It leads us down stimulating side streets after it has blocked off the main routes; it takes us off on unintended tangents and parentheses.

Mostly, though, I see shyness as neither a boon nor a burden, nor in terms of some calculus of profit and loss at all, but as part of the ineluctable oddness of being human. This makes it a fertile ground for exploring bigger questions about what it means to be a living, breathing, thinking self, aware that it is sharing a planet with billions of other such selves. Perhaps the oddest of many odd things about shyness is that, unlike other anxious states such as fear, shame and even embarrassment, it never strikes when we are alone. For however long it has existed, it must surely have added much to the sum of human loneliness. But it also lays bare how linked we are, how much we matter to each other.

2

THIS ODD STATE OF MIND

When his eldest daughter, Annie, was a year old, Charles Darwin noted how she fixed her gaze unblinkingly at a stranger's face, as if it were a lifeless object. She could not yet see that such faces belonged to other selves who might be looking at and taking note of her. He observed the first inkling of such awareness in his firstborn son, William, at two years and three months old. After Darwin had been away from home for ten days, he noticed that his son was uneasy around him and kept his eyes averted from his. The boy's downward glance, that classic sign of self-consciousness, revealed that locking his gaze with another's was now an encounter between two minds, each concerned with how the other might view it.

For Darwin this 'odd state of mind', shyness, was a great puzzle in his theory of evolution, for it held no obvious benefit for our species. It seemed like an unplanned by-product of the complexity of human consciousness, of us acquiring the ability to imagine how we might be imagined by other minds, but without ever being able to find this out conclusively (thank God, most of us would say).

As an evolutionary biologist, Darwin thought that shyness was a human universal, but he was not alone in thinking that his own countryfolk offered up some especially rich case studies. His Victorian bachelor scientist acquaintances, in particular, gave him ample occasion for a field study of that elusive human sub-species, *homo diffidentis*. As a young man, in 1831, just before he set off on the survey barque the HMS *Beagle*, Darwin went to the British Museum to see the renowned botanist Robert Brown. Thirty years earlier, when he was Darwin's age, Brown had undertaken a similar journey to the southern hemisphere, sailing around Australia on the famous expedition commanded by Captain Matthew Flinders, and bringing back specimens of four thousand species of plants. He told Darwin which microscope to buy, and in return Darwin said he would bring him back some orchids from Patagonia.

The American botanist Asa Gray called Brown 'a curious man in other things besides botany ... the driest pump imaginable'. He dressed entirely in black and carried his head down so that his jowly jawline vanished into his neck. A brilliant scientist, he had discovered 'Brownian motion', the tendency of pollen grains mixed with water to jiggle about under a microscope because they were hitting invisible atoms – a discovery that might have extended his fame beyond botany had he not hidden it in a privately printed pamphlet. For he jealously guarded his research findings as if he were Scrooge hoarding halfpennies. On the rare occasions Brown did publish, Gray wrote, he chose to 'enwrap rather than to explain his meaning', so that 'unless you follow Solomon's injunction and dig for the wisdom as for hid treasure, you may hardly apprehend it until you have found it all out for yourself'.

When Darwin returned from his *Beagle* voyage in 1836, Brown asked him rather fiercely what he meant to do with his stash of dried plants. Darwin was not keen to hand over anything to a man notorious for greedily guarding his own collections. But as a peace offering he gave Brown some fossil wood from the Andes, which mollified him. 'I think my silicified wood has unflintified Mr Brown's heart,' Darwin joked. He began calling on Brown for Sunday morning breakfasts, and his host 'poured forth a rich treasure of curious observations and acute remarks, but they almost always related to minute points'. Darwin's wife, Emma, found it exhausting trying to keep up a conversation with Brown at dinner, describing him and a fellow guest, the great geologist Charles Lyell, as 'two dead weights', whispering and muttering their way through the meal. Brown, she said, looked 'as if he longed to shrink into himself and disappear entirely'.

Darwin was more tolerant of the company of these mumbling men, for he too had to live with this 'odd state of mind'. All his life he had worked best alone, hated confrontation and suffered from psychosomatic ailments such as stomach cramps, vomiting fits and skin complaints. Like Brown, he procrastinated over publication, which meant he had one last reason to be thankful for his older friend's self-effacement. On 1 July 1858 Darwin presented his unpublished work on the theory of evolution by natural selection at a meeting of the Linnean Society, hastily arranged after he had been stunned to receive a paper through the post from Alfred Russel Wallace setting out the same arguments. Luckily, although the Linnean Society's meetings were arranged many months in advance, there had been a late cancellation caused by the very considerate death, on 10 June, of the advertised speaker, Robert Brown.

§

Darwin was twice lucky, in fact, because his rival in formulating a theory of evolution was shy as well. In his autobiography Alfred Russel Wallace writes that he became so as an adolescent, when he started growing very rapidly – reaching the great height for a Victorian of 6 foot 1 – and, as one of nine children in a genteelly poor family, had to wear clothes that were often shabby and too small and tight in the crotch. In January 1844, when he turned twenty-one, he made a frank inventory of his inadequacies: 'I

am shy, clumsy and lack confidence. I have no social sophistica-
tion … I am an abysmal public speaker … I have no wit or sense
of humour … I can recognize wit in others, which argues for a
capacity to develop it in my boring self.'

Well into his thirties he would dream of having to go to school
as a grown-up and opening his desk and rummaging inside so as
to hide his face, 'suffering over again with increased intensity the
shyness and sense of disgrace of my boyhood'. And yet Wallace
came to be grateful for what he called his 'constitutional shyness',
which he felt had gifted him long periods of solitary study and
a hesitancy over words that led him to avoid the verbosity that
marred so many scholarly works. (Perhaps: it seems to have had
the opposite effect on Robert Brown.)

But Wallace's shyness made him delay over publishing his
findings. Darwin's diffidence over the most contentious aspect
of *The Origin of Species*, meanwhile, led to him including only
one sentence on humans in its closing paragraphs: 'Light will be
thrown on the origin of man and his history.' Even after the book
appeared, Darwin's worries about how it would be received left
him covered in a nervous rash and suffering from headaches and
nausea. He became a virtual recluse, growing a bushy beard which
so transformed his looks that when he re-entered public life in 1866
not even his friends recognised him. In the sixth and final edition
of *Origin*, published in 1872, he became bolder and inserted a
single extra word at the start of the by now famous sentence on
humans: 'Much'.

In *The Expression of the Emotions in Man and Animals* (1872)
Darwin explored how humans and other animals manifest their
feelings. He observed that all our expressions of emotion have
equivalents in other animals, except one, which he called 'the
most peculiar and the most human': blushing. The consensus
on blushing in Darwin's time was that it revealed the moral and
spiritual dimension that separated us from the beasts. The German
philosopher Georg Wilhelm Friedrich Hegel had argued that the
transparency of the human skin, unlike the 'lifeless sheath' of

other animals, allowed both the movements of the blood and the workings of the soul to be seen, so that 'we have in this outward manifestation, as it were, the real fount of life made visible'.

In his book *The Physiology or Mechanism of Blushing* (1839) Thomas Burgess, a physician and expert on acne at the Blenheim Street dispensary in London, turned his attention to this 'beautiful and interesting phenomenon', which he called 'the lava of the heart'. He began by dismissing the colonialist prejudice that savage peoples were incapable of blushing and thus naturally shameless. He had observed that one of his black servants had scar tissue on her cheek which went red whenever he told her off, and had seen African albinos exhibited in Paris who had blushed spectacularly, not just on the face but on the ears, neck and breasts. Blushing, he inferred, was a universal trait, displayed by everyone except very small children and congenital idiots.

Burgess believed that, since blushing was universal, it was evidence of intelligent design by our creator. God had invented the blush so that our souls might display our moral lapses on our cheeks. Noting that Charlotte Corday, who murdered the French revolutionary Jean-Paul Marat, was said to have blushed after the guillotine had severed her head – whether she was embarrassed about killing Marat or about being beheaded was unclear – Burgess wondered if this meant that 'the stimulus which excites the blush has a higher or more elevated origin than that assigned to the animal or instinctive passions'. The flaw in Burgess's argument, as he himself conceded, was that timid people often blushed for no reason. Young people could seem abashed simply on entering a room or on being asked a routine question. He side-stepped this problem by inventing a new category, the 'False Blush', which had perverted the original intent of blushing and had no cause other than 'an extreme state of morbid sensibility'.

Darwin knew all this was nonsense. Blushing, he wrote, which 'makes the blusher to suffer and the beholder uncomfortable, without being of the least service to either of them,' had no moral or any other purpose. He noted cases of young women who had to undress in front of doctors blushing right down to their thighs, and found it extraordinary that the assumed opinion of others could excite such emotion and affect something so random as the circulation of the blood. Blushing, he decided, was just caused by the strange human capacity for 'self-attention'.

Darwin carried on being fascinated by this weird addendum to evolution, human self-consciousness, which meant that, aside from the involuntary act of blushing, we learned to stifle our most extreme emotional expressions. While infants routinely screamed for long periods, he observed, adults were taught to suppress these instincts, although to different degrees in different parts of the world. Some indigenous peoples wept copiously for trifling reasons. He had read of a New Zealand chief who cried like a baby because some sailors had spilt flour over his favourite cloak, and of Maori women proud of being able voluntarily to shed tears and wail theatrically when they met to mourn the dead. On the continent men also shed tears fairly freely, but Englishmen 'rarely cry, except under the pressure of the acutest grief'. Darwin put himself in this group. Only one thing, for the rest of his life, reduced him reliably to tears: a photograph of his beloved Annie, who had died at the age of ten, staring boldly and unblinkingly at the camera.

§

At the end of the eighteenth century foreign visitors to England had begun to note that its people were suffering from a queer and incurable condition. In London clubs and coffee-houses, once admired for their urbane talk, patrons sat in silence reading their newspapers, occasionally muttering to their neighbours under their breaths. Archbishop Talleyrand called it 'une taciturnité toute anglaise'. English reserve was seen as a strange amalgam of shyness, insecurity and conceit. In the 1820s the French traveller Édouard de Montulé remarked that this English coldness 'combined the theatrical *hauteur* of the Neapolitan with the severe pride of the Prussian'.

These travellers were unnerved by the silence of English public spaces. On the continent 'une conversation à l'Angloise' became a euphemism for a long silence. A German tourist, Ludwig Wolff, was astonished to hear no more than a hundred words spoken during a journey in a packed stagecoach from York to Leeds in 1833. English drivers rarely even talked to their horses, as their continental counterparts did. While French gastronomy was seen as a complete art of the table, good food being merely the garnish to conversation and conviviality, the English ate their meals to the unaccompanied sound of scraping cutlery. They had numerous social conventions for dispensing with words, such as placing a teaspoon in their cups to signal that they did not want more tea. Even drawing-room furniture discouraged talk, as the French politician Baron d'Haussez observed in 1833 of the 'immense and heavy *fauteuils*, which appear calculated to produce sleep rather than conversation'.

Foreign visitors also noted the English talent for privacy and enclosure. Houses were hidden behind iron fences and dense hedges, railway carriages were divided into small compartments and alehouses had partitions separated by green baize curtains on brass rails. Along the River Thames there were 'shades', stalls separated by wooden boards, in which men retired after working in the City to drink wine and cogitate alone, never speaking to their shade-abiding neighbours. In *The English at Home* (1861) the French writer Alphonse Esquiros called this phenomenon 'separation in union – the type of English life'.

Many felt that these strange behaviours were all symptoms of the same illness: anxiety about social class. When the English novelist Edward Bulwer-Lytton wrote in 1833 of 'the most noticeable trait in our national character, our reserve, and that *orgueil* … which is the displeasure, the amazement, and the proverb of our continental visitors,' he attributed it to the subtle social gradations in English society, the fact that class boundaries were shifting and social positions were difficult to judge, while aristocratic arrogance remained as strong as ever. English shyness was, he thought, a compound of vanity and anxiety, a reluctance to say anything that might expose one to social disdain. The same quality could be found all over England, and thus slowly 'from the petty droppings of the well of manners, the fossilized incrustations of national character are formed'.

§

In 1834, at the age of twenty-five, one such antisocial Englishman, Alexander Kinglake, set out on a journey through Europe and the Ottoman Empire. He had that combination of shyness and coolness which Bulwer-Lytton had just identified, and which seemed especially to afflict men taught in the English public schools and universities. Denied an army career by his poor eyesight, he took the brave step of going to the plague-ridden east when most Europeans had deserted it. After narrowly avoiding the plague in Constantinople, he made his way to the Holy Land and from Gaza began the hardest part of his journey: an eight-day slog across the Sinai desert, with a small entourage of English servants and Bedouin guides.

The English word 'solitude' derives from the Latin *sōlitūdo*, which, as the classicist Kinglake would certainly have known, also means 'desert'. Sinai was the unpeopled biblical wilderness where God spoke to Elijah in that 'still small voice', where the Israelites wandered for forty years and where Moses received the Ten Commandments. Kinglake confessed that it was a desire to be alone in this fabled place of silence and retreat that drove him, that he was one of those wandering Englishmen for whom injured pride had 'made the lone places more tolerable than ball rooms'.

For several days Kinglake and his tiny party worked their way through the sand dunes and wadis without meeting another soul. From morning to evening they sat aloft on their camels, their shoulders aching from the dual-swing rocking motion, their heads wrapped up against the scorching sun. Then Kinglake noticed a shimmering speck on the horizon through the heat haze. Three camels were approaching, two of them with riders. Eventually he identified an English gentleman in a shooting jacket, accompanied by his servant and two Bedouin guides. As they approached, Kinglake realised he felt 'shy and indolent' and had no wish 'to stop and talk like a morning visitor, in the midst of those broad solitudes'. His compatriot evidently felt likewise, for they simply touched their hats and carried on 'as if we had passed in Bond Street'. Their plan to ignore each other was only thwarted by their servants, who insisted on stopping. The stranger turned out to be a soldier returning to England overland from India. Clearly anxious to avoid the impression that he had stopped through 'civilian-like love of vain talk', he offered Kinglake an account of the plague in Cairo. Kinglake went on his way thinking this fellow 'manly and intelligent'.

If two Englishmen chance to meet somewhere on the other side of the earth, Alexis de Tocqueville wrote in *Democracy in America* (1840), even if they are surrounded by strangers whose language and manners they do not understand, they will 'first stare at each other with much curiosity, and a kind of secret uneasiness'. If one insists on accosting the other, 'they will take care only to converse with a constrained and absent air, upon very unimportant subjects'. It was as if de Tocqueville had been there in the Sinai, witnessing the awkward encounter of Kinglake and the soldier whose name he never learned but in whom he was delighted to find his own best qualities mirrored.

On returning to England in 1835, Kinglake began a book about his travels. He proved as diffident an author as he was a human being, spending several years writing it, abandoning it twice and, when it was finished, failing to find a publisher. Then, in 1844, he walked into the publishing house of John Ollivier on Pall Mall, and presented it to him for free, even paying £50 to cover his losses. The book was published the following year, anonymously, as *Eothen: or Traces of Travel Brought Home from the East*. The author's shyness even infected the folding plate in the frontispiece, a group portrait of Kinglake and his travelling entourage which he had painted himself, picturing them all from a distance so it was unclear which one was Kinglake. In the other coloured plate one could see, according to his biographer, the Victorian clergyman William Tuckwell, only 'the booted leg of Kinglake, who modestly hid his figure by a tree, but exposed his foot, of which he was very proud'.

There was nothing unassuming about the writing, though, which had a verve and swagger wholly absent in its author's person. One of the book's semi-comic (and semi-racist) conceits is that Kinglake's desire for solitude is constantly thwarted by the excitable natives he meets. 'His common talk is a series of piercing screams and cries,' he writes of the Bedouin, 'more painful to the ear than the most excruciating fine music.' To become an Arab, the reader just had to 'take one of those small, shabby houses in May Fair, and shut yourself up in it with forty or fifty shrill cousins for a couple of weeks in July'. Kinglake in fact offered no evidence for the noisiness of Arabs, other than that people often sound discordant when talking animatedly in a strange language. But he was reworking in whimsy a common trope in the literature of travel and empire: the contrast between the mature self-control of the white Englishman and the childish volatility of his colonial subjects.

For all Kinglake's insistence in *Eothen* that he is searching for monastic self-erasure, the personality that comes clattering through its pages is his own. He is that familiar figure, the Englishman abroad, building a high wall of *hauteur* around himself while letting in the odd light-shaft of self-deprecating humour. He is a very modern travel writer in his desire to detail his own thoughts and sensations rather than the landscape or antiquities he encounters. What matters to him, he concedes, is less what the silent Sinai or the sacred Holy Land is like than the fact that 'I (the eternal Ego that I am!) – I had lived to see, and I saw them'.

§

Eothen was a hit, and John Ollivier could hardly keep up with the demand for reprints. The author Sydney Smith wrote to Kinglake that his book was 'full of talent and will entitle you the next season to Oceans of Soup'. But instead of being a sought-after dinner guest, as Smith predicted, Kinglake made no attempt to capitalise on his literary triumph, or indeed make people aware that he was its author. In his mid-forties, as people started to twig that he had written *Eothen*, he began to be invited to balls and parties at London's great houses, but those who expected the effervescent company he offered on the page were soon disabused. Being short, short-sighted and shy, he found these events torture. He hated hearing his name proclaimed by masters of ceremonies as he entered ballrooms, thinking 'Mr Kinglake' sounded flat against 'his excellency' or 'his lordship', and that the women were rebuffing him by raising their fans perfunctorily.

He began arriving early so that no one would hear his name called out. As the first guest to arrive at the home of the singer Adelaide Kemble, he was met by Kemble's husband, John Sartoris, a host as taciturn as himself. They bowed, sat down by the fire and looked at one another in silence for ten minutes until Adelaide rescued them. Kinglake also stopped accepting invitations to country house weekends for, not having a valet who might have found this out for him from the other servants, he was confused about what guests were supposed to wear and where in the maze of rooms they were meant to meet.

He remained this strange mash-up of timidity and bravado. Petrified in polite company, he still thought nothing of nipping over to Algeria to assist the French general Saint-Arnaud in fighting an Arab rebellion, or accompanying his fox-hunting friend Lord Raglan to the Crimean War as a private guest, from where he had a ringside seat for the Charge of the Light Brigade. Ever concerned about losing face and quick to defend himself against the faintest slight, Kinglake was drawn to the increasingly outlawed practice of duelling. With its strict etiquette about the choice of location and weapons, the number of paces before firing and the role of the seconds, the ritual of the duel must have appealed to a man bewildered by social ambiguity. A letter of December 1837 had instructed his brother that, should he die in a forthcoming duel, he wished to be buried in whatever clothes he was wearing, 'for I do not wish to leave my grave toilet in the hands of Hags'.

In February 1846 Kinglake had again laid down the gauntlet, this time to one Edward FitzGerald, who he felt had insulted him by introducing him to his mistress. He sent a written challenge to FitzGerald to meet him in Calais, to escape British justice, for a change in the law the previous year had meant that if a man killed his opponent in a duel he could be tried for murder. Having crossed the channel and waited for eight days on the French coast, Kinglake finally accepted his adversary was not turning up and sailed home.

In 1857 Kinglake was elected Liberal MP for Bridgwater in Somerset. While delivering his maiden speech, in front of only a few dozen members, he broke down and had to abandon it. On the few occasions he spoke after that, his weak voice made little impact. Sir Robert Peel MP, son of the former prime minister, admitted that a well-received speech he made attacking the French emperor Napoleon III had been plagiarised from the preceding speech by Kinglake, which he had heard because he was sat on the same bench, but which the press gallery had not. Kinglake would write to *The Times* asking them to correct their misheard reports of what he had said in the Commons, with a ferocity he never displayed in the House. 'I did not say that "the Emperor of the French was bent forward like some mere dumb animal",' he wrote in one letter, 'I said that she (France) was led forward like some mere dumb animal who had been taught to pull a trigger and fire a musket without knowing why or wherefore except that she was under the orders of her master.'

Inarticulate and inaudible oratory was, according to Ralph Waldo Emerson, a fine English tradition. In *English Traits* (1856), in which he claimed to be able to trace the national reputation for taciturnity back seven hundred years, Emerson noted a perverted pride in bad public speaking in the House of Commons. The chamber seemed to be full of mumblers, whose voices sank into their throats, with no one around them brave enough to ask them to speak up. It was, he wrote of the honourable members, 'as if they were willing to show that they do not live by their tongues, or thought they spoke well enough if they had the tone of gentlemen'.

The historian David Vincent claims that the idea of English reserve crystallised in the middle of the nineteenth century as a way of justifying how British government worked. The elite public schools and universities nurtured the habit of saying one thing and feeling or knowing something else, which created a culture of 'honourable secrecy' that permeated government as its bureaucracy expanded. Important messages were not to be delivered in rousing speeches, but whispered in the corridors of power or behind closed doors. According to Vincent, this notion of honourable secrecy served as a convenient alibi for the civil service's parsimony with information and the growing power of the state, for it could be suggested that these simply reflected a 'gentlemanly distaste for unnecessary noise of any sort'.

When the *Times* journalist Michael McCarthy shadowed the Department of the Environment in the late 1980s, he found that civil servants were still using this esoteric code. Its key quality, he felt, was 'dynamic understatement'. Words that might seem bland to the uninitiated became charged with meaning if you were gentlemanly enough to be able to decode them. Hence the highest accolade was to say that something was 'rather impressive', but woe betide the official whose contributions were regarded as 'unhelpful' or 'unfortunate' or, on rare and heinous occasions, 'most unfortunate'. Even today, senior civil servants deploy a variant of this evasive vocabulary, with its suggestion that excessive keenness or candour is rather gauche and undignified. 'I am reluctant to support', 'I haven't formed a view yet' and 'I am happy to discuss' all signify dissent, while 'I'm open to this line of thinking' means 'yes'.

But this explanation for English reserve does not quite account for the protean character that was Alexander Kinglake. He may have been buttoned up, but he was also a late Romantic, a lover of Byron who loathed the airless respectability of English life and a maverick back-bencher, with no aspiration to hold high office or keep official secrets. His reserve suggested something stranger and more conflicted than establishment caginess. When the French philosopher Hippolyte Taine visited England in the summer of 1860, he noticed a shyness among its citizens that seemed similarly fine-grained in its emotional texture. As he observed in *Notes sur l'Angleterre* (1872), this led to odd inconsistencies. 'There are men well-educated, even learned, having travelled, knowing several languages, who are embarrassed in company,' he wrote. 'I know one of them who stammers in a drawing-room, and who on the following day has addressed eight meetings with great eloquence.'

Unlike many of his compatriots, Taine did not think these Englishmen's reserve was the result of an obsession with rank and class that had constipated their emotional lives. It was rather, he felt, that they were brimful of feelings, which were all the more affecting for bubbling up to the surface so rarely to disturb dead-calm waters. The English expressed their passions in ways overlooked by the inattentive, but those who watched carefully could see 'the emotions pass over these complexions, as one sees the colours change upon their meadows'.

Kinglake once told a few close friends of a dream he had years earlier, while he was a Cambridge undergraduate, in which he was attending an anatomical lecture in one of the lower school rooms at his alma mater, Eton. Seated as he was on the highest row of benches, it took him a while to realise that it was his own body being dissected by the professor. He was annoyed at being so far from the front that he could not see or hear very well. Kinglake thought it odd that, in a dream, 'a man may conceive himself to be in perfect possession of his identity, whilst separated from his own body by a distance of several feet'. Kinglake's unconscious, it seems, was giving his social fears an outlet. In his dreams the self he presented to the world was being mercilessly dismembered by others while his private self, feeling left out and ignored, looked helplessly on.

Kinglake spent his last three decades as a virtual recluse, completing a multi-volume, little-read history of the Crimean War. Towards the end of his life, in 1884, he declined an artist's request to sit for a portrait. 'I have all my life suffered from constitutional shyness,' he replied. 'I have never done more than overrule it, so to speak, for the time, without being able to conquer it.'

§

This was how the Victorians saw shyness: as an unwavering disposition, a force one could never defeat – as fixed and as little one's fault as a tendency to suffer from gout or piles. In an age like ours that believes in endless therapeutic experiments to remake the self, it is hard to get inside the head of this collective mentality, which saw shyness as just part of the genetic lottery, never to be overridden. A shyness deemed 'constitutional' could not be remedied, even when it insisted on leading you down the oddest avenues of behaviour.

If you walk the Robin Hood Way through Sherwood Forest today, you will find solid evidence of how odd such behaviour could be. In the middle of the Welbeck estate the bridleway starts to follow the line of a great earthwork scar in the middle of a field. This scar is peppered every few metres or so by what look like tiny greenhouses, made of thick glass covered by overrun grass, which the Ordnance Survey map calls 'Tunnel Skylights'. Underneath them lies a Victorian *grand projet*, a shrine to constitutional shyness.

The source of Lord William Cavendish-Scott-Bentinck's social phobia was unknown. In his twenties, as an army lieutenant, Tory MP and keen horseman, he had been known as handsome and charming. But after Adelaide Kemble turned down his offer of marriage in 1834 – being already secretly married to John Sartoris, the taciturn guest who refused to speak to Kinglake – he withdrew from public life. He still went to the opera, but occupied three stalls in order to have enough space around him.

In 1854, at the age of fifty-four, he became the fifth Duke

of Portland, inheriting the vast Welbeck estate within which to complete his disappearance from the world. It was common for aristocrats to refuse to acknowledge servants, and to require them to turn their faces to the wall when they passed them in corridors, but the duke preferred to make himself rather than his staff invisible. He gave all who worked there the order to pass him as if he were a tree. He had two letter boxes, one for incoming and one for outgoing mail, cut in each of the doors of the five rooms in the abbey he inhabited, so that he and his servants could send notes to each other. His doctor could only ask him questions through his valet, William Lewis, the one person permitted to take his pulse.

Three years into his dukedom he began his great work. Over 600 Irish navvies, many of them fresh from work on the new London Underground, began excavating the solid clay with steam ploughs, and over the next twenty years they built a 15-mile maze of tunnels and rooms under the estate. There were separate walking tunnels for the duke and for his estate workers, so he never had to chance upon them. This world below ground included several reception rooms, a billiards room and the largest ballroom in the country, lit from the roof by huge bull's-eye skylights and at night by thousands of gaslights. It held two thousand people, who could be lowered there twenty at a time via a hydraulic lift. But the duke never played billiards with anyone, or hosted any ball.

When he went to London he used the one-and-a-half mile tunnel running from the coach house to the estate's outskirts, the skylights throwing a ghostly glow down at intervals. The tunnel dipped down deep under a lake and came up near the Worksop road, from where the duke travelled a further three and a half miles overland, with his carriage's silk blinds drawn, to Worksop station. This lightweight coach was lifted on and off the train, with the duke still in it, and met at King's Cross by a coachman with more horses, who rode him to his Cavendish Square townhouse. The duke had the courtyard and back garden there enclosed with an 80-foot-high screen of ground glass and cast iron, so the square's other residents could not see in. This neurotic secrecy inspired rumours that he was hosting circuses or orgies in the grounds. The neighbours swore they could hear horses, whinnying and trotting on the gravel.

Building high walls around yourself is at least the rational act of a recluse. Why the duke chose to burrow underground as well is less clear, because the Welbeck estate was so vast it was easy to hide in a secluded wing, and the tunnel-building created such noise and mess that he was effectively declaring his shyness to the world. One rather sentimental theory is that he was building the tunnels to ease rural unemployment; another is that he wanted to extend the building without spoiling its façade, an explanation that the Pevsner guide dismisses outright, given 'the singularly unattractive frontages of Welbeck Abbey'.

The best explanation is that this is just how dukes behaved. Self-indulgence and eccentricity were part of the job spec. Many of them suffered from the building mania known as *aedificandi libidinem*; some made use of it to feed a shyness that an ungenerous observer might have thought closer to antisocial pride. The sixth Duke of Somerset, the 'proud duke', had a 13-mile wall built round his Sussex estate, employed outriders to clear the local lanes of hoi polloi when he went riding and communicated with his servants only through hand gestures. The eighth Duke of Bedford, the Duke of Portland's contemporary, rarely left his London home, and then only in a carriage with the blinds down. The eleventh Duke of Bedford stationed look-outs around his grounds to warn the electricians wiring Woburn Abbey that he was coming, so they could hide in cupboards.

This probably had less to do with a specifically English reserve than with an occupational hazard of the idle rich everywhere. Those who suffered from shyness and had near-limitless money to feed its whims seemed to be at special risk of ending their lives in silent, reclusive melancholy. While the Duke of Portland was building his tunnels, the shy King Ludwig II of Bavaria was protecting his privacy on a still more epic scale, building a series of fairy-tale palaces in the seclusion of the mountains, with tree houses, hunting lodges and artificial grottoes entered via open-sesame rocks dotted around the grounds for him to vanish still further from the world. Ludwig was always shy, but in early middle age he became fat and lost his teeth and, no longer meeting his own exacting aesthetic standards, stopped attending state banquets or military parades. In two of his castles he installed a 'wishing table' that could be lowered from the dining room via a trapdoor into the kitchen, laden with food, drink and cutlery, and returned to him without his having to be seen. Inspired by the sun king, Louis XIV of France, he now styled himself 'the moon king'. His refusal to go out in daylight led to his ministers hiring a psychiatrist to declare him mad and he was deposed, and drowned in mysterious circumstances.

But those who knew the Duke of Portland did not think him mad. He was known for being kind to his workers, albeit eccentrically, giving them each a donkey and a silk umbrella and building them all a roller-skating rink. According to an article in the *Derbyshire Times* in 1878, he loved 'to penetrate his magnificent domain by a series of burrows, and to startle his dependents by unexpected appearances from these subterranean depths'. If he came across a maid cleaning, he ordered her to go out and skate, whether she wanted to or not.

When the duke died, his three sisters had him laid out in state and invited people to view the body, just to show that the wildest rumours about his skin being disfigured by leprosy or syphilis were untrue. Arriving at Welbeck for the first time, the new duke and his stepsister Lady Ottoline Morrell found the front drive weed-strewn and covered with rubble, its trees decapitated and an exposed, flushing toilet in the corner of every bedroom in the abbey. Through a trapdoor from one of the underground tunnels, Lady Ottoline entered a huge room lined with mirrors and with a ceiling painted the colours of a setting sun. 'The sudden mood of gaiety that had made him decorate it as a ballroom must soon have faded,' she wrote, 'leaving the mock sunset to shine on the lonely figure reflected a hundred times in the mirrors.'

≋

The duke's invisibility inspired a public fascination that carried on after his death, the common condition of shyness being an insufficiently exciting reason for his behaviour. There was a persistent story that he had led a double life as Thomas Druce, who had emerged from obscurity to become the wealthy owner of an early London department store, the Baker Street Bazaar. In a case held at Marylebone and Clerkenwell Police Courts in 1908, the prosecution asserted that Druce was the fifth Duke of Portland, who did not die until 1879, fifteen years after Druce was supposed to have done, and that a fake funeral had been held, with a coffin full of lead and stones, so that the duke might relinquish the double life of which he had grown bored. The Druce family vault in Highgate cemetery was dug up and the coffin opened, disclosing what the judge called 'the silent but no less eloquent voice from the open grave': the shrouded, decaying body of Thomas Druce.

The sixth Duke of Portland, rightly contemptuous of the Druce case, had no time for outlandish theories. Using the same expression that Russel Wallace and Kinglake had used about themselves, he insisted his predecessor's behaviour arose 'merely from constitutional shyness'. Of course, most constitutionally shy people have neither the dedication nor the wherewithal to immortalise their condition in concrete and stone. In an age when dukes were rich enough to indulge their eccentricities almost without limit, this duke built an underground world that an archaeologist of the future might excavate for evidence of the strange habits of mind of the Victorian super-rich.

The sharp rise in death and estate duties in the first decades of the twentieth century brought this age of ducal prodigality to an end. Many of the great estates were sold, broken up and their mansions demolished. After the Second World War the Ministry of Defence took over Welbeck Abbey as an army training college, where the underground ballroom became a gym and recruits held midnight feasts in the tunnels. Dukes no longer had pockets deep enough to build second lives below ground. They hid instead behind the roped-off sections of houses they had sold to the National Trust, which opened them at weekends for two shillings and sixpence a head.

Our modern-day Dukes of Portland are those members of the international mega-moneyed class who build sprawling underground lairs in the poshest parts of Knightsbridge, Belgravia and Notting Hill. Here the £10m street-level mansions are merely the iceberg peak of a gargantuan underworld of multi-storey basements with gyms, bowling alleys, saunas, swimming pools and walk-in cigar humidors. You can tell where these underworlds are being built because the streets and squares are marked by angled conveyor belts carrying soil and rubble from the deep into skips, from where they are carted away to line the freeways of suburban golf courses.

This is just the rich behaving as they always did, using whatever legal means are available to maximise property value and indulge their desires. With no room to build outwards and no planning permission to build upwards, the only way is down. Unsurprisingly, the neighbours who have to put up with years of noisy building work see this kind of *aedificandi libidinem* as a figurative two-fingers to the world, a profligacy with no point other than its own display. And yet, even though I know they are right, part of me cannot help finding the thought of these underground worlds strangely sad. Trophy homes hidden from view, they are a reminder that no amount of money will allow us to escape from ourselves and our insecurities. With the burrowing duke in mind, I have an image in my head of shy hedge fund managers and private equity sharks, sitting alone in their home cinemas or laid out in massage rooms with no one to massage them.

Maybe there is something about this gravitropic instinct that betrays an introspective nature. The horribly embarrassed do, after all, say they wish the ground would swallow them up, like a mole duck-diving into the earth and leaving just a mound of soil behind. Perhaps the Duke of Portland was suffering, in the strictest sense of the phrase, from *nostalgie de la boue*, which has come to mean a longing for uncivilised life, but which literally means nostalgia for the mud of our beginnings, the primordial swamp from which all living things came. He wanted to escape from the world by returning to the earth.

§

This is the paradox of English reserve. Its exaggerated civility and emotional muteness seem designed to distance its practitioners from their more bestial selves, and perhaps from the more feral classes and races they deem beneath them. And yet it can also speak to a basic animal instinct, to hunker down and hide away from everything. The recurrence of this theme in the classics of English children's literature – the 'home under the ground' in Peter Pan's Neverland, the spaces under the floorboards of houses where the Borrowers live, the burrow beneath Wimbledon Common occupied by the Wombles – suggests that it speaks to a common desire. Shyness may have its roots in human self-consciousness, but it leaves us at the mercy of our animal emotions – making us, *in extremis*, shake with fear, run away and hide.

To the Victorians, one animal seemed to embody this kind of shyness in enthrallingly human form. When the first orangutans arrived at the London Zoological Gardens in Regent's Park in the late 1830s, many, including Darwin, were fascinated by these creatures, which seemed so like humans and yet so unfathomable. Wearing looks of settled sadness on their hairless, humanoid faces, they looked like more depressive versions of ourselves. Alfred Russel Wallace, who encountered them during a trip to Sarawak in Borneo in 1854 and even tried to raise a baby orang after he had shot its mother, thought them eerily similar to people, and they fuelled his sense that apes and humans shared an ancestry.

Orangutans were rarely spotted in the wild and were even more rarely seen in groups. Two or three might join up to pick a particularly rich crop of fruit, but they displayed none of the affable greetings and mutual grooming habits that more sociable apes did, and they returned to their solitude without farewells or signs of regret. The males, like reserved English gentlemen with no social skills, often inspired fear and repulsion in the females they sought to attract. Except when mating, they led lonely lives, spending much of their time breaking off branches to build themselves platforms high in the trees.

There were in fact good evolutionary reasons for the orangutan's shyness. The Bornean and Sumatran rainforests where the orang lived were dominated by the tall hardwood trees known as dipterocarps, which have inedible fruits, so the orang had to disperse and forage alone among the widely scattered fruit trees, which could only bear the weight of one bulky ape at a time. The tribespeople living on the edges of the forest, however, tended to anthropomorphise the orangutan's solitariness just as the Victorian English did. One creation myth had it that the orangs were all descended from a single tribesman who, shamed by some misdemeanour, had fled the village for the forest and never came back.

Those who saw orangutans in zoos also remarked on their shyness, which seemed to be of that especially English variety that cohabited with crankiness. An orangutan exhibited at the Royal Aquarium in Westminster in the 1880s was said to be

> fond of retirement, and when an opportunity offers will envelop himself from head to foot in his blanket, any attempt to remove which arouses a speedy retreat on the part of the offending person ... Although somewhat shy, he does not absolutely shun the public gaze, but generally looks straight before him over the heads of the crowd, as though searching for some object familiar to him.

In contrast to the orangutans, the chimpanzees who arrived at London zoo around the same time seemed to channel our more garrulous tendencies. The common idea that chimps were the most sociable of our ape cousins led to them starring in what became the zoo's most popular attraction, the chimpanzee tea party, dressed in their Sunday best and managing a rough approximation of table manners. And yet this was deceptive: the chimps were mercurial, and the females in particular could be as shy and morose as orangutans. A century of chimp research has since tried to decipher their grunts and squeals, or to teach them sign language, but our closest evolutionary cousins remain almost as remote from us as the red ape.

§

If you had happened to be wandering around London zoo one Thursday afternoon in July 1914, a month before the start of the First World War, you might have seen these two species, shy ape and shy Englishman, eyeing each other up. For a young poet, Siegfried Sassoon, was in the monkey house, staring dejectedly through the bars at the chimps and orangutans. One of them looked at him as if about to say something, he wrote later, but then 'sighed and looked away'. The others stared back with 'motionless morosity'.

Perhaps those sullen-looking apes were thinking that this stranger also had the pitiful mien of a caged animal. Sassoon had that quality of English reserve that Taine identified, the sense of an emotional life both bottled up and brimming over. His friends often characterised his shyness as slightly wild and creatural. The journalist and critic Robbie Ross likened him to 'a shy and offended deerhound'. Lady Ottoline Morrell thought only a French word would do: *farouche*, which comes from the Latin *forasticus*, 'out of doors', and means both timid and savage, like a wild animal. His comrades in the trenches nicknamed him Kangaroo. His cricket friends likened him to a heron or crane, lifting his thin legs up high as he languidly retrieved the ball.

Sassoon's trip to London zoo inspired a sonnet, 'Sporting Acquaintances', which records his failed attempt to converse with the chimpanzees and orang-utans and how strange it felt exchanging meaningful glances with them without being able to say a word. Its inspiration, though, was Sassoon's failed conversation not with an ape but with another human. He had gone to the zoo to brood, after a stilted breakfast meeting with a more famous and glamorous poet, Rupert Brooke.

Sassoon was almost unknown at the time, in part because he published his early poems under only his initials. Looking elegantly rumpled and still wearing a Tahiti suntan, the beautiful and confident Brooke inspired in Sassoon a resentful admiration, making him feel as if he was 'one more in the procession of people who were more interested in him than he was in them'. A shy man flattened in the force field of a charismatic, Sassoon imagined Brooke sighing with relief as they said goodbye and he went back to being his unrestrained self. Brooke, it seems, was polite enough and hardly to blame for the fact that people kept falling in love with him. By the time Sassoon's gently barbed account of their meeting was written he could not answer back, having died of blood poisoning in the Aegean on a ship bound for the Dardanelles.

Sassoon's personality, meanwhile, was said to have been transformed by his time as an officer in the Royal Welch Fusiliers, his anger at the death of his beloved comrade, Second Lieutenant David Thomas, in March 1916 turning him into 'Mad Jack'. But Sassoon never saw it this way; he thought of his shyness as a constant that followed him from boyhood to old age. There was something shy even about his bravery as a soldier, which took the form of patrolling the mine craters or wire-cutting in no man's land on his own, without telling his superiors.

In July 1916, during the Battle of the Somme, Sassoon singlehandedly attacked a German trench in Mametz Wood an hour before zero, peppering it with hand grenades and scattering dozens of Germans. But having secured the trench, he sat and read from a book of poems he had in his pocket, and his platoon failed to secure the advantage. He was recommended for a VC for this but failed to win one, probably because his gallantry was not conspicuous enough. Even Sassoon's account of the anti-war protest in which he threw his Military Cross ribbon into the River Mersey was subdued. 'The poor little thing fell weakly on to the water and floated away as though aware of its own futility,' he wrote.

Sassoon's denunciation of the war led to him meeting another paragon of English reserve. W. H. R. Rivers was a renowned scholar and psychiatrist who treated Sassoon at Craiglockhart War Hospital, near Edinburgh, for his diplomatically diagnosed 'shell shock'. Rivers was shy, stammering and a dreadful public speaker. His friend and fellow doctor Walter Langdon-Brown recalled that he once gave a lecture on the subject of 'Fatigue' and that 'before he had finished, his title was writ large on the faces of his audience'.

Rivers's shyness could not be dismissed as class *hauteur* nor, although he had pioneered the practice of anthropological fieldwork while living among the Toda people of southern India, as the neurotically over-civilised reserve cultivated by the imperial Englishman abroad. Rather, shyness had bred in him a loathing for snobbery and social façades. At Craiglockhart he rarely carried his swagger stick or returned salutes. Once, when he caught Sassoon using a visitor's hat as a makeshift football, Rivers simply fixed him with a benevolent half-smile and 'the half-shy look of a middle-aged person intruding on the segregative amusements of the young'. Rivers's shyness had given birth to a calmness and stoicism that few who knew him forgot, even long after he had died. All his life Sassoon had a compelling image of him in his mind, pulling his glasses up on to his head, wrapping his hands round his knee and listening intently to his patient. Sassoon was puzzled by this 'intense survival of his human integrity', the aura that someone so unassertive could retain even after death.

Brooke had been instantly magnetic; Rivers was so by slow increments. He made Sassoon see that shyness did not always have to be an inadequacy but could be a positive quality – something you *were* rather than something that stopped you being who you were. Shyness's energies are often reactive and damage-limiting: fearing that others will share our own disapproving thoughts about ourselves, our goal is often to not make a mistake, to avoid censure rather than go after praise. But not always, as Sassoon found in Rivers. If you could somehow prevent your shyness from clotting into this kind of neurotic risk aversion, it could help you face the world with an added layer of gentleness and curiosity.

※

One afternoon in Oxford in February 1919 Sassoon's friend Osbert Sitwell took him to meet a quite different type of shy Englishman. Being unfit for military service and feeling out of place in a London full of men in uniform, Ronald Firbank had moved to rooms on the High Street, opposite Magdalen College, in November 1915, and stayed there for the next four years. Here, while Sassoon was capturing German trenches solo, Firbank published a series of short comic novels at his own expense: gossamer-thin, waspish stories populated by libidinous cardinals and ancient dowagers. Sitwell had ascertained that, with no one to cook for him, Firbank lived on cold chicken and had in two years spoken only to his charlady and the guard on the London train. When Sitwell and Sassoon met him, Firbank was too nervous to sit still for more than a few seconds, and his few mumbled words were inaudible. But Sassoon was intrigued enough to invite Firbank to his rooms for tea, where his guest refused a plate of crumpets but 'as a gesture of politeness ... slowly absorbed a single grape'. His few words were interrupted by gasping sighs and a gurgling laugh.

Shortly after this meeting Firbank returned to London and resumed some of his pre-war haunts, attending private views and first nights assiduously. It seemed he preferred to act out his shyness in public and turn it into a piece of avant-garde performance art. For his discomfort in a theatre was so great that it became extremely conspicuous: he would stand up in the middle of an act, or vanish so far into his seat that he was virtually upside down. He was often found at the old Café Royal or the Eiffel Tower Restaurant, haunt of bohemian artists, sat from noon to midnight jotting down the odd line of dialogue in a notebook, drinking from a perpetually refilled brandy glass and pecking at a sliver of toast smeared with caviar. The waiters knew not to speak to him. Once, at the Café Royal, he had hidden under the table when the maître d' tried to engage him in conversation.

Firbank's assortment of gestures – admiring the backs of his hands, grasping his head, plucking at his tie – seem with hindsight to be the quintessence of camp, a word only just starting to acquire its current meaning. His painted nails and rouged cheeks should really have given the game away. But to his contemporaries these mannerisms seemed to signal only a kind of hyperbolic shyness. Effeminate behaviour, long before it became synonymous with homosexuality, denoted conspicuous idleness and aestheticism, a refusal to join in with the manly, bourgeois values of work and commerce. It was Firbank's attention-stealing shyness, not his undeclared homosexuality, that announced his separation from this 'straight' world. In his novel *The Flower beneath the Foot*, set in a vaguely Balkan country, shyness is spoken of in the hushed tones normally reserved for homosexuality. When Lady Something describes her daughter as being 'of the Violet persuasion', Queen Thleeanouhee replies indignantly: 'Where *I reign*, shyness is a quality which is entirely unknown …!'

It was odd that Sassoon, who had outstared the killing fields of the Somme, should find this fragile and foppish man so fascinating. Perhaps he admired the way Firbank flaunted his shyness rather than skulking round as Sassoon did, trying but failing to keep up his end of the conversation. Firbank's flat refusal to follow any social rules was in its own way admirable, and, while he would have been useless in a Somme trench, he had a different kind of tenacity. At a time when international travel was logistically difficult, this seeming social incompetent managed somehow to get himself from place to place, negotiating successfully with station porters and hotel staff. In an age when flying was the preserve of the intrepid, he regularly caught a plane from London to southern Europe or north Africa and back, earnestly announcing his itinerary in the *Times* court circular. *Mr. Ronald Firbank has returned to London after a prolonged tour in the East, and is making a few weeks' stay at 2, West Chapel-Street, Mayfair.*

Mr. Ronald Firbank has gone to Italy for the winter and will be for the next six months at the Palazzo Orsini, Rome. It wasn't clear to whom these messages were aimed, since Firbank hardly ever received visitors in London, or anywhere else.

As Rivers had done, Firbank offered up more primary source material for Sassoon's ongoing investigations into the curious condition of English reserve. T. E. Lawrence once said that if he were asked to 'export the ideal Englishman to an international exhibition', he would choose Sassoon. Born and raised in the Kentish Weald, educated at Marlborough and Cambridge, a country gentleman and fox-hunter, he certainly looked the part. But he was also homosexual, and a Jew, of Persian ancestry, who converted to Catholicism late in life. He wanted desperately to belong but, like many shy people, extracted a certain masochistic pride out of not belonging. For all his self-involvement, Sassoon also had a writer's fascination with other people and the poses they struck. While he seemed to others like the epitome of the reserved English gentleman, he was a careful dissector of the contradictions in this identity, the way that, in people like Firbank, it brought shyness and self-regard together in a surreal, half-acted personality.

Many of Sassoon's social circle were afflicted by this kind of English reserve – and like him they still seemed to enjoy a glittering social life, mixing in that upper-middle-class sphere in which high society met the arts. The artist Rex Whistler managed to be taken up by fashionable London hostesses and have many men and women fall in love with him, despite the fact that he said hardly anything, never replied to letters or answered the telephone and lost or forgot to cash many of the cheques he received for his work. Another of Sassoon's friends, the composer and artist Lord Berners, suffered from an extreme reserve that made him blink incessantly and laugh in a strangulated way like a blocked sneeze. Stories about his shyness, probably apocryphal, accumulated: that he wore a mask when out driving his Rolls-Royce, or would affect scarlet fever to keep a railway carriage to himself. Sassoon's friend T. E. Lawrence, meanwhile, managed to be both extravagantly reclusive and an Olympic-class networker who was always, Berners said, 'backing into the limelight'.

Sassoon seemed to have made it his life's work to learn how to be an Englishman by observing others performing the role. 'I wish I could understand why I enjoy adapting the attitude of a sort of social and slightly sinister Enoch Arden', he confided to his diary in 1925. In Tennyson's poem, Enoch Arden returns from sea after ten years of being presumed dead and never reveals to his wife that he is alive, because he loves her too much to spoil her new happiness with another man. He dies of a broken heart. All his life Sassoon talked of his 'Enoch Arden complex': his desire to stand back and watch others unseen, like a ghost.

§

In 1927 Sassoon briefly abandoned his habit of looking on from the edges and did something reckless: he began an affair with a beautiful young aristocrat, Stephen Tennant. Tennant had been earmarked for artistic greatness by his mother, Pamela, Lady Glenconner, a bohemian soul keen to distance herself from the family's fortune, earned from the manufacture of powdered bleach. She had published her eleven-year-old son's utterings in her book *The Sayings of the Children*. At thirteen he had his line-and-wash drawings displayed in a solo exhibition at a South Kensington gallery and reviewed kindly by strategically placed art critics. In his early twenties he wrote imperious style notes for the *Daily Mail*: 'Do not beam fatuously or leave a smile on your face or look breathlessly enthusiastic like a dog with its tongue out – it's a question of poise, not pose.' His hair was waved and sprinkled with gold dust; he wore magenta lipstick, mascara and gold earrings. At the family home, Wilsford Manor in Wiltshire, he and his fellow bright young things held pyjama parties and staged masques on the lawn dressed as nuns and shepherds. Someone less like Sassoon it seemed hard to imagine.

And yet they were not so unalike. As a student at the Slade School of Art, Tennant had skipped life classes because he could not face his fellow students, and had formed an *amitié amoureuse* with Rex Whistler. Evelyn Waugh later used Tennant and Whistler as his models for the shy Charles Ryder and the flamboyant Sebastian Flyte in *Brideshead Revisited*. For all his charm, Sebastian is the one who says he wants to run away from his family, and who ends his days as a recluse, a depressed alcoholic slowly dying in a Tunisian monastery.

Tennant had the same knack for combining outrageous behaviour with profound inhibition. In *Vile Bodies* Waugh had nailed the polarising private slang of the bright young things, in which everything was either 'divine' or socially mortifying: 'too, too shaming', 'perfectly sheepish' or 'shy-making'. Tennant lived by these extremes. The great moment of his life, he said, was when a coachload of tourists in St Moritz applauded him for being so beautiful. And yet he would hide in the toilets at The Ivy because he could not go into the restaurant before his friends had arrived. He loved Wilsford because, hidden in a mist-prone hollow in the Wiltshire Downs and hedged in by evergreen yews and oaks, it let him shut out the world. By 1929 Sassoon was virtually a live-in carer there, Tennant having taken to his bed, first with TB and then with an unspecific illness diagnosed as neurasthenia, that catch-all term for early twentieth-century melancholia.

In 1933, a year after Tennant had ended their affair simply by refusing to see him, Sassoon married Hester Gatty and found his own retreat about 30 miles away at Heytesbury House, a Georgian mansion near Warminster. The marriage soon faltered, but Sassoon came to love the remoteness of this place and the solitude of its woods. As a young boy in the late 1940s, Ferdinand Mount met the 'Hermit of Heytesbury' when he and his father were invited for tea. They wandered round the back of the house trying doors, finding their way eventually into an unlit drawing room that seemed empty, Mount recalled, 'until our eyes focused enough to see the celebrated gaunt hawk's profile outlined against the dying light'. Sassoon 'pushed a plate of dry cucumber sandwiches at us and began to talk in a shy undertone'.

All the stories about visiting Sassoon are like this. He invited almost everyone he met to tea, with the same grumble that no one ever came to see him. If they rang to confirm, he sounded edgy and regretful of having made the invitation, but told them to come anyway. At the appointed time they found the lodge unpeopled, and no one answering the door at the big house. They gained entry round the back and eventually discovered Sassoon in one of the rooms. At the start of any such encounter his shyness made him a bundle of self-concern with, according to his nun friend Dame Felicitas Corrigan, 'the emaciated face of an El Greco saint and the pent-up energy of a hydrogen bomb'. He would, without saying hello or looking at his guests, just start talking, into his lap or over their heads, about poetry, the servant problem, cricket or himself – as if he had been lecturing the air and they had just happened to catch him at it. His sentences were contorted and unfinished, and accompanied by nervous spasms and claspings of his face.

Those who made return visits learned that the trick was to catch his eye after an hour or so, and then swiftly interject so that conversation of a kind could occur. His friend Haro Hodson compared this indirect approach to gentling and bridling a horse. The adjective 'shy' first entered the English language in the thirteenth century to describe horses that were skittish, high-mettled or startled by strange noises and fast-moving objects, and the word did not migrate from horses to people until the early seventeenth century, being used twice by Shakespeare in *Measure for Measure*: 'A shy fellow was the Duke ... as shy, as grave, as just, as absolute, as Angelo.' Residual associations of shyness with the flightiness and stubbornness of horses remained until at least the end of the nineteenth century. According to an 1891 source cited in the *Oxford English Dictionary*, 'the wind is said to be shy when it will barely allow a vessel to sail on her course'.

Horse handlers still talk of 'head shyness', which can make brushing or bridling these animals a battle of wills. As soon as you pick up the reins, a shy horse will twig what you are up to and toss its head in circles or stretch it high and away from you – rather, in fact, like Sassoon jerking his head around, as if he did not want people to settle on any aspect of his face for long. Canny horse handlers will hold the bridle behind their backs until the horse lowers its head, and then seize it by the nose so that it opens its jaw in annoyance or surprise.

Eventually, like a halter-broken mare, Sassoon calmed down. The jerky movements receded, his sentences began to join up coherently – indeed he became astonishingly articulate, as if he were reciting perfectly turned sentences learned by heart – and he became blithely unaware of the darkening room, the ringing telephone, the kettle he had boiled half an hour ago. One of the Benedictine teacher-monks at Downside School, Dom Hubert Van Zeller, took some boys to visit him, and Sassoon became so entranced with his own monologue that he went on pouring tea into a cup long after it was full. Another time, while signing a book for one of the boys, he wrote 'To Siegfried … from Siegfried Siegfried.' Oddly, his diaries reveal that even in the middle of these torrents of self-preoccupied speech he was listening to each question he ignored and picking up every movement of his guests in the corner of his eye.

In his latter years his social life amounted mainly to playing cricket for Heytesbury village alongside his estate workers and the local farmhands. His hapless batting was tactfully hidden well down the order, but he insisted on fielding at the exposed position of mid-on, where he would let the approaching ball hit him hard on the shins before slowly picking it up. Since it was his land and he let the cricket club use it for free, no one could stop him leaving the pitch to lean on the fence or even walking off in the middle of a game if he got bored.

With its emphasis on good form, the things that were unsayable or did not need to be said, cricket was a sport that might have been devised especially for the reserved Englishman. A cricket match had a general air of calmness and quiet and unfolded slowly, enjoyed not for orgasmic moments like goals or tries but for its *longueurs* and its subtle shifts in the balance of power, as two teams felt their way to an advantage to ripples of polite applause. On a cricket field, nicely spaced out from the other fielders, Sassoon had just the right amount of solitude. In the after-match teas at the Angel Inn, he could handle the undemanding conversational currency that dealt in Somerset cricketers' batting averages and misty-eyed remembrances of old village matches. Anyone who tried to talk to him about deeper matters was quickly cut off.

§

Stephen Tennant, who dropped in on Sassoon sporadically in his early years at Heytesbury, had long since stopped calling. He was now in the grip of a shyness that, like Firbank's, had begun as a pose but turned into something painfully real. He had taken to his bed and there, propped up by pillows and surrounded by scent bottles and powder boxes, wrote exquisitely illustrated letters which one recipient, Stephen Spender, thought of as 'the essence of English retention – objects for private consumption, deluxe *samizdats*'. When Christopher Isherwood visited Tennant in June 1961, he described his strewing of books, clothes and jewellery all over the floors and furniture as 'partly like arrangements for still-life painting, partly like drunken unpacking'. Tennant had stopped looking in mirrors but would caress his once-revered cheekbones to be assured they were still there. Wilsford's garden was now a weedy wilderness, and a barricade of dock and nettles cut the house off from the nearby River Avon. The trees had died, throttled by the ivy the master of the house ordered never to be cut.

At the end of 1970 the novelist V. S. Naipaul and his wife, Pat, became tenants of Teasel Cottage, a bungalow in the manor grounds. Naipaul's patron Christopher Tennant, Lord Glenconner, had renovated the cottage for his younger brother because he thought Wilsford an extravagance for a single man with no income. Stephen had refused even to enter it. But he liked having an author as a neighbour and would send him, via his servants John and Mary Skull, the odd painting or poem. In fifteen years there

Naipaul never met Tennant, but acquired 'an immense sympathy' for him – partly, he conceded, because he remained a phantasm and he had no need to cater to his high-maintenance oddnesses.

In Naipaul's lightly fictionalised novel *The Enigma of Arrival* Tennant becomes a symbol for a country going quietly to seed. Like Naipaul, the book's unnamed narrator comes from Trinidad, goes to Oxford, becomes a writer and settles down in this emblematically English setting with his (also unnamed) landlord living in a nearby, semi-ruined manor. In 1949 or 1950 his landlord had simply withdrawn from the world, suffering from a malaise that the narrator sees as 'something like accidia, the monk's torpor or disease of the Middle Ages'. Naipaul's wife, Pat, is erased from the narrative, which leaves the landlord and narrator entwined in silent solitude, both as eager to be unseen as the other. Even though his landlord's fortune derives from Trinidadian plantations, the narrator feels kindly disposed and connected to him through the empire. For the narrator too is shy, ascribing it to 'the rawness of my colonial's nerves', which have remained even when all the usual anxieties about social gaucherie, sexual inhibition and unripe talent have faded with the end of youth.

The Enigma of Arrival contains very little dialogue, and the writing is hypnotically slow and self-conversing. The narrator measures out the seasons and agricultural rhythms in this melancholy, empty landscape in which, like the rural darkness that can cover the land in an instant, 'big things could happen almost secretly'. With no actual meeting with him to cloud the issue, the narrator begins to see the landlord's shyness as symbolic of this setting, and his slow decline as mirroring the death of the old rural ways in a new era of mechanised farming and urban living. He catches a glimpse of him only twice, once as a flash of thigh being sunbathed by its owner in his garden and then, in the passenger seat of a passing car, as a bald head with thin strands of hair carefully combed over it, a benign expression and a slow wave of the hand. In that wave, just his fingertips making an arc above the dashboard, the narrator sees 'the shyness that went at the same time with a great vanity … that wasn't so much a wish not to be seen as a wish to be applauded on sight'.

⦚

I have a memory of seeing a sketch from the 1960s BBC comedy show *Not Only … But Also* in which Peter Cook, playing Greta Garbo in a wig, beret and sunglasses, swept down a London street in an open-topped car with a megaphone bellowing 'I vant to be alone!' It puts me in mind of Tennant, who, even during his deepest hibernations, would make the odd trip into nearby Wilton or Salisbury in an instantly noticeable combo of taut pink shorts and camel coat. Having retreated from the world because it would not adjust to his exalted sense of himself, he could not stop his shyness segueing into showmanship.

But shyness can be an implement of passive-aggressive wilfulness and still be honestly arrived at. Tennant seems to have fallen for a common self-deception: being unable to stop nurturing and feeding his unhappiness because he thought it was what made him who he was. If his shyness was an act, it was one he believed in and kept up for years at great emotional cost. It was a word-and note-perfect piece of method acting of which Stanislavski or Lee Strasberg would have been proud. Like all these virtuosos of English reserve, he must have felt snared by his own shyness, but he could not shake it off. The mask had stuck to his face.

Tennant died in February 1987, a few weeks before *The Enigma of Arrival* was published. His house was sold to an American businessman, and all its contents were auctioned off in a marquee on the lawn. Everything in what Sotheby's billed as 'an English eccentric's dream house' went under the hammer, from the zebra-skin pouffes to the garden statuary that the auction house's director, Christopher King, had rescued after hours of thrashing through the undergrowth. Sylvia Blandford, Tennant's housekeeper-cum-nurse in his last years, expressed her relief that he was not alive to see all this, since 'he was such a private person, he didn't like anyone touching his belongings'.

Not everyone believed Tennant was so protective of his privacy. V. S. Naipaul's friend Paul Theroux revealed that he had been irritated by this 'idle, silly queen', who had led a meritless life but had convinced everyone he was *eccentric* – the word the English always gave to 'wealthy lunatics'. An American in long-term residence in London, Theroux had his own droll take on English reserve, that blend of 'shyness and suspicion ... wary curiosity and frugal kindness' which could, in severe cases like Tennant's, become a set of well-rehearsed, self-dramatising clichés. To Theroux, Tennant's yin-and-yang of emotional incontinence and shyness belonged to a vanishing age in which cosseted members of the upper-middle classes had their neuroses indulged by their loyal retinue.

Afflicted by English reserve myself, I am inclined to be a little more generous about it. The fact that extreme shyness can seem attention-seeking has always tended to arouse distrust in the non-shy. To an unfriendly observer it can look like inside-out narcissism, an overcooked performance, self-absorption masquerading as modesty. Since shyness rarely explains itself, it becomes a *tabula rasa* on which others can write their own meanings. The psychotherapist and writer Adam Phillips suggests that it has a bad reputation 'among the more glibly suspicious – among, that is, the psychologically-minded' because 'the ways in which shyness seeks and controls attention are always more vivid than whatever else the shy are so privately struggling with'. While we happily live with our own contradictory personality traits, we find other people's contradictions harder to accept, even though we should really know by now that consistency is a rare human quality.

It does feel that, in our increasingly confessional age, with its cult of sincerity and authenticity, people are becoming more suspicious of those who hold back, as if diffidence must be in some way fraudulent or cheapened by ulterior motives. A colleague of mine told me that he had given Daphne du Maurier's novel *Rebecca* to a friend, who had come back to him irritated and affronted by the unnamed narrator's shyness, which he dismissed as 'arrogance in low heels'. Shyness now often inspired such impatience, my colleague reflected, for it had 'lost its virtuous glow in a tell-all age'.

Of course, it is true that shyness can co-exist with self-absorption. It is based, after all, on feeling different from the crowd, and, however hedged round that is by self-doubt, it can amount to an inflated sense of one's own worth – a low-heeled arrogance. But being aware of this hazard certainly never helped *me* to avoid it. Nor do I think we can ever know enough about someone else simply to dismiss their shyness, or indeed any other part of their personality, as a sham. Separating someone's social performance from their authentic feelings is rarely straightforward, especially given the boundless human capacity for self-delusion.

Every self contains multitudes: we are all an amalgam of public and private versions of ourselves. A public self is also, in its way, real. Perhaps it is even more real than a private self, given the enormous effort we invest in its successful realisation. What a suffocatingly earnest world it would be if we all had to be an open book to everyone. There should surely be room in the gene pool for behaviour that is awkward or mulish, or that experiments with different ways of being ourselves, or that invites accusations of pretension or artifice – even if it involves ignoring passers-by in the desert, building ballrooms below ground or taking to bed for thirty years with our scent bottles. English reserve had its histrionic and affected aspects, and must have seemed like a put-on to those annoyed by it. But who really knows where a performance begins and ends? Genuine shyness, that truly odd state of mind, comes in many disguises.

3

HOW EMBARRASSING

In the first years of the Second World War, a man known as 'the Prof' stalked the corridors of Bletchley Park mansion wearing an air of deep unease. He could not even bring himself to look at people he knew as they passed each other, his gaze staying fixed on the nearest wall, which he touched lightly with his fingers as if wanting to cling on to something. The new Government Code and Cypher School at Bletchley was an industrial operation, as busy as a small town, with hundreds of secretaries and code-breakers scuttling between the prefab huts and the teleprinters in the main building. For the first time in his life the Prof was confronted by large numbers of women. 'I once offered him a cup of tea but he shrank back with fear,' recalled Sarah Norton, who worked near by, in Hut 4. He coped with these young women in corridors, she said, by 'shambling down to the canteen in a curious sideways step, his eyes fixed to the ground'.

Alan Turing was cursed with that peculiarly middle-class English talent for social embarrassment. You would not guess it from photographs, which reveal a boyish face turned in matinee-idol half-profile, his hair neatly gelled, but if you met him in the flesh Turing looked eternally awkward. He was covered in ink stains, his fingernails were bitten raw, his tie was badly knotted, his jacket buttons were in the wrong holes and his hair stood on end except for a too-long fringe which he had to toss back and out of his eyes. It was as if he saw his body as a mere encumbrance he had to lug round to service his enormous brain. For while this body was uncoordinated and embarrassable, his brilliant mind worked as reliably as a computer – that machine he hadn't got round to inventing yet.

According to his mother, Sara, Turing was a vivacious boy who suddenly became, at the age of ten, remote and withdrawn. She blamed this on their painful partings when he was dropped off at prep school at the start of a new term and he would rush down the drive in pursuit of his parents' retreating car. 'He appears self-contained and is apt to be solitary,' wrote Turing's housemaster at Sherborne. 'This is not due to moroseness, but simply I think a shy disposition.' Sherborne presumably aggravated this disposition when, in his first year there, he had to participate in an initiation rite in which he was forced into a waste paper bin and kicked across the common room by the other boys, who also liked to trap him under the floorboards. Sherborne, like many English public schools saturated with the Victorian ideals of muscular Christianity, believed it better to be a good mixer than a swot, especially a swot in the philistine sciences. In one of his reports Turing's headmaster accused him of having no 'esprit de corps' and cautioned that 'if he is to be solely a *Scientific Specialist*, he is wasting his time at a Public School'.

As a young man, Turing's ability to turn his forensic mind to dissecting his own awkwardness made him a skilful semiotician of the social life to which he was so ill-suited, a sort of code-breaker of human behaviour. While studying at Princeton in the mid-1930s, he tried to decrypt American manners. The American habit of saying 'aha' while listening to someone else, because they thought silence might be rude, unnerved him – as did the startlingly informal tradespeople, such as the laundry van man who put his arm on Turing's shoulder while speaking to him. 'Whenever you thank them for anything, they say "You're welcome",' he wrote to his mother. 'I rather liked it at first, thinking I was welcome, but now I find it comes back like a ball thrown against a wall, and become positively apprehensive.'

§

While at Princeton, Turing published a classic paper, 'On computable numbers', the first attempt to describe what a computer might look like. Just a dozen years later, in June 1948, his small team at Manchester University persuaded such a machine to work. Turing became a fervent proselytiser for artificial intelligence, believing that this 'mechanical brain' would one day compete on equal terms with a human brain. He even thought it would be able to write sonnets as well as Shakespeare, although he conceded that the comparison was a little unfair because a sonnet written by a machine would be better appreciated by another machine.

In 1952 he and his colleague Christopher Strachey created a computer program, using sentence-building algorithms and synonyms from *Roget's Thesaurus*, that could write love letters. 'Darling Sweetheart,' went one, 'You are my avid fellow feeling. My affection curiously clings to your passionate wish. My liking yearns to your heart. You are my wistful sympathy: my tender liking. Yours beautifully …' This bit of whimsy had a poignant undertow. Turing could never write such a love letter himself – not just because he was shy, but because he was gay. Homosexuality was illegal, and a letter might have incriminated him.

Computer code relies on a kind of logic that trades in form rather than meaning. Using such formal logic, we cannot infer a falsehood from a true set of premises, even if we have no idea what those premises mean – which allows us, for example, to make algebraic calculations or follow the unchanging rules of chess. For this type of thinking Turing showed that a machine, even a primitive

1940s one, could outstrip our feeble brains. But humans are not automatons, solving problems by algorithm. They have inherited that peculiar offshoot of human evolution, self-consciousness, which allows them to imagine what others might be thinking of them, and to dream up embarrassing scenarios that might not even be close to happening. A computer is unembarrassable for, while it may be hyper-intelligent, it is too rational to care what a person, or indeed another computer, thinks of it. A computer cannot be shy.

If anyone was proof of the human brain's chaotic non-computability, it was Alan Turing. Early one morning in the autumn of 1950 his colleague Max Newman's young son discovered him on the doorstep of their house in his jogging clothes. Turing explained that he had set out on a run and on the way decided to invite the Newmans for dinner. Not wishing to disturb them, he was trying to scratch his invitation on a rhododendron leaf with a twig. No computer could ever have replicated such a stupid-brilliant intuitive leap.

Unlike computers, people are both intelligent and unintelligent, prone to irrational thought patterns that create the very situation they want to avoid. Turing's efforts to escape attention succeeded only in attracting it and making him more embarrassed. His contorted efforts to avoid eye contact in corridors just made him more noticeable. He sought solitude in running, but, dressed in a pair of ancient flannel trousers tied at the waist with rope, sometimes with an alarm clock attached, he could not have been more conspicuous. He carried this alarm clock on trains in lieu of a wristwatch, startling everyone in the carriage, including himself, when it went off.

Mathematics offered a possible escape route. In his book *A Mathematician's Apology*, written in 1940, the Cambridge maths professor G. H. Hardy had celebrated the remote and beautiful uselessness of numbers, and expressed the hope that his discipline would remain 'gentle and clean' and play no part in the war. Turing attended Hardy's lectures at Cambridge and knew him slightly at Princeton, but their mutual reserve ensured they were never friends. Hardy's shyness was similarly cultivated in rough public-school life – in his case, at Winchester. Like Turing, he would pass acquaintances in the street without acknowledging them and loathed having his picture taken. He had no mirror in his rooms, not even a shaving mirror, and on entering a hotel room the first thing he did was to cover up the mirrors with towels – despite the fact that, as his friend C. P. Snow pointed out, 'all his life he was good-looking quite out of the ordinary'.

Turing was certainly drawn to Hardy's idea that mathematics was a consolingly parallel universe of abstract relationships, a refuge from the baffling social conventions that blighted his relations with others. But, in the end, he was far too interested in the real world and in other people to be Hardy's true disciple. Turing's shyness, like so many people's, was erratic. He could be nervy and confident, shy and sociable, serious and witty, embarrassed and unembarrassable, depending on the setting.

Turing's work reflected this conflicted personality, being highly abstract and theoretical and yet also directed out at the world. His interest in combining pure mathematical logic with practical problem-solving turned out to be a perfect preparation for codebreaking. And so, to G. H. Hardy's chagrin perhaps, mathematics ended up having a decisive effect on the war after all. At Bletchley the Nazi war machine found itself outflanked by a motley band of maths wranglers, chess champions and crossword fanatics, with Turing as their reluctant front man, stalking the corridors looking down at his shoes.

§

Turing believed that a computer's mechanical brain, interacting rationally with the world by ticking through its algorithms and dispensing intelligence like a vending machine, was not so very different from a human one. But just as he was predicting that computers would one day think like us, another highly original mind was beginning its own very different soundings into the inimitable strangeness of human self-consciousness. A few days before Christmas 1949 a young doctoral student, Erving Goffman, arrived by boat on the small Shetland island of Unst. He stayed for the next year and a half, claiming to be an American studying the economics of crofting. In fact, he was a Canadian studying people.

Unst is the most northerly inhabited island in Britain. Goffman settled in the main village of Baltasound, first in the hotel and then in a tiny cottage he bought from a local crofter. The island's population of about a thousand was an enclosed community, with outsiders kept at a distance. Visiting seamen were offered no more than a brief nod or a word about the weather, and tourists found themselves cut out of conversations by a private code of gestures and dialect words.

But this stand-offishness was not just reserved for visitors. The islanders were also shy of each other, and so self-effacing that they rarely used the word 'I' in conversation. If they received a compliment, women would either cast their heads down in discomfiture or interrupt the perpetrator by rushing at him with waving arms. When the island's young men sailed off for the mainland, or to join the merchant navy or the whaling expeditions, there were no tears, nor were these shed at funerals. The only time the island's women cried was in the darkened community hall during film showings by the Highland and Islands Film Guild. The shyest islanders of all were the children. When the primary school had visitors, the pupils would cover their faces with their hands, scrutinising the stranger through their fingers. They thought they could make themselves invisible by making others invisible to them. 'Shetlanders take some knowing,' wrote W. P. Livingstone, in his 1947 guide *Shetland and the Shetlanders*. 'It is the children who defeat one; well-behaved, they are excessively shy, and it is a triumph if you get a word from them.'

The shyness of Shetlanders was sometimes explained by their Nordic ancestry: the islands had been under Norse rule until 1472, and Unst is closer to Bergen than to Aberdeen. Nordic people have a reputation for shyness – a product, perhaps, of a Calvinist Protestant tradition that shunned brazenness and ostentation, the freezing temperatures that necessitated taciturnity when outdoors, and the ethnic homogeneity which meant that shared experiences and feelings needed only to be implied rather than said out loud. Henrik Ibsen, who drank heavily to cure his own shyness, described the people of his home town of Skien in Norway as 'afraid openly to surrender to a mood or to let themselves be carried away; they suffer from shyness of the soul'. The Shetland character, it was said, retained a similar Viking reticence nursed in the cold, dark winters and unpeopled wilds of Ultima Thule.

A more specific cause of their shyness, which Goffman alighted on, was the historical relationship between the crofters and the laird. Until the 1895 crofting act, the landlord could hike rents without warning. Crofters feared that any show of wealth on their part might lead to a rent increase, and so they hid any evidence of how much they owned and, more generally, of what they thought and felt. Their behaviour at auctions was symptomatic. Household furnishings were worth a lot second-hand on Unst because of high freight charges from the mainland, so auctions were big events. But bidders risked showing their neighbours how much money they had, or they might find themselves competing with a friend for the same lot. So they used unobtrusive signals meant to be seen only by the auctioneer, such as lifting a hand half-way out of a pocket or catching his eye with an equivocal look. This meant that the auctioneer often made mistakes, and people were sold things they had no idea they had bid for.

Goffman wondered if the self-consciousness he observed might also be due, paradoxically, to the lack of privacy on Unst. The island was just 12 miles long and 5 miles wide, mostly low-lying peat moorland, with little vegetation and no trees, so crofters could easily see the state of each other's crops and livestock, and the mistakes they made when farming them. Since they did not like having visitors without advance warning, they would look out of the kitchen window every quarter of an hour or so, or when they heard the croft collies barking, to see if anyone was approaching. They deployed a tool every islander owned: a pocket telescope.

One situation, though, demanded sociability. Since Unst's roads were never crowded, when people crossed paths on them they could not convincingly pretend not to have seen each other. The solution was to exchange a few innocuous words. *'Ae, ae.' 'Ae, ae.' 'Foine day.' 'Foine day.' 'Voo is du?' 'Nae sae bad.'* Only two groups were excused having to acknowledge others like this on Unst's roads: children under the age of fourteen, and anyone inside one of Unst's fourteen motor cars. Motorists were obliged simply to lift one hand off the wheel and smile when they passed someone. This was the only occasion on Unst, Goffman noted, when men smiled in greeting. Similar exchanges occurred if people found themselves sat next to each other at social events in the community hall. *'Good crowd.' 'Aye, fine crowd.' 'So.' 'So so.' 'Well, well.' 'Well, well.'* If anyone heard an opinion they did not agree with, they relied on what Goffman called 'terminative echoes', ways of ending the conversation civilly. *'There's something in what you say.' 'I dinna kin.' 'It's past spaekin about.'*

Unst had several people with deformed faces or cleft lips and palates, whom the other islanders found it hard to talk to without being distracted by their looks. These people kept out of sight and were described as 'shy', but Goffman thought they had sacrificed themselves for the community's sake, withdrawing from situations in which they might cause embarrassment and disrupt the smoothness of social occasions. The islanders also had a ready supply of ruses to get round their shyness: icebreakers such as guess-the-weight competitions, whist and musical chairs, and foolproof conversational topics such as the birth of lambs and foals, or the catch of the island's two fishing boats. The most reliable antidote to shyness, brewed in nearly every home, was beer.

※

Goffman's fieldwork, written up as his PhD thesis for the University of Chicago, 'Communication Conduct in an Island Community', formed the basis for his research on embarrassment, which took up much of the rest of his life. Embarrassment, he argued, grew out of 'unfulfilled expectations'. Any social encounter consisted of people projecting claims to be an acceptable public self – someone reasonably courteous, coherent, presentable and aware of social codes – and having those claims verified by others. Embarrassment occurred when something threw doubt upon those claims and the encounter was shipwrecked on assumptions that no longer held. The person who regularly failed to convince his peers in this way, Goffman wrote, 'truly wears the leper's bell'.

The physical symptoms of embarrassment – blushing, blanching, stuttering, sweating, blinking, shaking and even fainting – were bad enough. But embarrassment was a social calamity as well, being evidence of low status, moral shame and other unwelcome traits. Hence the frantic efforts to conceal it with false smiles, fake laughter and averted gazes. Goffman thought that embarrassment was alarming because it exposed the precariousness of the social order. Since everyone had to verify whether everyone else had an acceptable social self, embarrassment was contagious, spreading out in ever-widening circles of unease like ripples on water. Oddly, it was only the minor shame of embarrassment that was infectious, and witnessing others suffer more serious humiliations inspired simply *Schadenfreude*.

Goffman revealed little about himself. Even as he emerged as an academic star, he seldom spoke at conferences, gave interviews or allowed his publishers to release his photo. One rare biographical morsel he served up was that his interest in human interaction stemmed from his shyness as a young man, aggravated by his being only 5 foot 4. At the local dance hall in Dauphin, Manitoba, he would stand in the doorway between the bar and the dance floor, unable to afford another drink and too embarrassed to ask a girl to dance. Here, on the edge of things, his career as a watcher of social rituals began.

Goffman seems to have felt rather at home among the shy Shetlanders of Unst, mucking in by cutting peat for winter fires and joining in at the community hall socials, where he was admired for being able to take the ultra-strong home-made beer which the men nipped outside to swig. But mostly he kept his distance. 'My real aim,' he wrote on the first page of his PhD thesis, 'was to be an observant participant, rather than a participating observer.' Perhaps it was Goffman's shyness that led him to avoid the direct interviewing most sociologists did, and to rely instead on overheard conversations and discreet surveillance. This suited the islanders, who felt inhibited by people note-taking on their conversations and did not like touching on personal issues. Goffman's thesis records that he did only a few interviews on matters which 'the islanders felt were proper subjects for interviews'. After returning to America, he was never again so at ease with strangers. His later books appear to have involved no fieldwork at all, other than reading other people's work.

The world according to Goffman, where an embarrassed person had to be avoided like a lurgy victim to save others from the stain of awkwardness, sounded bleak. But it was also a world in which people colluded sweetly to shield each other from ridicule. Our collective investment in the polite fictions of social life can be a torment but can also inspire a touching solidarity. In *The Expression of the Emotions in Man and Animals*, Darwin tells the story of a shy and nervous man who had a dinner held in his honour. When he rose to give his speech, which he had learned by rote, he said not a word while behaving as if he was speaking animatedly, and clearly believing he was. His friends 'loudly applauded the imaginary bursts of eloquence, whenever his gestures indicated a pause, and the man never discovered that he had remained the whole time completely silent'. Darwin could see, like Goffman, that we were bundles of insecurity, serial appeasers, joined in a benign conspiracy with the rest of the human race not to discomfort each other.

We will go to ornate lengths not to embarrass ourselves and those around us, often inadvertently embarrassing ourselves more in the process. The comedian Michael Bentine once claimed that his paternal grandfather, Don Antonio Bentin Palamerra, vice-president of Peru, was too self-conscious to disrupt proceedings to leave the Chamber of Deputies to relieve himself, and would keep a fast horse and carriage ready to hurry him home at the end of each session. The strain on his kidneys and bladder was such that, according to Bentine, he contracted renal carcinoma and died, as president-elect, aged fifty-five. Embarrassment is such an abysmal fate that people will die in order to avoid it. The American doctor Henry J. Heimlich, in his description of the manoeuvre named after him, observed that 'sometimes, a victim of choking becomes embarrassed by his predicament and succeeds in getting up and leaving the eating area unnoticed. In a nearby room, he loses consciousness and, if unattended, he will die or suffer permanent brain damage within seconds.'

§

It is sometimes supposed that embarrassment is a recently acquired condition, a product of our excessively civilised and thus anxiety-inducing modern societies. Our sense of the word 'embarrassment' – emotional discomfort arising from social awkwardness or self-consciousness, as opposed to its original meaning of a hindrance or impediment – did not find itself called for in English until the middle of the eighteenth century.

In his book *Humiliation*, William Ian Miller, a scholar of saga-era Iceland, argues that, in such pre-modern cultures, shame was less an inner feeling than a social condition, as conspicuous as a physical deformity. The world of the Icelandic sagas is one in which shame is so tangible that men will kill and maim each other in response to the smallest refusal to show respect. No one is shy in such a world, for everyone knows and agrees what shame looks like, and so there is no need to agonise over it in some tortuous interior monologue. In *Njál's Saga*, Kol, after having his leg hacked off by Kolskegg, looks calmly at the stump and says, 'That's what I get for not having a shield.' In *Egil's Saga* the eponymous warrior comes close to killing a young poet, Einar, for having the cheek to present him with an overly valuable gift. The difference today, Miller writes, is that shame has receded and embarrassment has grown. While we are more able to retain our self-respect in the face of others' disdain, we are also more likely to feel ashamed when others might see no reason for us to be.

The German-British sociologist Norbert Elias has argued that, until the last few hundred years, life was essentially lived in public. Families would eat and sleep in the same room, strangers would happily share a bed and it was normal for people to urinate or defecate in full view of others. Then, from the sixteenth century onwards, a 'civilising process' began to take hold across Europe. The medieval code of manners, called 'courtesy' because it was practised by court nobility, morphed into 'civility', meant to be practised by everyone. Rules about eating in company, spitting, nose-blowing and going to the toilet became more demanding and self-constraining. Elias finds evidence for this shift in new guides to manners such as Erasmus's *On Civility in Children* (1530). Erasmus's standards seem fairly relaxed by today's lights. A young man, he wrote, need not *ventris flatum retineat* (suppress his farts), for 'in doing so he might, under the appearance of urbanity, contract an illness', and, in the absence of a cloth, he should blow out his snot and tread it into the floor. But in these modest beginnings Elias sees the start of a process by which bodily functions and uncouth behaviour became gradually invisible in polite society.

Elias suggests that a key factor was the rise of the nation state and its claiming of a monopoly on the use of violence. In private life, evenness of temper thus came to be prized over physical coercion. As social life became less dangerous, and feasting and dancing were less likely to end in arguments and fighting, what Elias calls the 'shame-threshold' advanced. Physical and psychological barriers grew up around people, especially among strangers in public, and there were more opportunities for awkwardness about when these boundaries could be crossed. A person feared that, if they crossed this shame-threshold, they would lose love and respect, and they began to internalise what they imagined to be the negative judgements of others. The shame-threshold advanced into our hearts and minds.

It is a persuasive-sounding account. But Goffman's work on Unst casts doubt on Elias's idea that embarrassment is a recent invention, and that people intermingled less inhibitedly in small-scale, pre-modern societies. On the contrary, the smallness of Unst seemed to have cultivated a claustrophobic social awkwardness. Everyone knew everyone else too well. They lived much of their lives in public, watched and judged by those around them, and it made them cling tenaciously to their little pockets of privacy.

§

Perhaps the truth is more that embarrassment is endlessly omnivorous and adaptable. It can thrive in the austere communal life of remote Scottish islands, and it can thrive in the social worlds that have travelled furthest along what Elias called the civilising process. For over-evolved gentility and airless formality are also great incubators of shared awkwardness.

One of the sharpest observers of this kind of social world was, while Goffman was studying shyness in Unst, living quietly among the English middle classes. Elizabeth Taylor was Alan Turing's exact contemporary, born just a week apart from him in the summer of 1912. Instead of going to Cambridge like him, in the early 1930s she went to work for the code-breaker Dilly Knox as the governess of his seven-year-old son Oliver. Oliver Knox, who ended up working at Bletchley Park like his father, recalled Taylor as 'walking decisively, if with the suggestion of a stoop, this being (as I now think) perhaps symbolic – her diffidence the thinnest of veils covering a decisiveness, a positiveness, even a detached sort of cruelty'. In 1936 Taylor married a prosperous sweet manufacturer from High Wycombe and they moved to the Buckinghamshire village of Penn. An impeccably mannered woman of her generation and class, she rarely strayed from writing about life in these nicely kept home counties villages, with their neat little geranium urns, flagpoles and weeping copper beeches.

In Taylor's excruciating story 'The Letter-Writers', a shy, single woman, Emily, has been writing to an expat novelist,

Edmund Fabry, for a decade. Gathering up news and tidying it into sentences for him takes up most of her life. Now he has arrived in England from Rome and has arranged to come to her village. The meeting is calamitous. The cat eats the lobster she has prepared for lunch, she gets nervously drunk, and a neighbour who is a comical busybody in the letters turns out in real life to be merely tedious. The breezy façade Emily has made out of ink and paper is revealed as just that, and all conversation peters out. The story ends with her sitting down to write Edmund another letter after he has left, as if nothing has happened.

Emily's relationship with Edmund was mirrored in Taylor's own correspondence with the writer Robert Liddell, who lived a safe distance away in Athens (although they did meet a few times, quite successfully). It lasted from 1948 to 1975, a month before she died, when she was too ill to pick up a pen. Writing letters was Taylor's way of coping with her shyness, which had worsened when, as a young woman, she was badly burned by a firework that stuck in her coat collar. It left scars on her neck that were barely visible but which made her, in company, clasp her hands together to stop herself hiding her face.

All through history, letter-writing has offered salvation for the shy. A key moment for these shy letter-writers came in the 1840s, when the British government assumed a postal monopoly and introduced three things – prepaid stamps, sealed envelopes and street post-boxes – that guaranteed the privacy of the mail and ended the tradition of the postmaster or postmistress being the main source of local gossip. The London middle classes soon began the tradition of chiselling little rectangular openings in their front doors so they could receive letters without even having to talk to the postman. By the 1930s, when Taylor began her letter-writing life, the Royal Mail had a national next-day delivery service that was a logistical miracle. Its night mail trains crisscrossed the country and its red Morris Minor bullnose vans rolled along every British street, bringing every kind of letter from bank statements to shy lovers' avowals.

A correspondence via the Royal Mail had the potential for slow-growing intimacy, enhanced by that deliciously expectant wait between sending and receiving which email and text messages have since destroyed. Taylor's own epistolary friendships progressed by these careful increments. As she got to know her correspondent better, she replaced the surname with the forename, then 'yours sincerely' became 'with love', and finally 'dear' became 'dearest'. Women especially seemed to thrive in the ripening closeness of this kind of relationship. 'A great many of the most accomplished letter writers have been women,' argue Frank and Anita Kermode in the preface to their *Oxford Book of Letters*. 'It is in the business of such easy, delicate self-exposures that women seem to succeed best.' In Taylor's story Edmund Fabry similarly notes that letter-writing is an art 'at which Englishwomen have excelled'.

For years Taylor visited a rather grand and intimidating older writer, Ivy Compton-Burnett, at her flat in Braemar Mansions, South Kensington, always asking taxi drivers to drop her off a few streets away so she could ensure she was not too early. Each luncheon was an awkward and wooden occasion, with Taylor fretting about the flaky pastry from her Banbury cake cascading on to her knees, the shakiness of her hand as she helped herself to raspberry fool or the superannuated cheese her host liked to serve, which made her guests fear that the flat's dodgy drains had finally given up the ghost. At the end Compton-Burnett would whisper, 'Would you like to …?', and Taylor would say 'no' before hurrying to the ladies at Harvey Nichols in Knightsbridge.

The only thing that helped her through these occasions was the thought that she could tell Liddell about them later, in letters written from notes made on the train back from London Euston to High Wycombe. Liddell and Taylor agreed that what they most envied about children was their ability to cry, or be sick, when they were bored by or upset with other people. Deprived of this outlet by shyness and social convention, Taylor used letter-writing to cathartically dissect her social embarrassments. When another of her pen friends, the interior designer Herman Schrijver, died, she said how much she missed telling him things and wished 'one could write letters to the dead'.

⁂

In the early spring of 1946 Taylor went to see a film that affected her deeply. It was *Brief Encounter*, in which Celia Johnson played the role of Laura Jesson, a suburban wife so restrained she pretends to listen to a tiresome acquaintance rather than say a last farewell to her lover. As Laura in voiceover begins her confession of her chaste affair with Alec Harvey, the camera zooms in on Dolly Messiter, who becomes a grotesque, Beckettian mouth, chuntering away oblivious to the distress she is causing. The film is about being shy in such a world where conversation is a face-saving ritual, where people cover up their awkwardness by talking at each other about things that don't matter. Laura and Alec's relationship begins with this sort of non-talk: *How kind it was of you to take so much trouble. It's clearing up, I think. Yes, it's going to be nice. Well, I must be getting along to the hospital. Now, I must be getting along to the grocers!*

In a 1953 essay the film critic Roger Manvell wrote that British film-makers faced a particular dilemma: our national reserve veiled the strong emotions we feel. Relying as all film-makers did on self-revelatory speech and action to tell a story, they had the delicate task of 'stripping the mask of shyness from our brows and revealing the warmth and the tenderness, the strengths and the weaknesses beneath'. In *Brief Encounter* the director, David Lean, had achieved this by filtering emotion through 'eloquent silences' and 'the clichés of accepted behaviour'. The film's emotions were all muted, suggested through crushed handkerchiefs and quivering mouths. Such understatement was, for Manvell, 'as indigenous as our green, sweet and rain-quenched landscapes'.

'I believe we would all behave quite differently if we lived in a warm, sunny climate all the time,' Laura says in the film. 'We wouldn't be so withdrawn and shy and difficult.' Alec tells her he has fallen in love with her shyness, but her own feelings for him compete with her embarrassment at feeling them, and mostly her feelings lose. When she first realises she is in love, on the train home, she scans the carriage and sees a vicar looking straight at her, blushes, opens her library book and pretends to read.

Brief Encounter is like *Anna Karenina* strained through the fine sieve of English shyness. Unlike in Tolstoy's novel, the affair is unconsummated, the heroine stops just short of throwing herself under an express train and she goes back to her husband and children. The uninitiated could find this English middle-class restraint ludicrous. When the film previewed in Rochester, a largely working-class audience laughed at the love scenes and shouted, 'Isn't 'e ever goin' to 'ave it orf with 'er?' German audiences greeted the film with boos and catcalls. A British Military Government report from Berlin stated that they 'profess total inability to understand the moral scruples on which the plot hinges'.

Taylor wrote her own story of an unconsummated affair, *A Game of Hide and Seek*, after seeing *Brief Encounter*. The novel's romance unfolds in the same furtive places as the film: railway station buffets, park benches and on streets in 'the darkest place between two lamps'. The film's daylight locations – Boots lending libraries, Kardomah cafés, matinee cinemas – were the housewifely world Taylor knew so well. She felt linked to Celia Johnson, whom she even looked rather like, because much of the film was shot in Beaconsfield, where she had her hair done and went shopping, and Johnson was seen coming out of the grocer's shop and café she frequented.

Taylor spent days just walking round these Thames Valley towns on her own, sitting in the Tudor tearooms and public gardens and browsing in the antique shops her characters might visit. She took boat trips along the Thames and gazed at the exposed houses whose neatly shaved lawns went right up to the riverbank, and caught snatches of conversation coming from verandahs. She went to pubs on her own and, while nursing a gin and tonic, listened in to conversations, the Erving Goffman of middle England.

In 1961 the author Elizabeth Jane Howard interviewed her on

a new BBC TV book programme called *Something To Read*. The interview was scheduled to last eight minutes; erring on the side of caution, Howard prepared thirty questions. Not cautious enough, as it turned out. They were done in a minute and a half, because Taylor, looking to her interrogator 'like a trapped and rather beautiful owl', answered yes or no to all of them. Afterwards, as the two women sat in the BBC canteen in Manchester sipping from cardboard cups of instant coffee, Howard, a fellow sufferer, failed to breach Taylor's high wall of reserve.

'I just wanted to see my novels in print, because I felt they weren't there until they were printed,' Taylor said in one of her very rare interviews. 'I want to make a world that doesn't exist, a world for people to look at.' But compared with the release she got from letter-writing, she found the process of sending her books out into the world horribly embarrassing. Her daughter Joanna only found out about her mother's first novel from a friend at school. 'My hands become ice at the thought of my book being published,' Taylor wrote to the novelist Elizabeth Bowen, 'and I do hope that, like silicosis, it is an *occupational* disease.'

She poured into her novels all her dislike of simulated sociability. Awkwardness and embarrassment are, Meg and Patrick in *The Soul of Kindness* decide, 'under-rated forms of suffering'. 'I never think embarrassment is a trivial emotion,' agrees Beatrice in Taylor's story 'Hester Lilly'. Her women live Laura Jesson-like lives of stockbrokerish comfort and silent anguish, baking sponges for coffee mornings, hosting bridge evenings, attending summer fêtes and gymkhanas and enduring formula luncheons that always start with sherry and end with fool. One of her opening sentences beautifully condenses the way that people steel themselves to join in these rituals: 'In the morning, Charles went down the garden to practise calling for three cheers.'

She dreaded reviews, because if they were unkind she felt embarrassed seeing people afterwards, even if they were unlikely to have read them. She was an epic blusher. She blushed at the thought of discarded drafts of her work which no one had seen and that she had long since thrown away. She blushed when men, mistaking her for Elizabeth Taylor the film star, wrote asking for pictures of her in a bikini. She blushed at parties when people said simply that they had read her books. She blushed at the thought of the letters she had written even after she had ensured they were burned, not wishing to be posthumously mortified by her gossipy self. 'I do not think I am modest,' she said in her last interview. 'I am just terribly embarrassed.'

§

Taylor's story 'The Blush' ends with the main character 'glad that she was alone, for she could feel her face, her throat, even the tops of her arms burning, and she went over to a looking-glass and studied with great interest this strange phenomenon'. Blushing is a sign that our bodies will not always do our minds' bidding, and can even become less compliant the more we try to control them. Somewhere at the heart of embarrassment seems to lie this fear that our bodies may let us down at any moment and reveal us to be nothing more than animals ruled by our biological urges.

In the tribal communities of the Mount Hagen area of Papua New Guinea, those who suffer the 'big shame' (*pipil mam*) of being caught defecating or having sex can be driven to suicide. Their only other option is to atone for their shame by sacrificing a pig and praying to the ghosts. Such shame about being seen copulating, even with one's spouse, occurs throughout Melanesia. The anthropologist Bronislaw Malinowski, conducting fieldwork in the Trobriand Islands in the western Pacific in 1915, heard of one man so ashamed of being caught having sex in his garden that he killed himself with derris root fish poison. These acts seem to be shaming not because one has been discovered doing something immoral but because the self has been exposed in its natural, animal-like state.

We are human because we are humiliatable. Civilisation is a slim veneer that can quickly peel away to reveal the shitting, pissing, puking animals that we are. The anthropologist Clifford

Geertz once suggested that the Balinese term *lek*, usually translated as 'shame', would be better rendered as 'stage fright', because
the Balinese are terrified of being stripped of their social roles.
When their public persona is breached, they become 'suddenly and
unwillingly creatural, locked in mutual embarrassment, as though
they had happened upon each other's nakedness'.

Embarrassment is felt by everyone, but we do not all think
and talk about it in the same way. Every culture has its own rich
emotional lexicon, its subtly different words and senses for that
universal feeling. Many south-east Asian languages have a single
word conflating shame, shyness and embarrassment, while not
being quite synonymous with any of them. The Malayan word
malu, for instance, signifies a kind of virtuous embarrassment
that needs to be instilled in children by their elders so they understand what civilised behaviour is. A Malay word for the genitals
is *kemaluan*, which uses the root *malu* and means 'thing or object
of shame'. Male elders will tease toddler boys until they expose
their penises. When they do, the elders laugh at them for having
no *malu*, and a lesson is learned.

Michael Young, who conducted anthropological fieldwork in
Kalauna village on Goodenough Island, Papua New Guinea, in the
late 1960s, noted that the tribal word *wowomumu* covered a wide
spectrum from shyness to mild embarrassment to deep shame. In
Kalauna, courtship was a nervous affair which required a young
man to chew betel nut with his girlfriend one or two nights a
week in her father's house while he waited for her to propose to
him. Even after they were married, the couple were shy around
each other. Although the wife would cook for her husband from
the time she came to join him in his parents' hamlet, they would
eat separately for several months, as embarrassed about eating
together as sleeping together. To have a child during the first year
of marriage was shameful, for this was a sign of a wanton sexual
appetite, as was a wife who laughed too much. A man's relations
with his wife's family, however warm they became, were never
entirely free of *wowomumu*.

This kind of shyness is both a feeling and an ethos, an attitude one deliberately assumes in order to show respect for and deference to others. The Hindi word *lajja* conveys a similar sense of an honourable embarrassment meant to be knowingly displayed as a sign of humility and good manners. A woman shows *lajja* by covering her face or leaving the room to avoid talking to her husband's elder brother or father, or another man to whom he should defer. The iconic, if somewhat counterintuitive, representation of *lajja* is of the mother goddess Kali brandishing a decapitated head, with her foot on the chest of a man lying on the ground beneath her. She has defeated a demon who could only be killed at the hands of a naked woman but, embarrassed by her nakedness, she has gone on a crazed rampage. Her husband, Siva, has tried to stop her by prostrating himself among the corpses by her feet and she has accidentally trodden on him. She is showing *lajja* at this disrespectful act by stretching out her tongue and biting it. Women still do this in parts of India to show they are embarrassed.

§

If something is of great significance within a culture, that culture develops a fertile and refined vocabulary around it. Common Ground, the British organisation that celebrates local distinctiveness, once listed the many different Welsh words for rain. These included *dafnu* (spotting), *brasfrwrw* (big spaced drops), *hegar law* (fierce rain), *lluwchlaw* (sheets of rain), *chwipio bwrw* (whiplash rain), *pistyllio* (fountain rain) and *piso* (pissing down). The Welsh have many words for rain for the same reason that the Bedouin have many words for camels: these phenomena are so common in these parts that a nuanced language emerged to account for their minute variations. Perhaps the intensity of embarrassment varies similarly, leading to the proliferation of words with subtly distinct meanings in the parts of the world where it is felt most potently.

The Nordic countries rival south-east Asian cultures in the subtlety of their language of embarrassment. A shy Finnish historian I met once told me all the different Finnish synonyms for 'embarrassed'. *Nolo*, the most common word, had a negative sense, for instance in the phrase '*Vähän noloa!*' (How embarrassing!). 'Nobody wants to be *nolo*,' he said, 'because it also connotes being pitiful.' But there were other words, he added, that roughly tallied with embarrassment – *kiusaantunut*, *vaivaantunut*, *hämillinen*, *hämmentynyt* – which evoked a more general sense of confusion or discomfort and had a neutral or even positive meaning. Another word, *myötähäpeä*, the vicarious embarrassment one feels for others, was *Schadenfreude*'s kinder cousin. He told me that a common explanation for the Finnish embrace of the tango, which became a national passion after Argentine musicians brought it to Europe in the 1910s, is that it gave Finns a licence to touch and to communicate feelings they were too embarrassed to form into words.

In 1964 the American psychiatrist Herbert Hendin was studying suicide in Scandinavia and reported that the Swedes he interviewed were peculiarly prone to embarrassment. Interviewed for a second time, Swedish women would often be embarrassed at having revealed so much about themselves previously. They blushed spectacularly, from hairline to neck, when required to discuss their emotions. Swedish men were even more embarrassed when talking about their feelings, and in defence assumed 'an attitude of intellectual curiosity rather than emotional involvement'.

In his study of his country's collective mentality the Swedish ethnologist Åke Daun observed a similar sheepishness. Many Swedes, he noted, would rather take the stairs than share a lift with a slight acquaintance, for fear of being unable to think of anything to say. They found it hard to make eye contact during conversations. They rarely gave speeches without writing out every word and reading it aloud, and Swedes often joked that being asked to deliver the customary vote of thanks to the host for a meal made them instantly lose their appetite. The Swedes' embarrassability extended to their most extreme life experiences. Women giving birth tried to scream with pain quietly. Afterwards they would ask the midwife if they had made much noise, and were pleased if they were told they had not. At funerals it was OK to snivel a bit if you were a woman, but 'cries of despair are embarrassing and are remembered long afterwards'.

The film director Ingmar Bergman, the son of a Lutheran minister, attended many Swedish funerals as a boy, and noticed that no one ever cried, even when the coffin was taken away. He was so intrigued by the decorousness of these rituals of mourning that pretend funerals became his favourite game. When the prime minister Olof Palme was shot dead on a Stockholm street in 1986, many Swedish observers pointed out how unusual it was to see their compatriots weeping in public at the news. And yet, according to a poll conducted by Gunnel Gustafson of the University of Umeå, first-generation immigrants in Sweden admitted to crying at Palme's death far more than native Swedes (44 per cent compared to 24 per cent). Gustafson's study was based on a similar one conducted in Chicago after John F. Kennedy's assassination, when 53 per cent of Americans said they cried.

Perhaps one day a cartographer of shyness will be able to trace these enclaves of extreme embarrassment by designing a colour-coded map using those smart big-data visualisation tools that can map everything from voting patterns to cancer rates. Deep red would naturally be used for the most chronic cases of embarrassment, shading incrementally from orange into unembarrassable yellow the nearer you got to the Mediterranean. When the writer Susan Sontag lived in Sweden in the late 1960s, she charted such a gradual dilution within the country itself, suggesting that people became more outgoing the further south from Stockholm you went. The citizens of the southernmost province of Skåne, she discovered, were known to Swedes as 'reserve Danes', famous for their 'positively Latin jollity'.

※

Erving Goffman sailed 4,000 miles to Unst to study embarrassment, but he could just as easily have driven a few hundred miles from Chicago into the plains of the upper Midwest and found abundant research material. Just as in Shetland, the shyness of the people of this region is often accounted for by their Nordic and northern European origins. When the homesteaders arrived there in the late nineteenth century, men outnumbered women ten to one, and bachelor farmers worked alone, fighting locusts, prairie fires and blizzards, with no trains, cars or radios to lessen the loneliness. The Norwegian-American writer Ole Rølvaag, in his bleak tales of plains winters, immortalised the gallant reticence of these male settlers who were too busy 'proving up' – gaining title to their land within the five-year period of the Homestead Act by working on it and building a home – to learn social niceties or find a wife. The phrase 'Minnesota nice' came to denote this Unst-like inclination to emotional restraint, to nod politely and truncate conversations with terminative echoes like 'not too bad' or 'you betcha', delivered in the sing-song intonation of the Nordic languages.

In my last years at primary school my favourite reading matter was, I now realise, a masterly distillation of this kind of upper Midwest stoicism: the dozens of cheap Coronet paperbacks, with pages as coarse as blotting paper that I made dog-eared through re-reading, of Charles Schulz's *Peanuts* comic strips. I also loved the animated Charlie Brown TV specials that were shown in the daytime during the school holidays, with their minor-key Vince Guaraldi jazz soundtracks and their eschewal of canned laughter, which seemed to cast a Linus blanket of melancholy over proceedings. Peter Robbins, who provided Charlie Brown's voice, said his lines with an unaffected clarity of feeling. He sounded not like the precocious stage-school children who seemed to populate other American TV shows, but like a boy with real failures and frustrations. Through *Peanuts* I learned of the American tradition of grade-school children exchanging Valentine cards openly with their classmates, instead of shyly and anonymously, as in Britain. This bare-faced bartering in the stock exchange of social approval, and Charlie Brown's futile wait for a card from the Little Red-Haired Girl to whom he was too shy to speak, seemed crueller than the most Gothic fairy tale.

At high school in St Paul, Minnesota, in the 1930s, Charles Schulz had suffered that familiar shy see-sawing between feeling horribly invisible most of the time and horribly visible some of the time. He found it painful even to greet a classmate in the corridor. As a young man, he was deeply self-conscious when travelling to Chicago to sell his comic strips to syndicates, because his sample panels were drawn on huge rectangular boards, the size of which provoked comments from fellow passengers. Even after he became famous, trips away from home filled him with terror, and he often did not show up for public engagements. Sometimes his wife, Jeannie, would drop him off at the airport only to find that he had beaten her home in a taxi.

Charlie Brown is Schulz's shyness in cartoon form. As a boy, Schulz thought his face so bland that, were he to bump into a classmate in downtown St Paul, they would not recognise him. This odd train of thought was what inspired Charlie Brown's anonymous round head, its only mark a squiggle on his brow that is either a wisp of hair or an eternal worm of worry. Schulz's virtuosic little twist was to give him a dog, Snoopy, who is a brilliant, wordless communicator – quite unlike the boy who supplies his meals and whom he calls 'that round-headed kid'. A constant theme in *Peanuts* is Charlie Brown being reminded of his own insignificance. In one of the surreal extended storylines Schulz specialised in, his hero, not wanting to appear at summer camp with a rash, wears a brown paper bag over his head. His bag-wearing self makes more impact than his normal self and is elected camp president.

Schulz came to believe, in a classically Minnesotan form of self-laceration, that his own inhibitions were merely upended narcissism. 'Shyness,' he wrote, 'is the overtly self-conscious thinking that you are the only person in the world; that how you look and what you do is of any importance.' But the lesson of *Peanuts* is quite the opposite. Who, after all, is a better model of humanity: Lucy van Pelt, who shouts at the world with bone-shuddering conviction, or Charlie Brown, whose shyness has made him a gentle, fair-minded stoic?

When it appeared on a page of noisy comic strips all jostling for attention, *Peanuts* drew the eye with its clean lines and white spaces, the boldness with which it had so little going on. In the winter months, when the arctic winds blow down from Manitoba, Minnesota's many lakes and ponds are covered with ice thick enough to support skating, ice fishing and even huts. The mood music of Minnesotan weather in *Peanuts* – the softly falling snow-flakes, the frozen ponds on which the characters skate silently and the stone-faced snowmen they build and befriend, only for them to melt away – is part of a general ambience of stillness and quiet.

In *Peanuts* problems remain unresolved and words unspoken. The signature note is the bathetic non-ending, a final panel with Charlie Brown exhaling a *sigh*, smiling wonkily with sweat beads shooting off his face or blushing in a way that fills his head with diagonal lines. Schulz knew that shyness has no narrative arc: the shy just have to carry on being shy. A daily comic strip was his way of managing this, communicating with the world remotely for nearly half a century, by creating his own world with a few bold pen strokes in four little boxes, and signing his name at the end.

※

Growing up in the suburbs of Minneapolis St Paul in the 1950s, a gangly, awkward boy called Gary Keillor, with 'a powerful wish to be invisible', read and loved *Peanuts*. A Minnesotan stoic like Charlie Brown, he had the added problem that his family were Exclusive Brethren, a fundamentalist sub-sect of the Plymouth Brethren, which meant he was not allowed to invite friends into his house. As well as frowning upon parties, dancing and alcohol, the Keillors had no television set, for the word of the Bible was all and temptation came via sight. So Gary sought solace in the invention that had also consoled the young Charles Schulz in the 1930s: radio. He commandeered the curved handle of a vacuum cleaner as a microphone and imagined he was speaking to millions of listeners.

When he began radio announcing at the University of

Minnesota, the now renamed Garrison Keillor found he had acquired, from years of osmotic radio listening, a mellifluous timbre with a pleasing dying fall, one that made him sought out ever after for voiceover work. He discovered that a low-key, moseying-along voice worked better on radio than a boomingly oratorical one. Tongue-tied in real life, he became proficient at radio's synthetic spontaneity, dropping well-timed 'y'knows' and 'kindas' into the middle of his sentences.

He found in this practised artlessness a way of turning himself into someone else, a man who could speak without being inter-rupted or worrying about people yawning or looking at their watches. For radio, like Cicero's letter to Lucius Lucceius, is a medium without blushes. Carried through the air on invisible electromagnetic waves, it combines a reassuring anonymity with the intimacy of one voice talking to another. In 1969, when Keillor took over the morning show at Minnesota Educational Radio, he found he enjoyed this virtual, faceless relationship with his listeners, feeling like 'the shepherd of lovely but temporarily unhappy people'.

The following year he had the most joyous breakthrough of his professional life, one that was to be as significant as his radio career in the semi-surmounting of his shyness. He got his first acceptance letter from the *New Yorker*, the magazine he had unearthed as a teenager in the periodicals room of Minneapolis Public Library. It was for a 400-word cod newspaper article about a sixteen-year-old boy whose parents were so worried about his shyness that they moved in a local prostitute.

The *New Yorker* was edited by the surpassingly shy William Shawn, who worked at the magazine for fifty-four years and ensured his name never once appeared in it. When, in 1965, Tom Wolfe wrote a notorious attack on the magazine for the *New York Herald Tribune*, he made fun of Shawn's inability even to say hello in the corridor and his habit of inviting writers to lunch and saying nothing, and implied that the *New Yorker*'s dullness and ponder-ousness mirrored its editor's personality. But many shy writers, including Elizabeth Taylor and Garrison Keillor, had cause to be grateful for Shawn's diligent reading of unsolicited stories and careful editing. He would erase excitable words and add commas that – in the words of another acutely shy *New Yorker* writer, E. B. White – fell 'with the precision of knives in a circus act, outlining the victim'.

White's own rules about good writing, which had a decisive influence on *New Yorker* style and which Keillor signed up to keenly, were formalised in his classic *The Elements of Style*. This handbook was based on an earlier model written by Will Strunk, his old professor at Cornell, which White saw as an essay on the 'nature and beauty of brevity'. Good writing did not offer the writer's opinions gratuitously, *The Elements of Style* ruled, because this implied that 'the demand for them is brisk, which may not be the case'. For White, the best prose combined simplicity and self-concealment and was 'both a mask and an unveiling', particularly for the personal essayist, 'who must take his trousers off without showing his genitals'. A writer's voice was a vehicle for disguised egotism, and tact and taste were vital elements in the disguise. This thinking was made flesh in a magazine which, from its elegant calligraphic lines to its tinder-dry wit, was all about subsuming the awkward and inept individual into an anonymous, collective urbanity. The *New Yorker* was a prophylactic against embarrassment.

On 6 July 1974 Keillor's *A Prairie Home Companion*, a parody of the live variety shows he had listened to as a boy, began on Minnesota Public Radio. Not until the end of the decade, by which time half a million Minnesotans were tuning in, was the show's most famous element installed. 'It's been a quiet week here in Lake Wobegon, on the edge of the prairie,' Keillor would always begin, before launching into a shaggy, scriptless yarn about an imaginary prairie town north-west of Minneapolis. This town was full of shy people and, like Goffman's Unst, was a place where embarrassment arose not from stranger anxiety but from long acquaintance. Even close friends stood an arm's length apart; romantic passion was voiced as mild interest; the Fearmonger's Shoppe had been serving 'all your phobia needs since 1954'; and the town's timidest citizens were the Norwegian bachelor farmers, who ate shy-busting Powdermilk biscuits and hung out at one end of the town's only bar, like 'perpetually disgruntled, elderly teenagers leaning against a wall'.

A Prairie Home Companion became a national cult, with millions of Americans sat beside their radios at 5 p.m. Central Time each Saturday to hear Keillor begin the show with a husky rendition of the Hank Snow song 'Hello Love'. Now, duetting with musical guests and performing his own monologues dressed in a tuxedo with bare-ankle trousers, sneakers and loud red tie, he seemed to have left embarrassment behind. Only those watching in the audience as the show was broadcast would have noticed his habit of staring down at his socks.

It is hard to unlearn a childhood aptitude for embarrassment, whatever adult reassurance we receive and however much credit we accumulate in the bank of *sang froid*, for it only takes one embarrassing episode for us to be suddenly and hopelessly overdrawn again. One day Keillor was with his massage therapist and felt his speech slurring and his mouth growing numb. Not wishing to make a fuss, like Heimlich's embarrassed man choking to death, he drove to the hospital on his own. 'To pick up a phone and call 911 for an ambulance would be, well … it seemed not quite justifiable to me,' he said later. When he reached the emergency room, he waited in line to be seen, a true Minnesotan, too embarrassed to say he was having a stroke.

§

Unlike Scandinavians or south-east Asians, Americans have no carefully calibrated language for describing different kinds of embarrassment. They have a reputation for seeing shyness as un-American. Their cultural heroes are seemingly self-sufficient, outdoorsy types: pioneers, backwoodsmen, cowboys, baseball players – exemplars of what Theodore Roosevelt called 'the strenuous life'. But does this make them any less likely to be embarrassed? Many of America's most illustrious citizens, and not only those from Minnesota, have been unable to look another human in the eye. Nathaniel Hawthorne, who left the road for the surrounding fields if he saw anyone approaching the other way, diagnosed himself as 'a mild, shy, gentle, melancholic ... hiding his blushes under an assumed name'. Emily Dickinson addressed her house visitors from behind a half-closed bedroom door. Ralph Waldo Emerson, convinced of his own 'porcupine impossibility of contact with men', identified a strain in his country's culture which cultivated 'eternal loneliness ... how insular & pathetically solitary, are all the people we know!'

Whether or not it was part of this same tendency towards pathetic solitariness, a century later America gave birth to that now thriving sub-species of the shy, the nerd. 'In Detroit, someone who once would be called a drip or a square is now, regrettably, a nerd,' declared *Newsweek* in 1951, while Alan Turing, who certainly fitted the profile, was inaugurating the computer age. But nerds did not properly emerge as a socially awkward, techno-literate subculture for another two decades. On 5 March 1975, just as the über-cool Fonz was popularising 'nerd' as a term of opprobrium in *Happy Days*, about thirty people gathered in a garage in the southern Californian suburb of Menlo Park for the first meeting of the Homebrew Computer Club. In the same way that Nordic embarrassment thrived in the sub-Arctic chill, nerds required a supportive ecosystem. And Menlo Park was in the middle of the Santa Clara Valley, which was steadily replacing its orchards and market gardens with microchip factories and electronics firms.

Each session of the Homebrew Computer Club had a 'random access period', when anyone could say what they liked to the group. One of its members, Steve Wozniak, looked at first glance like a familiar type: the American science-fair kid made to feel suddenly invisible in sixth grade as the harsh rituals of adolescent dating began. Too shy to speak even in this congenial company, he communicated by demonstrating his models and sharing his designs. But while he might have seemed solitary and shy, his instincts, like Turing's before him, were basically social. At a time when computers communicated only through punch cards and flashing lights, he wanted to make them of wider benefit to humanity. His way of being noticed by others was to create something that would be useful to them and give away his expertise as a gift. Later that year, after building the first ever computer with a keyboard and monitor, he photocopied the design and gave it to his fellow Homebrewers for free – at least until his friend Steve Jobs came up with a different business model.

In the early 1980s, by which time the home computer that Wozniak had more or less invented had found its way into millions of teenage bedrooms, the word 'nerd' finally entered the common idiom, along with related phrases such as 'nerd pack', which referred to both the plastic containers that stopped pens from marking clothes and the groups of uncool kids in American high schools who carried them in their shirt pockets. The nerd diaspora had spread out from the Santa Clara Valley, now renamed Silicon Valley. In the 1990s, as more people learned html and turned the internet into a global common room, the word was recovered as a badge of pride. Bands such as Weezer, They Might Be Giants and Nerf Herder were grouped together as 'nerd pop', and 'nerdcore' arose as a subset of hip-hop. T-shirts declared the wearer, in confident slab serif, to be a GEEK or a NERD.

Nerds became cool – and, often, very rich – because their antisocial pursuits turned out to answer a human need to share information without the embarrassment of actually meeting face-to-face. Since nerds were the few people who could understand the computer code that enabled this to happen, they were as useful in the new world of the microchip as Turing had been at Bletchley. The difference was that they were writing code, not deciphering it. Computers are hardly any closer to Turing's ideal of being able to think like people. But we can now set them to work as virtual Cyrano de Bergeracs, surrogate selves to whom we outsource our most awkward encounters. Our modern cure-all for embarrassment is technology. The multi-tasking minicomputers we still call 'phones' keep us in constant touch with each other, but they also allow us to regulate our sociability like a thermostat.

Texting, which the Finnish company Nokia introduced into its phones in the mid-1990s almost as an afterthought to replace the old-fashioned and not very popular system of paging, is a primitive technology. It uses that basic primate attribute, the opposable thumb, and is essentially a time-consuming and energy-inefficient substitute for talking. But texting quickly took off among taciturn young Finnish men because it was a way of talking to others, especially girls, without the signals being scrambled by blushing faces or tied tongues. In a country with 85 per cent membership of the Evangelical Lutheran Church, the cellphone became the favourite confirmation present for fifteen-year-olds. Two sociologists from the University of Tampere found that a Finnish boy would rarely tell a girl he loved her, but would text loving messages, taking up to half an hour to edit and redraft, and writing in English because he found it easier to express strong feelings in another language.

Other scholars of cellphone culture have shown that text messages performed a similar role in the Philippines, which quickly took over from Finland as the texting capital of the world. Cellphones arrived in the Philippines around 1996, and within five years the number of handsets had grown to 7 million and the country was accounting for 10 per cent of the world's text messages. In part this was because the Philippines was a poor country, landlines were rare and texting was cheap. But it probably also had something to do with what Filipinos call *hiya*, another of those south-east Asian words that combine shyness and embarrassment without quite meaning either.

Filipino courtship rituals are traditionally coy and convoluted. The man, who is meant to do all the running while the woman plays hard to get (*pakipot*) in order to preserve her honour, is often *torpe*, too sheepish to admit his feelings. And so elaborate, hedge-betting rituals have evolved. The man might begin with *harana*, the Spanish-influenced serenade of courtship sung beneath his beloved's window on hot Filipino nights, with his friends brought along for moral support as well as close harmonies. Things might then move on to 'teasing' (*tuksuhan*) by mutual friends or using a 'human bridge' (*tulay*) between the likely lovers, until such time as they can be persuaded to go out together on their own. The cellphone has allowed young Filipinos to circumvent these face-saving routines and instead test the waters by text.

※

So it is the world over: texting lets those more dextrous with their thumbs than their tongues be more intrepid than in real life. That ping or whistle announcing a text's arrival is less insistent than a phone ring. It does not catch us by surprise or demand we answer it instantly. It lends us space to digest and ponder a response, keeping the world on a leash. Kisses added to the end of a text, a speeded-up version of that delicate *pas de deux* from 'yours sincerely' to 'with love', can be quickly recanted if they fall on flinty ground. The Japanese have even improvised a menu of shy or embarrassed-looking emoticons which use asterisks and semi-colons to make blushing cheeks or sweat drops. A short text message can encompass a cosmos of nuance. Blending intimacy with artifice, it lets us say the things that embarrass us face-to-face and to experiment with suaver versions of ourselves.

When I overhear unguarded conversations in train carriages or see someone barking at a hands-free set in the street, for all the world as if they were a lunatic shouting at an imaginary foe, I wonder whether the cellphone has destroyed the division between private and public life and whether embarrassment is now extinct. But then I see young people slyly texting in their laps or under tables, their faces flickering minutely at a confidence passed on via the glowing screen. And it occurs to me that, for all this yattering away in public, human ingenuity has conjured up the cellphone to solve a simple and eternal problem. We want to say what we think and feel to people's faces, to open our hearts to them. But we are all just really embarrassed.

4

TONGUE-TIED

One day in March 1918, towards the end of his period of anthropological fieldwork in Melanesia, Bronislaw Malinowski joined
a boat trip to Gumawana village at the south-east edge of the
Amphlett islands, off the coast of Papua New Guinea. On these
islands he encountered a people who were 'shy, yet arrogant to
anyone who has any dealings with them'. They could grow very
little on their own rocky soil, so the women made decorative clay
pots and the men exchanged them with neighbouring islanders for
pigs, sago and betel nuts.

When Malinowski's boat anchored, the men approached in
their canoes, proffering pots. But when his party waded ashore, the
islanders panicked and the young women fled and hid in the bush
beyond the village. Even 'the old hags', as Malinowski charmingly
described them, hid in their huts. In order to lure the women out to
make pots, his party had to bribe them with tobacco. Meanwhile
the men 'sat dully on stones, *independent, sulky, unfriendly – true
islanders!*' Malinowski found that all strangers, not just white

Europeans, inspired such shyness in the Amphlettans.

During his time in Melanesia, Malinowski came to think that all humans were prone to shyness and had evolved ways of alleviating it. In his classic essay 'The problem of meaning in primitive languages' he identified a genre of informationally empty talk among non-intimates that was as commonly used by remote tribespeople as in an English drawing room. He called it 'phatic communion': 'phatic' from the Greek *phanein*, to show oneself, and 'communion' because he saw it as establishing an initial bond that could later be consummated by the breaking of bread.

Having learned enough of the local languages to take notes on conversations, Malinowski was surprised how much of the talk he overheard was a seemingly pointless flow of words. The stock Melanesian phrase 'whence comest thou?' was strikingly akin to the English 'how do you do?' in being said simply to fill the disagreeable silence at the start of a conversation. These opening gambits soon dissolved into expressions of preference or dislike, accounts of trivial events or statements of the obvious. In phatic communion, words served as a social glue to bind speakers briefly together, for all humans seemed to find it unnerving when a pall of silence fell between them, the unspeaking stranger being the special enemy of 'savage tribesmen' and 'our own uneducated classes'.

Many years later the anthropologist Robin Dunbar found hard evidence for Malinowski's theories. He and his graduate students at the University of Liverpool listened in to conversations in cafeterias, trains, pubs and crowds milling round during fire drills, and found that two-thirds of the talk was neither intellectual nor practical, but seemingly trivial gossip about other people. Dunbar suggested that, just as monkeys groom each other to preserve alliances and pecking orders, so language was a sort of 'vocal grooming', suitable for the larger, more scattered groups in which humans lived. Human speech did not evolve, as most people had thought, to exchange useful information about how to spear mammoths or start fires. It was a form of soothing human contact, made of words instead of arms and warm bodies.

In *The Descent of Man* Charles Darwin noted a similar discomfort with silence among other social animals, such as wild horses and cattle, who would stop their contact calls, the random grunts or whinnies they make while foraging and eating, to alert the group to danger. More recently, the ethnomusicologist Joseph Jordania has suggested that early humans used humming as a contact call. That supportive 'hmmm' we deploy when listening to someone else may be an evolutionary hangover from its associations with this kind of reassuring noise-making.

※

Cultures with a reputation for shyness, such as the Nordic countries, seem to have a higher tolerance of silence. The Swedish ethnologist Annick Sjögren, raised in France, noticed that in her adoptive country the spoken word 'weighs lightly' and is no sooner dispensed than it will 'vanish into thin air'. French conversation is a rhetorical performance, detached from oneself, so one can say things without thinking, simply enjoying the sound of the syllables on one's tongue, without being afraid that one will be called to account for it. In Sweden, by contrast, what one says is a personal marker, and words are pondered carefully for their meaning. Small talk is *kallprata*, literally 'cold talk', and Swedish words for the talkative such as *pratkvarnar* (chatterboxes), *pladdermajor* (babblers) and *frasmakare* (phrasemongers) convey a suspicious attitude to talking for its own sake. 'Talking apparently never ceases to be a problem for the Swedes: a lean across an abyss,' reflected Susan Sontag after living in Stockholm at the end of the 1960s. 'Conversations are always in danger of running out of gas, both from the imperative of secretiveness and from the positive lure of silence. Silence is the Swedish national vice.'

The Swedish and Finnish words for shyness, *blyg* and *ujo*, carry positive associations, suggesting someone who is unassuming and willing to listen to others. Many Finnish proverbs point to the value of choosing words carefully and not saying any more than one needs to: *One word is enough to make a lot of trouble. Brevity makes a good psalm. A barking dog does not catch a hare. One mouth, two ears.* According to the Finnish scholars Jaakko Lehtonen and Kari Sajavaara, in an essay on 'the silent Finn', the overuse among their compatriots of what linguists call back-channel behaviour – nodding, eyebrow-raising, saying 'hmmm' while the other person is speaking – is considered intrusive and the preserve of drunks.

The Finnish film-maker Aki Kaurismäki's characters are similarly sparing with speech. They work away silently in dull jobs at supermarket checkouts or kitchen sinks and drive through the country's backroads, chain-drinking vodka while exchanging cryptic grunts. In *The Match Factory Girl* (1990) thirteen minutes pass, in a film just sixty-eight minutes long, before anyone speaks. Leading up to this momentous event, the eponymous heroine spends a day in the factory, goes home to cook and eat a meal with her parents, and attends a Finnish tango where the men ask women to dance by silently touching their hands, while she is ignored and sits holding her handbag in her lap. Eventually she goes into a bar and says three words: 'a small beer'.

Even in the Nordic countries, though, silence can carry awkward or hostile subtexts. In his autobiography, Ingmar Bergman attributes his stammering as a boy to the fact that grown-ups would not speak to a misbehaving child until they were visibly contrite – a cold shoulder far more painful, he recalls, than the ensuing interrogation, wheedled-out confession and ritual fetching of the carpet-beater. The Swedes have a phrase for it: *att tiga ihjäl* ('to kill by silence'). Different cultures may view shyness in a different light, and may differently assess what comprises a healthy balance between talking and listening. But silence can be deadly in all of them.

※

Just before 10 p.m. on 18 June 1940, four days after the fall of Paris, a man skilled in the art of the deadly silence sat in front of a microphone in studio 4B at Broadcasting House in London's Portland Place. He was dressed in full French military uniform down to his leggings and thigh boots, having fled to England the previous day as his country brokered a humiliating armistice with the Nazis. The BBC engineer asked him to say something to test the sound level. He stared intently at the microphone and, in a deep, resonant voice, said two words: 'La France'. He then sat in complete silence until the red light flashed to signal that they were live, and he began an emotional plea to his compatriots. 'Has the last word been said? Must hope disappear? Is defeat final?,' he said in French that managed to sound hard-edged and guttural and yet also stirring and lyrical. 'Whatever happens, the flame of French resistance must not be extinguished, and it will not be extinguished.' The French have come to know the cadences of the 'appel du 18 juin' even better than English speakers know Winston Churchill's 'finest hour' speech, delivered in the Commons earlier that day.

Charles de Gaulle's mesmerising personality flowed from his tongue. Even in extemporised addresses or when answering questions from journalists, he spoke in jewel-like sentences as if he had already drafted and redrafted them in his head. 'Magnificent personality he sounds,' wrote Vere Hodgson, a welfare worker from Notting Hill, in her diary, after listening to de Gaulle on the radio. 'His voice is thrilling, and his answer to Pétain made me shiver in my chair. Such tragedy too in his tones.' It was his lapidary sentences and sonorous delivery that allowed this low-ranking officer, barely known in France and unknown in Britain, with an army of just a few thousand soldiers behind him, to rally his compatriots and lead his nation in exile.

But these extraordinary public performances were interspersed with long periods when he would simply say *oui* or *non* or nothing at all. In the French pub on Dean Street in Soho, where the scattered colony of exiles from across the channel congregated, it was always crowded and noisy, the *bonhomie* overseen by a jovial patron, Victor Berlemont. When de Gaulle went there, he sat silently with a glass of wine while the French soldiers stood to attention and the room fell into an awkward hush.

It was as if de Gaulle's bursts of eloquence required long periods of silence to recharge his energies and store up more words, or perhaps he had decided that if he could not speak in poetry he would rather not speak at all. Most tongue-tied people cannot, as de Gaulle did, suddenly become fluent at will. Unable to think clearly when talking to others, we mangle our syntax, stumble over consonants and function far below our mental powers. Our fear is that we are boring others – which makes us throw away our words quickly or trail off at the end of sentences, so the fear becomes self-fulfilling. And yet de Gaulle never seemed to have this problem. He was silent or silver-tongued, nothing in between. It was maddening and magnetic, this refusal to make the most cursory effort at small talk and then to speak, on his own terms, so beautifully.

In May 1943 de Gaulle moved his HQ to Algiers, wanting to be on French territory. Lady Diana Cooper, based there while her husband Duff was British representative to the French committee of liberation, found that table talk with de Gaulle 'flowed like glue'. The Coopers christened him Charlie Wormwood after wormwood and gall, the symbols of bitterness in the Book of Lamentations. At formal dinners he and his wife, Yvonne, were a life-sapping pairing. He was from Lille and she was from Calais, and they both lived up to the reputation of the northern French as reserved, like their neighbours across the channel. G. K. Chesterton thought the 'shyness and moody embarrassment' of the English were also displayed by the northern French, with whom they shared an ancestry and history, for both lacked 'the rapid gestures of the South'. The de Gaulles certainly lived up to this stereotype, recoiling at the tactility of Mediterraneans and disliking the familiar French 'tu', which they did not even use with each other all the time.

On Whit Sunday in June 1943 the British minister in Algiers, Harold Macmillan, had a meeting with de Gaulle and afterwards suggested they drive to the coastal town of Tipasa for an afternoon off. There Macmillan stripped naked and went for a swim. De Gaulle declined to join him but 'sat in a dignified manner on a rock, with his military cap, his uniform and belt'. Macmillan, who threw up before giving speeches but otherwise hid his shyness well, was fascinated by 'this strange – attractive yet impossible – character'. His wife, Dorothy, was stuck with looking after Yvonne. She said later that talking to her was 'like digging at clay with a trowel'.

§

De Gaulle's shyness was quite genuine and much more than just rudeness. After being captured at Verdun in March 1916, he acquired over the next two and a half years of war a reputation among his fellow prisoners for natural leadership. So Ferdinand Plessy, a fellow POW at Ingolstadt and then Wülzburg, was astonished when one evening de Gaulle confessed to him that he was shy. Plessy could not square this with his friend's natural eloquence and air of authority. But then he reflected that de Gaulle knew how to keep his distance. He remembered that the prisoners' shower room had no partitions, just a duckboard with sprinklers overhead, and he had not once seen de Gaulle naked.

De Gaulle hated his large nose, sticky-out ears and receding chin and rarely looked in mirrors. He knew that, at nearly 6 foot 5, he walked a thin line between grandeur and ungainliness. 'We people are never quite at ease,' he told the French politician Louis Joxe. 'I mean – giants. The chairs are always too small, the tables too low, the impression one makes too strong.' His sight was poor and to read anything he had to wear bottle-bottom glasses, which he loathed. He so hated the telephone that not even his aides dared call him at his work desk, and his home phone was deliberately installed under the stairs so he had to contort his body to use it.

He could see that his shyness meant he would have to carefully cultivate a public, rhetorical style. In notebooks written as a POW he was already sketching this out. 'One must speak little. In action one must say nothing,' he told himself. 'The chief is the one who does not speak.' Unable to conduct social niceties, he acted only on the grand scale, veering between eloquent monologue and gravid silence. In fact, this public role extended so far into his private life that it was hard to know where the latter began. His son recalled that de Gaulle would emerge from his bedroom each morning in jacket and tie, and that the only time he had ever seen him in a state of undress was after his prostate operation.

If de Gaulle was devoid of personal vanity, he certainly nurtured a giant, impersonal superiority complex, referring to himself in the third person because he felt that France's representative on earth deserved such respect. In the name of French prestige he insisted on leading the First Army into Paris in an open-topped car when, on 26 August 1944, the capital was liberated. Although he knew the city was still full of Germans and French collaborationists ready to take pot shots, he then went up to the Arc de Triomphe to lay a wreath on the Tomb of the Unknown Soldier and lead the singing of the Marseillaise. He walked the length of the Champs-Élysées down to the Place de la Concorde, where a car was waiting to take him to Notre-Dame, which was crammed full of people wanting to give thanks for the city's liberation.

As de Gaulle got out of his car in the Parvis Notre-Dame, the first shots came from the rooftops overlooking the square, with bursts of answering fire from the gendarmes. De Gaulle entered the nave with snipers firing from the high galleries and the congregation throwing themselves on the ground and hiding under the pews. His minders tried to hustle him away, but he shook them off and walked slowly down the centre aisle, his shoulders back and his arms outstretched, as if the hail of bullets were no more than a slight drizzle and it wasn't worth putting up his brolly. 'Nothing could be more important,' he wrote of this moment in his memoirs, 'than for me not to yield to the panic of the crowd.'

As gendarmes worked their way through the cathedral, watching for flashes from above and firing at them, bullets ricocheted off the cathedral's pillars and chips of stone flew through the air. There was no electricity for the organ, and so the shots rang out *a cappella*. 'The advantage of having an unattractive face is that it allows one to hide, and to master, the emotions that one might reveal in public,' de Gaulle said later. As he walked down the aisle, and smelt the incense mingling with the whiff of cordite, he let his features settle into this unrevealing mask. Stirred by de Gaulle's silent courage, the congregation calmed down and rose to sing the *Te Deum*.

⁂

From Homeric epic to Shakespeare's *Henry V*, classic literature is full of loud-mouthed generals delivering stirring battle cries. Being slain in combat is also typically an occasion to say a few words: the laconic dying utterance is a leitmotif, for instance, in the Icelandic sagas. Real-life soldiers tend to be more taciturn. On the battlefield words weigh heavily. Better to say nothing than give a wrong order and send your comrades to their deaths. This verbal parsimony can linger after the battles are over, for people who have seen the worst of war are often the most reticent about it. There are no adequate words to describe a comrade's blown-off face or shell-mangled body, and those who have witnessed such things feel unable to cross that inevitable gulf of incomprehension that divides them from non-combatants. As Siegfried Sassoon observed in his poem 'Survivors', muteness and stammering were common symptoms of soldiers suffering from shell shock. One of the early names for shell shock was 'shell shyness'.

One day in Cairo in 1941, Charles de Gaulle met a soldier even shyer than himself. He was taken in to the office of Archibald Wavell, the British commander-in-chief, Middle East. The two men shook hands without speaking, and there was silence for several minutes. Wavell's chief of staff, Major-General Sir Arthur Smith, tried to retrieve the situation by suggesting that Wavell show de Gaulle his wall map. The two men studied it silently for some minutes before they shook hands again and de Gaulle left – not a word having been said by either of them.

Wavell's crushing silences were as notorious as de Gaulle's. He would listen to his staff while doodling on a notepad as they delivered messages or reports and then say in a dry, raspy voice, 'I see', or 'I should do that, if I were you'. In a series of lectures on 'Generals and Generalship' delivered at Trinity College, Cambridge, in February 1939, Wavell had argued that, while a commander should impress his personality upon his troops, he should only address them if he felt able to manage a fitting oration; a bad speech might lose his men in a few minutes. A soldier demanded competence of his leader, and such small anodynes as the harsh conditions of war could afford. Only after these basic needs were met did he look for thrilling oratory, and he could live without that if he had the rest. Certainly, the wall of reserve that lay between Wavell and his troops did not stop him conveying wisdom, integrity and even charisma. Diana Cooper, who had felt so depleted by de Gaulle, said of Wavell that she 'might fall in love with him if I got over my fear of his silences'.

As a brigade major in the Ypres Salient in the First World War, Wavell visited every part of the front line and listened carefully to his men – the antithesis of the red-faced, barking generals in Sassoon's poems. His shyness had made him a contrarian, suspicious of masculine bluster and the overconfident parroting of fixed ideas. He deplored the way that men were dying because high command clung mulishly to unsheltered and boggy trenches and refused to move back or sideways to more solid chalk or better-defended positions. The massacre at Bellewaarde Ridge in June 1915 convinced him of the stupidity of static trench warfare and massed attacks by foot soldiers against entrenched positions and of the need to find more creative ways of waging war. During this battle he lost his left eye. His habit ever after of looking intently at people with his one good eye while not speaking, his glower augmented by the monocle placed over it, fed his reputation for impassivity and unreadability.

Later in the war Wavell served in Palestine under the then commander-in-chief of the Middle East, General Allenby, whose novel use of military deception he came to admire. In October 1917 Wavell witnessed the famous ruse in which a bloodstained haversack full of false papers was left for the Turks to pick up, misleading them about which flank the British were about to attack in Gaza. He was also inspired by the unorthodox tactics of T. E. Lawrence, another soldier whose deep introversion had incubated a lateral mind. In 1920 Lawrence wrote a pioneering treatise on guerrilla warfare, 'The Evolution of a Revolt', which argued that armies should not be static but drift around like a gas, intangible and invisible. 'Armies were like plants, immobile, firm-rooted, nourished through long stems to the head,' he wrote. 'We might be a vapour, blowing where we listed.'

The historian Nicholas Rankin argues that the British talent for military deception so brilliantly fulfilled in the two world wars grew out of a national character that valued self-deprecation and concealment. The native tradition of speaking cryptically and masking seriousness with irony or jokes as 'a cover for shyness or sentiment' allowed the British to excel in the dark arts of espionage, the code-breaking of Bletchley Park and military tactics based on forgery and false rumour.

When Italy entered the war on 10 June 1940, Wavell had only 36,000 troops stationed in Egypt against 150,000 Italian troops in Libya. The Axis powers were on an unbroken run of victories, and another rout seemed likely. Wavell concluded that the enemy would have to be met with unconventional thinking. In late summer he had an intelligence officer, Dudley Clarke, posted to his staff and asked him to set up 'A' Force, an organisation dedicated to the art of military deception. Clarke had encountered Wavell three years earlier, when he first came under his command in Palestine. During a long drive from Jerusalem to Haifa, Wavell asked him when he had joined up, and Clarke replied '1916, sir'. An hour later, Wavell said, 'I meant when did you join this Headquarters?' Clarke came to value this unwillingness to waste words, and besides he was reserved as well, preferring to glide in and out of rooms unnoticed – a 'Military Jeeves', in the words of one of his superiors, who solved problems with 'a sphinxlike quality of sardonic humour and absorbent watchfulness'.

While they waited for reinforcements to arrive, Wavell and Clarke now began to turn their English flair for shyness and social disguise into a military strategy. Their plan was to use concealment and artifice to make the Italians think the region was swarming with Desert Rats. A small team of camouflage experts, headed by the magician and illusionist Jasper Maskelyne, assisted them. They made inflatable warships and papier-mâché horses, and turned trucks into tanks by covering them with painted canvas. They tied telephone poles to oil drums and threw netting over them, to make what looked like big guns from the air. They dolled up patches of desert to look like airfields and roads. They raced camels dragging harrows across the desert to kick up dust clouds like those created by tanks. Meanwhile, the ack-ack guns kept the Italian planes at high altitude, so they could not inspect this imaginary army too closely. The literal-minded Marshal Rodolfo Graziani, Italy's commander-in-chief in North Africa, fell for it. On 13 September the Italian Tenth Army crossed gingerly into Egypt, but after just 50 miles it stopped at the small coastal town of Sidi Barrani and dug in.

※

Wavell's long periods of silent reflection had turned him into a careful student of war. He knew that a good general relied less on the *coup d'oeil* in the heat of battle than on mundane things such as reconnaissance, administration and attention to detail about transport and lines of supply. But his shyness also hid, or perhaps begot, a talent for taking risks. Shy people are good at waiting and thinking; a few of them are also good at translating that eventually into action. These few people tend to be excellent at waging war, which involves long periods of boredom interrupted briefly by bloodshed. Wavell believed that a general had to be a gambler in these decisive moments, for he had learned from the last war that speed and movement counted more than firepower. The Palestine campaigns had shown the value of a mobile cavalry; how much more formidable, he thought, would be his nifty little Bren gun carriers racing across the desert. He knew the desert war would rely on fleetness of both movement and thought, because it would be fought less over territory and more like a naval battle, with mechanised armies chasing each other over sand rather than sea.

On 9 December, with reinforcements having arrived but his army still greatly outnumbered, Wavell counterattacked. His first triumph, made easier by his natural reticence, was to have kept this a complete surprise. The Egyptian prime minister commended him on being the first man to keep a secret in Cairo. With typical undersell, Wavell told the war correspondents that 'this is not an offensive ... you might call it an important raid'. Instead, his army began a stunning advance. Those who knew Wavell's restraint in person were astonished by his boldness in battle. After taking Sidi Barrani easily on 11 December, the British cleared all Italian forces out of Egypt in four days. By the new year they were deep into Libya, and by February, when the British defeated the Italians at Beda Fomm, they had conquered the whole of Cyrenaica and were on the verge of overrunning the last of the Italian forces. 'Wavell's Thirty Thousand' were now as famous as the Battle of Britain's few.

But five days after Beda Fomm, with Wavell's army poised to conquer Tripoli, Churchill ordered him to halt the advance and send his best troops to defend Greece against the Axis powers. The result was a disaster, with the British forced to evacuate to Crete and then from Crete itself. Meanwhile, a little-known German general, Erwin Rommel, had arrived in Tunis with the newly formed Afrika Korps. By the end of April he had pushed the Desert Rats all the way back to the Egyptian border, leaving Tobruk under siege.

Wavell's relations with the volatile and voluble Churchill were poor. His shyness, which had served him well in giving him the space for silent thought and allowing him to turn a problem round in the light and view it from another angle, now became a shortcoming. Churchill demanded action on every front and regarded Wavell's hedge-betting communiqués as evidence of undue caution. He wanted him to support the Free French plan to invade Syria and Iraq, held by French forces loyal to the Vichy regime – which was why de Gaulle had been in Cairo and why Wavell was not keen to see him.

Noel Annan, who worked as a military intelligence officer in the War Office and knew both Churchill and Wavell, thought it a contrast between two public school types: the old Harrovian prime minister, buccaneering and impatient of protocol, and the Wykehamist soldier-scholar, careful and reserved. But it was also a contrast between Churchill the crowd-pleasing politician, aware that war was partly about propaganda and placating allies, and Wavell the close-mouthed general concerned only with the rightness of military strategy. This lay at the heart of their worst quarrel, over whether to hold Tobruk. For Wavell the port was militarily unimportant; for Churchill it was a symbol of resistance and crucial to morale. On Wavell's trips to London, Churchill questioned him fiercely and was annoyed by his stumbling, mumbling answers. Ian Jacob, later director-general of the BBC, who attended these meetings as a war cabinet secretary, said it was 'hard to make anyone understand how tongue-tied Wavell was, and therefore how little impression he gave of intellect and character'.

Wavell got on well with Joan Bright, who worked in the Cabinet War Rooms. She was friendly and discreet, a former girlfriend of Ian Fleming often thought to be the model for Miss Moneypenny, and she could draw people out, although even she found Wavell hard work. He invited her to the United Service Club on Pall Mall for lunch, which they ate silently. As they walked back across St James's Park, equally silently, Wavell suddenly turned to her and asked why the prime minister disliked him. She told him bluntly that he did not talk enough. He began to explain, haltingly, that when he was very young, his mother had him brought down to the drawing room to speak to guests, and this hated party act had destroyed forever his ability to talk easily on demand. His mother had literally taken the words out of his mouth. Privately Bright thought this 'too ordinary an excuse – there are few mothers who do not do this for their children'.

After the disastrous failure in June 1941 of Operation Battleaxe, a Churchill-inspired plan to relieve Tobruk, the prime minister relieved Wavell of his posting and demoted him to commander-in-chief, India. The war correspondent Alan Moorehead, saddened by the news, likened Wavell to the defender of Moscow, General Kutuzov, in Tolstoy's *War and Peace*: old and one-eyed, a philosopher of human nature, modest and aware of complexity, unlike the vain and coldly calculating Napoleon. 'His fine head, his lined and leathery face, even his blind eye, give you the feeling of strength and sagacity and patience,' wrote Moorehead of Wavell, 'though there is little in what he says normally to suggest any of those qualities.'

The third Battle of El Alamein is now remembered as a watershed victory of the war, with General Montgomery as its Admiral Nelson. Montgomery was arrogant, egotistical and Wavell's complete opposite. The self-proclaimed saviour of the British army, he drove from unit to unit as if he were campaigning for election, making barnstorming speeches about hitting Rommel for six – a bullshitter who imbued his troops with confidence and gave them the partly self-fulfilling impression of having engineered a sea change.

'It may almost be said, "Before Alamein we never had a victory,' wrote Churchill later. 'After Alamein we never had a defeat."' But neither claim was true. Well before El Alamein, Wavell had all but destroyed Italy's Tenth Army, shattering Italian morale and Mussolini's vision of an African empire. As the architect of the first big allied victories, he delivered vital uplift when the Axis seemed invincible. His march across the desert can also now be seen as the first great deceptive campaign, one that institution-alised deception as a war strategy and culminated in the more celebrated strategic deceits before D-day. If the English genius for military deception was cultivated from English shyness, then Wavell was its embodiment.

But well before he died in 1950, Wavell's role in the war was fading from memory, bumped aside by his self-promoting successors, largely because he himself stayed silent. He did not say a word to support or exonerate his war record – not even in written prose, at which he was a model of eloquence and clarity, quite the opposite of his speaking self. Instead he invested his energies in compiling an anthology, *Other Men's Flowers* (1944), of the poems he knew by heart. A bestseller, it was an odd book to be compiled by such a shy man, for it affirmed the value of poetry as public communication rather than interior mental journey, and criticised T. S. Eliot in its opening pages for 'sinn[ing] against the light of poetry by wrapping his great talent in the napkin of obscurity'. Wavell pointed out that poetry was in origin a declamatory art and, with typical magnanimity, praised the 'characteristic gusto' with which Churchill recited verse. Here also lay a tinge of regret, for while he knew reams of it by rote, Wavell only said poetry out loud while riding a horse or driving alone, and wished he could fly solo so he could 'declaim it in the skies'. Otherwise, for fear of being overheard, he would not even risk reciting it in the bath.

※

One person who never had any trouble talking to Wavell was the queen, because she knew she just had to broach his favourite topic, the Black Watch, of which she happened to be colonel-in-chief, and he would relax. The king had no such luck and called Wavell 'the oyster' because he was so hard to prise open. But George VI could equally have been describing himself. Like Wavell, he talked fairly fluently about his pet subjects, such as factory assembly lines and breeding game birds. But he never mastered small talk, a greater failing in a monarch than a soldier. His fear of not knowing what to say was aggravated by his fear of not being able to say it. Since the age of seven he had suffered from an appalling stammer.

Early theories about stammerers saw them as almost literally tongue-tied – because their tongues were either too hard and thick, as Aristotle thought, or too moist and cold, as Francis

Bacon believed. With the rising interest in psychiatry in the late nineteenth century, stammering came to be seen as a symptom of nervous debility and shyness. To want to speak, but to contrive not to, seemed like a classic instance of the counterproductive, irrational impulses of the unconscious mind. Nowadays we tend to see stammering once again as a mechanical problem, a neurodevelopmental disorder that emerges, for unknown reasons, in about one in twenty young children. And yet it still seems rooted in the uniquely human capacity for self-reflection, which is why stepping outside that self can offer temporary relief. Stammering actors rarely suffer while playing a role; nor do stammerers when they sing or speak in a different language. The stammering Henry James was fluent when speaking French, and he could chant his favourite poems to friends.

As with overthinking one's shyness, overthinking one's stammer only makes it worse, creating a vicious circle of disfluency. Like shyness, it is curiously intermittent, so that stammerers who feel they have conquered it can find that it returns unbidden at the most inconvenient times. If shyness is not a cause of stammering, then stammering is certainly a cause of shyness, for many sufferers choose not to speak for fear they will be unable to.

As a young boy, George VI, then Prince Albert, would like the other royal children have to learn a poem by rote on the occasion of his grandparents' birthdays and recite it to assembled guests. This terrifying ordeal confirmed him in his desire to remain silent whenever possible. As a naval cadet he was marked down as stupid because he could not say 'quarter' and thus failed to respond when asked what half of a half was. On one occasion, in his twenties, he was so nervous when addressing an audience of farmers in the Midlands that he emitted a wordless mumble for several minutes while his equerry stood by his side wondering what to do. After this, Prince Albert settled for seeming rude. When people were introduced to him at functions, he would shake hands and move mutely on.

It was not unknown for kings and princes to say hardly

anything. Charles I, another shy, stammering youth who grew up in the shadow of a more glamorous older brother, could rely on Van Dyck portraits or Ben Jonson masques to underline the grandeur of his monarchy. The shy, German-speaking George I always began his speeches to parliament with a short sentence in English, before handing the script to his lord chancellor, who read the rest. Prince Albert's misfortune was to come of age in the new regime of mass media democracy, when the royal family had to legitimise its power with the spoken word. For a shy prince, radio and film presented endless potential for humiliation and disgrace.

※

At the opening of the British Empire Exhibition in 1924, King George V's speech at Wembley Stadium had been heard by millions of listeners. In May 1925 Albert, now Duke of York, succeeded his older brother as president of the Exhibition and had to make a brief speech introducing the king at Wembley as it reopened for the year. He fretted about it for months, going over the lines endlessly in his head: 'Your Majesty, as President, I ask you graciously to declare open again the British Empire Exhibition …'

Just before noon on 9 May he stood on Wembley's royal dais and waited for the 1,200-strong Brigade of Guards to finish playing the national anthem. This kind of pomp and ceremony unnerved him. All his life his most hated duty was inspecting troops, having to examine the polish on boots and the sharpness of creases while knowing that the soldiers were all watching him. Now the troops went rigid and a deep hush fell over the stadium as 90,000 people waited for him to open his mouth and for sound to come out. It began badly. The loudspeakers were giving feedback and he had the ill luck, which can befuddle even the most confident, of hearing his own voice a beat after it left his mouth.

People who don't stammer, especially those who cruelly ape those who do, think it is just about repeating the start of a word. But a stammerer wrestling with a word is more likely to make no noise at all, or a sucking sound, as they inhale air instead of letting their voice travel upwards through the diaphragm on an outward breath. The duke's speech was full of such excruciating pauses as his facial muscles worked overtime but no sound came out. As with many stammerers, the constant jaw-tightening meant that talking exhausted him. The Wembley speech was being broadcast live across the country, over the wireless as well as through *Daily Mail* loudspeakers installed in public places. It was the first time his people had encountered his stammer. While the rest of the Wembley crowd squirmed in sympathy for the duke, an Australian called Lionel Logue turned to his son and said quietly that he thought he could cure him.

Logue was a pioneer in the new field of speech therapy. During the war he had treated soldiers afflicted with speech disorders as a result of shell shock and gas attacks. One of his patients was John Wheeler-Bennett, who was left with a stammer after his Kent prep school was bombed in 1916. 'Only those who have themselves suffered the tragedies of the stammerer can appreciate to the full their depth and poignancy,' Wheeler-Bennett wrote from the heart half a century later, in his biography of George VI. 'The bitter humiliation and anguish of the spirit ... the shrinking from help prompted by pity.'

In his small consulting rooms at the cheap end of Harley Street, Logue encountered quiet misery daily. One of his patients, on her commute home to Earls Court from the City, would go on a different line back to Hammersmith and walk from there, rather than attempt the hard 'k' in 'Court' when buying a ticket. Another, scared of speaking to bus conductors, would ensure she always had the exact fare in small change. Perhaps the Duke of York was listening, on 19 August 1925, three months after his Wembley disaster, to a BBC radio talk by Logue about stammering titled 'Voices and Brick Walls'. 'I know of nothing which will build so huge a brick wall as this defect,' Logue told listeners. 'The ordinary procedure of buying a train ticket, or asking to be directed in the street, is untold agony.'

Most of us know the film version. In *The King's Speech*, Logue insists on holding sessions at his consulting rooms rather than the duke's home, and on being on first-name terms with 'Bertie', even calling him 'mate'. Logue then draws the duke out, much against his will, to discuss personal matters: his overbearing father, the nanny who preferred his brother and pinched him to make him cry, the painful metal splints he was made to wear for his knock knees. Logue gets the duke to cut loose, to say 'shit fuck bugger' to fill in the pauses in his speeches. For his stammer is the result not merely of 'mechanical difficulties', as the duke insists, but deep-rooted repressions. The film champions the informal, modern values of Logue, this 'jumped-up jackaroo from the outback', against upper-class English stiffness.

But the real Logue was no tea-and-empathy therapist. His methods were practical, teaching his patients to breathe properly and relax the muscles so that they did not spasm. His was no miracle cure, and not all of his patients got better. One of his failures was the novelist Nicholas Mosley, who went to him as a seventeen-year-old Eton schoolboy to little effect, except to be embarrassed at being made to speak with the up-and-down modulations of a ham actor. Mosley went on to be an army officer, where lives depended on his ability to deliver orders. Stammering through drill practice on the parade ground, he worried he 'might unwittingly become like the Emperor Christophe of Haiti who used for his amusement to march his crack troops over a cliff'. And yet, fighting his way up the spine of Italy with the London Irish Rifles in October 1944, Mosley led a near-suicidal charge across open ground against a German-occupied farmhouse at Monte Spaduro, near Bologna, and ordered the advance without a stutter. 'In matters of life and death, you don't stammer,' he said later. 'It's the yackety-yack of life where you stammer.' His impediment remained, re-emerging disastrously later in life during a lecture at the Edinburgh festival that he had to abandon.

The appeal of stammering to the cinematic imagination, with its narrative logic that demands a crisis and a solution, is that it feels like an obstacle to be decisively overcome. In reality, as Mosley's story reveals, the stammerer has to cope with the untidy coming-and-going of symptoms. In modern stammering therapy the word 'cure' is rarely used. Most young children who stammer grow out of it, but of the one in a hundred who are still stammering in their teens, few do.

The real king's speech got slightly better under Logue's tuition. But Logue still had to close-read the text of any speech the king had to make, finding alternatives for bothersome words, such as those starting with *s*, *f*, *g* and *k* – the last of these a special torment because the king often had to refer to the queen and the kingdom (which Logue replaced with 'her majesty' and 'our realm'). For the rest of his life the king dreaded the state opening of parliament, which meant delivering a speech while seated, constricting his breathing. He told Logue of an anxiety dream, which he woke up from in a cold sweat, in which he was in the House of Lords with his mouth opening and shutting but nothing coming out. All his life he feared the radio microphone and that flashing red light which told him to start speaking. He was often photographed sitting in front of one of the bespoke royal microphones mounted in art deco oak cases. But he loathed these most of all, saying the design reminded him of the Cenotaph, and they were always replaced by normal microphones for the actual broadcast.

Even when the king mastered his stammer he spoke monotonously, with a lisp, and with the generally poor vocal skills of the shy man who always expects talking to be a trial. In the film, George VI overcomes his stutter in a rousing broadcast on the day war breaks out, the people roaring their approval from the Mall while Beethoven's Emperor Concerto soars in the background. It is like the Arthurian legend of the Fisher King, whose impotence renders his kingdom a barren wasteland, and who must be restored to potency to lead his people into war. If you listen to the real king's speech delivered on that day, though, it proceeds by what Logue called 'three-word breaks', developed to carry him along in strategically placed breathing pauses. When this technique worked, it gave his speech an accidental gravity, a pleasing series of ascensions and dying falls. When it failed, as here, the king could only manage a word at a time and the breaks came in odd places: 'In this grave … hour … perhaps … the most fateful … in our history … I send … to every household of my people … both at home … and overseas … this message.'

There was no Hollywood ending. Stammering, like shyness, is a life sentence. 'The King broadcast a speech last night which was badly spoken enough, I should have thought, to finish the Royal Family in this country,' wrote the poet Stephen Spender – a man not insensitive to shyness, who found it hard even to go into pubs on his own – in his diary. 'His voice sounds like a very spasmodic often interrupted tape machine. It produces an effect of colourless monotony … First of all one tries to listen to what he is saying. Then one forgets this and starts sympathizing with him in his difficulties. Then one wants to smash the radio.'

Throughout the war people listened gingerly to the king's broadcasts, wondering if he would get through them. In John Boorman's autobiographical film *Hope and Glory* (1987), set in semi-detached London suburbia during the war, the twelve-year-old Bill Rohan and his family have finished their Christmas dinner and are listening to the king's message. As he makes it to the end, Bill's father Clive says, 'He was a lot better this year.' The rest mumble agreement, but Bill says, 'You said that last year, Dad.' His father replies: 'The land and the King are one, my son. If he stutters, we falter. He's getting better, and so are we.' The national anthem strikes up on the wireless, and they all stand anxiously to attention. The monarch's stuttering reflects a nation similarly stuttering in response to mortal danger; Churchill's voice, booming hearteningly out of the radio later on in the film, marks the turning of the tide.

This was Erving Goffman's theory of social embarrassment proven on a national scale. Everyone was conspiring to conceal an awkward situation that did not in fact need to be concealed, for they were all well aware of it. The king's stammer was the nation's open secret. The press hardly mentioned it – when they did, they said it was a small handicap that happily had now been surmounted – and the Archbishop of Canterbury, Cosmo Lang, caused huge offence before the coronation by mentioning it in the mildest terms. Newsreel film of the king's speeches was often censored to spare everyone's discomfort. Yet Mass Observation, a social research organisation that specialised in unearthing unspoken public sentiment, found that his stammer was at the forefront of people's minds when they listened to him, making them feel both anxious and protective. Many, like Bill's dad in *Hope and Glory*, told themselves it was getting better.

When the king addressed the nation on VE day, his longest ever broadcast at thirteen minutes, Mass Observation found many listeners worrying about his stammer and finding his halting delivery both painful and touching. One woman interviewed said she felt, like most people she knew, 'admiration for the way he faces his difficulties, fear that he shall trip up, and a kind of personal embarrassment when he seems likely to do so'. A Mass Observation investigator heard the VE day broadcast in a Chelsea pub with the room hushed like a church. Whenever the king halted over a hard word, her young Marxist neighbour tutted loudly and was 'the centre of looks of intense malevolence from all corners of the room'.

The king's task, which was to pretend he didn't have a stammer when everyone knew he did, was far from being the most heroic sacrifice of the war. But there was still a kind of valour in his so unfailingly doing the homework set by Logue – gargling with warm water and standing at open windows intoning tongue twisters like 'She sifted seven thick-stalked thistles through strong thick sieves' and 'Let's go gathering healthy heather with the gay brigade of grand dragoons' – just so he could do his bit to sustain this collective fiction. It is an obligation to others to which even the shy and the stammering have to sign up: an agreement to use the tongues in our heads to make sense of the world together with words, to ensure that the silence between us is not too deadly.

When Clement Attlee came to Buckingham Palace to kiss hands with George VI in July 1945, there was another long and painful silence. Attlee at last broke it by saying, 'I've won the election.' The king replied, 'I know. I heard it on the six o'clock news.' Again seemingly unaware that he was just as hard to open up, the king christened his new prime minister, perhaps the shyest in history, 'clam'. Attlee's best and most fitting *bon mot* came when advising Harold Laski, the Labour Party chairman, that 'a period of silence on your part would be welcome'. His own periods of silence were lengthy and not always welcome. Wilfred Fienburgh, who worked at Labour Party headquarters, said that talking to him was 'like throwing biscuits to a dog – all you could get out of him was yup, yup, yup'.

But Attlee's shyness also seemed to let him quietly assemble information and then snap into action. It probably made him seem more incisive than he was, for instead of thinking aloud he would, after much deliberation, just announce his decision by Olympian fiat. Attlee's three stock answers to interviewers were 'Yes, 'No' and 'I don't know'. It is hard to imagine someone so monosyllabic surviving in today's twenty-four-hour news culture, when politicians are meant to dress down, pepper their speech with glottal stops and be ever-ready with an anecdote about meeting the ordinary voter washing his Ford Sierra or walking on Hampstead Heath. This carefully coiffured casualness has done little to correct their public image as liars and chancers.

This informalising of political rhetoric is part of a more general drift in cultural life. In the post-war years an increasingly secular society adopted a new article of faith: better communication. The war effort had put a high value on teamwork and encouraged psychologists to study group dynamics. Human relations management theory argued that workers were more productive when they felt consulted in decisions. Educational research stressed that groups learned more by talking than passive listening. Workplaces discarded their more formal hierarchies in favour of an ethos of collaboration and talking things out. Just as surely as church spires were built to reach heavenwards in hope, so the architecture of modern life supported this article of faith that if we carried on talking, a point would come when all would be understood. The open-plan office, although its real purpose was to reduce rent costs by getting rid of redundant square footage taken up by linking corridors and partition walls, was justified with evangelical invocations of the creativity of chance conversations.

More recently, universities have been consumed by the same rhetoric that talk is an unalloyed good. Their libraries are no longer silent cathedrals but social hubs divided into 'quiet zones' and 'social learning zones'. Having conducted unofficial fieldwork in these zones over a number of years, my provisional research findings are that 'quiet zones' rarely are, and that the merits of 'social learning' over the dully traditional arts of reading and contemplation remain at best unconfirmed.

I wonder if this is why the stammer has acquired the romantic lustre that lends itself to Hollywood endings: other forms of inarticulacy are ever more infra dig. In a recent fly-on-the-wall TV series set in a Yorkshire school a shy boy with a crippling stammer was taught how to read aloud for his English oral exam by a teacher using a trick he had seen Logue deploy in *The King's Speech*, when he makes the duke recite from *Hamlet* while distracted by a gramophone playing music through headphones. It was a memorable and moving piece of television, much replayed and discussed. But it made me wonder if stammerers get a routinely kind hearing not always granted those who are merely unwilling or incoherent speakers. Only those who are tragically deprived of the ability to speak receive our automatic sympathy, for being able to do so is the *sine qua non* of modern life.

In his book *Speaking into the Air* the philosopher John Durham Peters claims that we now live by a dialogic ideal, a belief in the possibility and desirability of humans attaining a pure meeting of minds through better communication. He traces this ideal as far back as Saint Augustine, for whom the model of perfect communion was the angel, a term that comes from the Greek *angelos*, meaning messenger. Angels, Augustine said, could commune instantly and telepathically without the obstacle of distance or the imperfections of language. The new media of the Victorian era revived this long-held dream of angelic contact. A romantic aura surrounded new inventions such as telegraphy and the telephone, which were linked in the public mind with fads like mesmerism and telepathy, and with the ideal of empathetic connection developing within psychology, as part of a single dream: communicating with others perfectly.

For Durham Peters this search for perfect communication is a fool's errand, for not everything important can be put into words or shared with others. Much that is meaningful in our lives is beyond the reach of language, he writes, such as 'the dreams I forget on waking; the conversations children have with their "air friends" when they are alone; the sound of the heartbeat in my ears as I lie upon the pillow'. The dialogic ideal has no respect for the inaccessibility of other people and is 'a pogrom against the distinctness of human beings'. The failure of communication, with its attendant awareness that we can never truly know anyone else, teaches us the humility to accept the otherness of others and allows for 'the bursting open of pity, generosity, and love'.

§

Like Durham Peters, I find it hard to sign up to the modern shibboleth that it is always good to talk. In an age that seems to be driven by the dubious belief that pouring one's heart out is the best way of purging oneself of anxiety or disappointment, I wonder if there is something to be said for the lost art of bottling things up. A problem shared may be a problem halved, but it is also a problem made real, brought into the world of concrete and communal meaning. Something you thought about saying, but didn't, can be forgotten when the mood passes, dismissed as the *ignis fatuus* it perhaps was. But something you said out loud, and that someone else answered with that reassuring echo of nods and hums that feels like empathy, is harder to put back in the box and forget about.

In a culture that values talk as an end in itself, the risk is that we will unburden ourselves to each other, in ever louder voices, without stopping to think about how much sense we are making or if anyone is really listening. Once, in a seminar, I spotted one of my students deploying a graceful gesture that involved extending his arm at 90 degrees, slowly unclenching the fist and gazing upwards, as if he had released a helium-filled balloon and it was escaping into the air. I asked him what this meant and it turned out to be a youth-culture meme, the 'awkward balloon', the release of which signified that an uneasy silence had fallen. I wasn't clear whether the gesture was meant to exacerbate or dissipate the awkwardness, but the meaning was the same: silence is awkward and to be avoided. I did not say to him – for, naturally, being tongue-tied, I couldn't think of a reply until later – that, in small doses, awkward silences might be useful. In a world of constant babble, such discomfiting hiatuses might inspire a thoughtfulness about how much we can ever really know each other.

The cry 'no one understands me', often voiced by the shy, if only in their own heads, rarely sounds appealing to any listener. But the shy and tongue-tied can also be more aware than most that no one really understands anyone. They have a salutary sense of the limits of language and are unafflicted by the hubristic delusion that we can ever make ourselves truly understood. Speech is an extraordinarily sophisticated human skill, requiring one's brain, breath, tongue and teeth to work in unison in order to bring the amorphous workings of the mind into verbal coherence. Such a demanding trick could never be pulled off perfectly. The inarticulate know that language is an evolutionary make-do, aimed at reaching fleetingly across the unbridgeable mental divide between us all. In that sense we are all tongue-tied; some of us are just more tongue-tied than others.

I am often told I am a good listener, but I am inclined to think that the standard of human listening is so low that to earn this accolade – particularly among my own largely benign but verbose tribe, *homo academicus* – requires you simply to allow your conversational partner to speak while you deliver the odd raised eyebrow or non-committal grunt. As I nod sagely and wonder once again how to disentangle myself from someone else's monologue, Malinowski's words spring to mind: 'The hearer listens under some restraint and with slightly veiled impatience ... For in this use of speech the bonds created between hearer and speaker are not quite symmetrical, the man linguistically active receiving the greater share of social pleasure and self-enhancement.'

There is something we cling to in any unhappy situation that stops us escaping from it. I suspect that what sustains the shyness of many people is that conceited part of us that finds much social conversation to be an empty ritual, a mere filling in of awkward silence. The socially confident can seem to us not to be listening to each other at all, but playing a game of conversational catch, exchanging words like a ball thrown through the air. The shy are not just bad at small talk; we are against it on principle. We feel we have some special flair for avoiding the platitudinous, what Cyril Connolly called that 'ceremony of self-wastage' that takes place whenever fluent conversers assemble and dispense their energies in 'noises upon the air'.

We are wrong, of course – or at least we are searching for an unattainable truth. Not all conversation can be momentous or profound, because our inner lives will always be richer than our ability to articulate them, and talk is about creating common ground out of words, a shared reality that is, like all shared realities, fuzzy and flawed. Just as Malinowski found in Melanesia, some kinds of talk are nothing more than their pleasing surfaces, and are no less real for that. All of us, including the shy, might as well seek meaning and take delight in those surfaces – because looking for depth in them is like trying to walk through a looking glass into a world that doesn't exist.

5

STAGE FRIGHT

Dirk Bogarde always blamed his shyness on the fateful moment when, aged thirteen, he acquired a baby brother. To lighten the domestic load after this unforeseen arrival, and to knock some sense into a boy doing badly at school, Bogarde's father sent him to live with his aunt and her husband in Bishopbriggs, near Glasgow. He had been at his new school just a few days when his classmates, affronted by his posh English accent, stuffed his head down a toilet. Bogarde always claimed that his three Bishopbriggs years were the formative ones that made him accept loneliness as his natural state. He began building a wall round himself, learning to speak cryptically and cry discreetly, without moving a facial muscle. He likened himself to a hermit crab, tight in his scavenged shell. 'Like the ones I had scrabbled about for in rock-pools at Cuckmere Haven in the happier days, I was safe from predators,' he wrote, 'and by predators I meant everyone I met.'

When Bogarde became an actor, he realised too late that his shyness was unconquerable and that this was 'the wrong profession for such a malady; for malady it was which crippled me before I walked into a crowded room, theatre, restaurant or bar'. In 1955 he began touring in Ugo Betti's light comedy *Summertime*, directed by a young Peter Hall. His starring role in the hit film *Doctor in the House* had turned him overnight into a matinee idol, his every entrance and exit in the play greeted with screams from young female fans. He had special trousers made with a side zip because, if these women ever got near him, they were apt to rip open his flies. None of this did much for his already suffocating stage fright.

In November *Summertime* opened at the Apollo on Shaftesbury Avenue. It was a year before *Look Back in Anger* transformed the post-war theatrical landscape, and this avenue still dominated British theatre, its first nights an occasion for evening wear, furs and tiaras. A West End theatre was a daunting space for actors who arrived there from the large provincial Alhambras and were struck by how intimate the auditoria were, with audiences close enough to the stage that you could see their faces even in the dark. Every night, before curtain up, Bogarde would throw up in a dressing-room bucket.

'You can't be as frightened as I am now and still be alive,' he told one reporter. 'This is as near death, execution and everything else that I've ever come across ... That terror releases a million things in your brain, titchy things in the soul, which come flooding in as a kind of antidote to the poison of terror.' It would be easy to dismiss this as prize luvviedom were it not for the fact that Bogarde had known more respectable kinds of fear, having fought on D-day and in the battle for Normandy, witnessed the bloody aftermath of bombing raids in France and liberated Bergen-Belsen. All of these he endured, but after three weeks in the West End he was ill and had to be replaced.

Meanwhile, the seventeen-year-old Anna Massey was making a more successful West End debut at the Cambridge Theatre in another light comedy, William Douglas-Home's *The Reluctant Debutante*. Massey also suffered from stage fright, which became so severe that the skin on her hands started peeling off. It did not help that while she was appearing in *The Reluctant Debutante* she was a reluctant 'deb' for real, part of that soon-to-be-defunct tradition in which young women had to curtsey to the queen at court and then spend the social season attending balls and parties. As a perennial wallflower, she suffered stage fright in these settings as well. At one party, hosted by the Duchess of Argyll, she waited by the front door to be collected an hour early, so mortified was she to be sat on the sidelines while the prettier girls were whisked on to the dance floor.

Although *The Reluctant Debutante* was a huge hit, running for two years in the West End and then transferring to Broadway, and her own performance as the spirited *ingénue* was much praised, it did little to boost her confidence. She tried all manner of cures, from beta blockers to hypnotherapy, but nothing shifted her stage fright, which she blamed for her hair turning prematurely white. Only one thing helped a little: turning off her dressing-room tannoy so as not to hear the expectant buzz in the auditorium.

Bogarde was quite wrong to see his stage fright as evidence that he had entered the wrong profession. Far from being the preserve of the shy, stage fright is the shyness everyone gets, the common cold of self-consciousness. The most assured can suddenly succumb. Laurence Olivier had a first-time attack while appearing in *The Master Builder* at the National Theatre at the age of fifty-seven. Convinced he would forget the next line, he felt his throat closing up, his teeth clenching and the audience spinning in his eye sockets. Soon after, playing Othello, he dreaded being on the stage alone and begged Frank Finlay, playing Iago, to stay in the wings during his soliloquies. Olivier's stage fright afflicted him like a rare, inexplicable virus. He was a charismatic extrovert, and he could find no parallel in anything he had felt before, on or off stage. The fear took him five years to shake off. Whereas Massey tried to forget the audience was there, Olivier found it helped to peek from behind the curtain before the play began and curse the 'bastards' making their way to their seats, using this confected anger to conquer his nerves.

Bogarde fixed on a more radical solution. After appearing on stage once more, in Jean Anouilh's *Jezebel*, he was diagnosed with pleurisy and double pneumonia and nearly died, and decided to cut his losses and abandon the theatre for good. Always ambivalent about the profession, at the end of the 1960s he retired to Clermont, a farmhouse on a hill in Provence, and began to think of himself more as a writer than an actor. From here he wrote long, gossipy letters to hundreds of people, tapped out on his old Adler typewriter. In these epistolary friendships, his well-hidden desire to be noticed and needed could at last emerge. As one of his correspondents, Penelope Mortimer, told him in a letter, he was 'a great believer in long distance and remote devotion'.

In 1983 he was due to return to Britain to perform in a TV adaptation of Arnold Bennett's *Buried Alive*, a novella about a famous painter, Priam Farll, who out of shyness assumes the identity of his valet, Henry Leek, on the latter's death. While Leek is buried in Westminster Abbey under Farll's name, Farll melts into the Putney streets to live out Leek's shadowy life. Bogarde was perfectly cast, but he pulled out and the project fell through. He never got over his stage fright.

※

Although the ancient Athenians knew all about stage fright, the phrase itself is a late Victorian invention. Over the previous century and a half there had arisen a series of theatrical conventions which, in the pursuit of a sense of drama and occasion, created a greater feeling of separation between audience and performer and thus greater potential for anxiety in the latter. Only in the mid-eighteenth century, for instance, did audiences begin to listen to a play in reverential silence, when David Garrick, during his tenure at the Theatre Royal Drury Lane, trained them to stop talking and bombarding the stage with fruit, and banned them from sitting on the stage. It was during this era that the thrusting forestage, which immersed actors in the audience, began to recede until the main acting space had withdrawn behind the barrier of a proscenium arch.

Improved lighting widened still further the gulf between audience and actor. The arrival of gas lighting in the early nineteenth century allowed auditorium lights to be extinguished at once without a team of candle-snuffers, although the black-out was not total because pilot lights had to stay on. By the 1820s most London theatres had limelights, which burned quicklime in an oxyhydrogen flame to illuminate star actors with an incandescent white beam. Then, in 1881, Richard D'Oyly Carte installed electric lighting in his new Savoy Theatre and others soon followed. The auditorium could now be plunged into complete darkness and stage lighting was more penetrating, with spotlights creating a narrower, sharper beam cut off from surrounding shadow. As the heroic loneliness of the actor intensified in this light, so did the potential for *Lampenfieber*, the illuminating name that Germans give to stage fright.

While the modern theatre built up these physical and mental divides, music was acquiring its own equally daunting performing conventions. 'The audience intimidates me,' a young Frédéric Chopin told Franz Liszt in 1835. 'I feel asphyxiated by its breath, paralysed by its curious glances, struck dumb by all those strange faces.' It was Liszt who, in 1839, greatly increased the potential for such anxiety by inventing the form of the 'recital', with the pianist striding out from the wings to take his seat and playing for a whole evening, sat in profile so they could see both his dazzling fingerwork and his face.

Clara Schumann had begun playing scoreless as a child prodigy in 1828, but Liszt turned memorising into a theatrical performance, as if the piece were the virtuoso's own spontaneous creation. Like a rock star, he would sometimes fling his score into the audience along with his gloves. Many thought that playing by rote was conceited and disrespectful to the composers. In 1861, performing Beethoven sonatas in London, the pianist Sir Charles Hallé had to revert to using a score (or pretending to) after being criticised for playing from memory. By the end of the century, though, scoreless playing had become the unwritten and nerve-racking convention.

At the same time, the new discipline of sociology was identifying the fear of being on public display as a general feature of modern city life. In his 1903 essay 'The metropolis and mental life' Georg Simmel argued that the city combined intimidating anonymity with enforced proximity to the strangers with whom we shared its spaces. On streetcars, omnibuses and underground trains, people dead-eyed each other without exchanging a word. Being seen and silently assessed by one's fellow citizens was the inevitable lot of the modern metropolitan, who had developed a 'blasé attitude' as a defence mechanism. This inner boundary of reserve among city dwellers was so strong that they often did not know by sight their neighbours of many years, and it led small-town people to dismiss them as cold and uncongenial. But without this reserve, cultivated in the permanent stage set of the modern city, Simmel believed that the urbanite would be 'completely atomized internally and come to an unimaginable psychic state'.

Another new field of inquiry, psychoanalysis, recognised the fear of performing in public as one of the most common forms of shame in modern social life. In *The Interpretation of Dreams* (1900) Sigmund Freud identified a common embarrassment dream which always took the same form: the dreamer was naked in public, unable to move and escape this distressing situation, and surrounded by indifferent strangers. The embarrassment at being naked was somehow made worse by its being played out in front of an anonymous crowd who, far from being scandalised by one's nakedness, could not care less.

The first psychiatric investigations of shyness tended to conflate it with stage fright. In his 1901 book *Les Timides et la Timidité* the Parisian psychiatrist Paul Hartenberg wrote that for a young man 'it is a big deal just to enter a salon' for 'he dies of the fear that there might be something in his outfit that is not absolutely impeccable'. In 1903 his fellow Frenchman Pierre Janet named a condition, *phobie des situations sociales*, to describe the fear of being watched while doing routine things such as writing, talking or playing the piano. One of Janet's patients was a fifty-two-year-old man who was afraid of walking across Parisian squares. In their vicinity he started shaking, could not breathe and heard a voice telling him: 'You're going to die.'

Stage fright was as much a physical as a mental malady. In 1907 the American psychologist Josiah Morse listed the somatic symptoms: abdominal constrictions, palpitations, cold sweats, trembling, chills, rising gorge and occasional vomiting. For its victims stage fright seemed to be a spontaneous and unstoppable emotional reaction 'like the vertigo which is produced by looking off great heights and precipices'. Other sufferers compared it to seasickness. In extreme cases the parasympathetic nervous system shut down the metabolism and increased gastric activity, and the truly stage-frit suffered that loosening of the sphincters which is presumably the origin of the phrase about having 'no guts'. Morse believed that stage fright was part of the more general condition of timidity, which expressed itself in 'various degrees of stupidity or mental confusion' and 'a chaos of feelings or stupor'. Its only real difference from timidity, he argued, was that 'there is no element of shame in stage-fright, for there is no blushing. One blushes before a single person, never before a thousand.'

The violinist Eugene Gruenberg was well acquainted with stage fright, for he performed with the Leipzig Opera Orchestra and the Boston Symphony Orchestra, both of whose audiences had a reputation for being demanding. In an essay on stage fright written in 1919 he blamed it on the architecture of modern theatres and concert halls, which made the performer skulk in subterranean green rooms 'like a culprit, waiting for his decapitation'. But he also thought that anyone could be struck by this 'stage-fright bacillus': a surgeon before an operation, a young woman entering a ballroom, a waiter serving at tables. For Gruenberg theatrical or concert-hall stage fright was simply an acute instance of the dramaturgical nature of modern life, which forced us to become social performers and brought us into contact with unknown and often hostile others.

What would you do if your consuming ambition was to be a concert pianist and yet you suffered from crippling stage fright? It is a surprisingly common predicament. In 1905 a fifteen-year-old English girl called Agatha Miller boarded at a Paris pension, where she was taught piano. Slated to perform in the end-of-term concert, she was seized by fear and plagued by anxiety dreams in which she arrived late, the keys of the piano stuck together or it turned into a church organ which she could not play. In the end she became so ill that she was forbidden from performing. Even when she was allowed to play in public, her nerves defeated her.

Young women of Agatha Miller's generation and class had to perform their genteel social roles flawlessly and unfailingly. Many found it so draining that they had to 'retire' for a couple of hours in the afternoon to recuperate. The intensely shy Agatha found this kind of role play especially exhausting. For her first season as a debutante, her mother took her to Cairo. One officer returned her after a dance, telling her mother that she danced well but 'you had better try and teach her to talk now'. She found it impossible to keep up her end of a conversation and feared drying, just like an actor forgetting her lines. She had the bad luck not to like either alcohol or tobacco, those then near-universal props for feigning self-possession. At cocktail parties she looked for somewhere to hide her full glass of wine while envying those women nonchalantly flipping away cigarette ash as they talked.

According to Erving Goffman, the unending performance that is social life breaks down only in an extreme crisis. At this critical moment, he writes, 'the flustered individual gives up trying to conceal or play down his uneasiness'. He collapses into tears or fits of laughter, faints, flees from the scene or becomes rigidly immobile. Once this Rubicon is crossed, 'it is very difficult for him to recover composure. He answers to a new set of rhythms.' This is what happened to Agatha late one Friday night in December 1926, when she suffered a severe attack of stage fright that shadowed the rest of her life. Her novel *The Murder of Roger Ackroyd* had appeared earlier that year and made her famous under her married name, Agatha Christie. But she was still grieving from her mother's death, and her husband had just confessed he was having an affair. At their house in Surrey she packed a case, got into the two-seater Morris she had bought with her royalties and drove off into the dark. The car was found abandoned next morning near Guildford. She had taken a train to Harrogate and, under a pseudonym, booked into the Hydropathic Hotel.

By withdrawing so dramatically from the world Christie had succeeded only in attracting its attention. Her abandoned car became a tourist site, with ice-cream vans parked around it. The police dragged nearby lakes and rivers and scoured the North Downs with tracker dogs. When she was finally spotted by the Hydropathic Hotel's bandsmen, the press turned from suspecting her husband of murder to accusing Christie of being a self-publicist. In fact, she was horrified at the attention. The brief reference to it in her memoirs is to feeling 'like a fox, hunted, my earths dug up and yelping hounds following me everywhere'. Her biographer Laura Thompson suggests that her loathing of publicity began here and was an attempt finally to refute the idea that her vanishing had been a canny career move.

During a happy second marriage, to the archaeologist Max Mallowan, her shyness abated, but even he noticed in her 'an inbuilt armour off which any questionnaire was liable to glance like a spent arrow'. Accompanying Mallowan on digs in Syria and Iraq in the 1930s, she commended herself on overcoming her debility, until an encounter with a curt male colleague of her husband's once again made her, she wrote, 'completely imbecile with shyness'.

Christie was not the first or last writer to overcompensate for her inarticulacy in the flesh with fluency and prolificacy on the printed page. But she was unusual in creating a central character so starkly her opposite. The woman who conceived the hyper-confident Poirot, an actor *manqué* who treated the apprehending of the villain as an opportunity for bravura intellectual display, was the same one who took over from Dorothy L. Sayers as chairwoman of the Detective Club with the proviso that she would never have to make a speech. 'If you are doubly burdened, first by acute shyness, and secondly by only seeing the right thing to do or say twenty four hours later, what can you do?,' she wrote in the *Daily Mail*. 'Only write about quick-witted men and resourceful girls whose reactions are like greased lightning.' To her diary Christie confided that she thought Poirot 'an egocentric creep'.

It is odd, given her stage fright, that after the war she should turn to writing plays for Shaftesbury Avenue, her ebullient producer Peter Saunders nursing her through what she called her 'shy fits' on first nights. In April 1958, when *The Mousetrap* became the longest-running production in British theatre, with 2,239 performances, Saunders invited nearly a thousand people to a party at the Savoy Hotel. Ever since her grandmothers had taken her to Gilbert and Sullivan operettas at the Savoy as a girl, she had seen it as the essence of glamour. Poirot and his sidekick Hastings dine often in the Savoy Grill and Christie said she had once seen a man who *was* Poirot having lunch there. These associations only made her more anxious about attending the party. 'See you at "Hell at the Savoy" on Sunday,' she wrote to her agent.

Saunders asked her to arrive early so she could have photographs taken with a birthday cake and the play's cast – another ordeal, for she was phobic of cameras and self-conscious about having become very overweight. Arriving alone in her best bottle-green chiffon dress and elbow-length white gloves, she tried to enter the room where the party was and the doorman, not recognising her, refused her entry. The bestselling author in history, paralysed by her 'miserable, horrible, inevitable shyness', meekly turned away and had to be rescued later from the lounge. 'I still have that overlag of feeling that I am *pretending* to be an author,' she wrote in mitigation. 'Perhaps I am a little like my grandson, young Mathew, at two years old, coming down the stairs and reassuring himself by saying: "*This is Mathew coming downstairs!*"'

Christie found a means of side-stepping her stage fright. A fast writer, she had learned to touch-type to keep up with her flow of ideas, but by her early sixties she found it tiring to sit at a desk all day. Dictating her words to someone, even to her trusted secretary Charlotte Fisher, made her self-conscious and she kept stumbling and losing her rhythm. So she became an early adopter of a new invention: the portable tape recorder.

Speaking into a machine can be awkward for a shy person, because at some point you will hit the playback button and be confronted with that disconcerting sense of near recognition you feel when hearing your own voice. Your recorded voice is yourself as others hear you, through the air rather than through the bones of your skull, which is why it sounds so high-pitched and odd. But a tape recorder, whirring and wheezing away, is at least a respectful audience. It never scowls, folds its arms or heckles. If you lose your thread, you can click the pause button, as Christie often did, and gather up your thoughts.

A few years ago Christie's grandson Mathew Prichard – the one who talked to himself while coming downstairs – found a cardboard box of twenty-seven unlabelled tapes, thirteen hours of recordings of reflections for her autobiography. He feared her old Grundig Memorette machine had been ruined by leaking battery acid. But a technical friend fiddled with it, and her voice came through loud and clear, talking gaily about her pre-war travels in the Middle East. 'I must have behaved rather as dogs do when they retire with a bone,' Christie was saying of her habit of writing furtively. 'They depart in a rather secretive manner and you do not see them again for around a half-hour. They return self-consciously with mud on their nose. I think I must have done much the same.'

With only a machine for an audience, Christie's voice did not sound as though it belonged to someone shy at all. It was clear, unhurried and slightly grand, rolling its Rs and clipping its conso-nants with relish, rather like Margaret Rutherford, who played the redoubtable Miss Marple on film. Christie's only nervous tic was a slight cough in mid-sentence. She sounded like an old-school headmistress addressing her girls with just the right blend of warmth and firmness. It was the sort of voice you never hear any more, right out of deepest England.

§

While Agatha Christie was conversing with her trusty reel-to-reel, another failed concert pianist was embracing similar remedies for stage fright. One of the great virtuosos of his age, the Canadian Glenn Gould, had come to feel that concert halls were circuses, 'a comfortably upholstered extension of the Roman Colosseum', where the audience was subconsciously overcome by bloodlust and wanted to see the soloist fail. But he longed to abolish applause as well, thinking it lured pianists into show-off rubatos and glissandos. For concerts, Gould dressed in an ill-fitting lounge suit instead of the usual black tie, loped on to stage with his hands in his pockets, conducted himself with a spare hand and hummed along with the music. These apparently attention-seeking tics were really about immersing himself in his playing and shutting out the audience. On the rare occasions when performing that he looked right into the auditorium, he seemed momentarily shocked to see people there.

Gould was not alone among his peers in showing this combination of anxiety and obduracy in front of an audience. Many pianists of his generation also loathed giving concerts, battling with stage fright or shyness or succumbing to mysterious illnesses. In 1964, aged thirty-six, the brilliant American pianist Leon Fleisher had his career curtailed by a strange condition that shaped his right hand into a claw. After contemplating suicide, he managed to forge a second career playing repertoire for the left hand only. His condition was only diagnosed much later as a neurological disorder called dystonia, eventually cured by a pioneering course of Botox. He feared it had been caused by a lifelong search for perfection which had brought him 'great despair, self-pity and unhappiness allied with commensurate ecstasies'. Another celebrated American pianist, Gary Graffman, who suffered from dystonia and other involuntary jerks and contortions, wrote that 'instrumentalists' hand problems – somewhat like social diseases – are unmentionable ... Admitting difficulties is like jumping, bleeding, into piranha-filled waters.'

A rotund powerhouse of a man who played piano as if possessed, John Ogdon was shy and withdrawn away from the recital hall. His friend Brian Masters described him as a 'shambling shell' whose trick when conversing with someone was simply to nod and smile sweetly. He chain-smoked but barely inhaled, deploying the cigarette mainly as a device to ward off conversation, and his voice on the rare occasions he did use it was 'marshmallic and mild'. In 1973, perhaps owing to the pressure of performing 200 concerts a year around the world, he suffered a manic-depressive psychosis, became angry and violent with his wife and tried to kill himself. He received electric shock treatment, which ruined his playing technique forever.

Set against this roll call of illness and failure, Gould's point about the toxic nature of these performing rituals begins to seem less eccentric. In 1964 Gould himself retired from performing, aged thirty-two, and retreated into the safe, windowless cocoon of the recording studio. The microphone, he felt, had a clarity and richness with which the concert hall's blunt-edged acoustics could not compete, and the long-playing record granted a new power to listeners, liberating them from the audience-conquering pomposity of the great concertos and the virtuoso's pointless splashing around of notes.

In the new age of the mixing desk, Gould predicted, concert-going would be 'as dormant in the twenty-first century as, with luck, will Tristan da Cunha's volcano'. His stage fright had turned him, *ex post facto*, into an evangelistic media futurologist in the McLuhanite mode. He began to lead a nocturnal existence, waking up in mid-afternoon and confining his social life to rambling, dead-of-night phone calls with long-suffering friends – he believed you could have more rewarding relationships if you filtered out the visual interference – before settling down to work until dawn on his tape recorders and splicing machines.

Gould was very taken with the Canadian thinker Jean Le Moyne's idea of the 'charity of the machine'. Le Moyne thought that in the future all machines – radio, TV, telephones, cars, trains – would form part of a network, a single organism that functioned as a 'second nature'. While Le Moyne's contemporaries worried about the alienating, robotic impersonality of machines, he believed instead that they might create a space for collective humanity to express itself without the distracting noise of egotism and self-consciousness. People show their better natures, he felt, when they are not in close proximity to each other. His theories about an integrated network of machines are now seen to have anticipated the internet, although even Le Moyne might have struggled to argue that people's better natures are displayed there.

Gould had loved the radio since he was a boy and as an adult had it on all the time, even as he slept. 'It's always occurred to me that when those first people sat glued or wired to their crystal sets,' he said, 'what they really were recognizing was ... the sheer mystery and challenge of another human voice being five blocks away and being heard.' In 1965 he made his first radio documentary for the Canadian Broadcasting Corporation, *The Search for Petula Clark*. Through the prism of Clark's music, which Gould discovered while driving the long number 17 highway in Ontario and enjoying its superb wireless reception, the programme celebrated the mobile solitude of the long car journey with a radio as your only link to the rest of humanity.

On Lake Simcoe, 90 miles north of Toronto, Gould had a winter-proofed cottage which his family had owned since he was young. As a boy he had cycled into the nearby farmland and sung to the cows, and claimed never again to have encountered such a congenial audience. He loved what he called the 'Ibsenesque gloom' of the north's wild landscapes and gunmetal-grey skies. He associated Beethoven with driving through snow on the way back to Toronto on Sunday afternoons, listening to the New York Philharmonic on the radio, and he always preferred the northern European composers – Orlando Gibbons's austerely beautiful counterpoint, Bach's immaculately crafted mathematics, Sibelius's tone poems – to the more impassioned Mediterraneans.

He went on to make a number of radio documentaries about the far north, which has a similar imaginative pull on Canadians as the west has on Americans. *The Idea of North* (1967) was based around a 1,015-mile journey he took on the Muskeg Express from Winnipeg to Churchill in sub-arctic northern Manitoba. The programme mixed and overlapped human speech in a way that he called 'contrapuntal' and which was inspired by his solitary journeys north, when he whiled away time at truck stops eavesdropping on conversations, learning to hear the lilting cadences of northerners' speech as a kind of music.

This idea of the north as a place where you could escape other people was, as Gould well knew, a romantic fallacy. His interviewees, old hands who talked about life in the northern third of Canada, often said that the isolation and harshness of the environment meant that people stuck closer together and relied on each other more. Gould, who did not even like the cold very much, knew that you could just as easily live a hermit-like existence in a hotel suite with room service. But his romantic attitude to the far north embodied two notions he held dear: that solitude was a precondition for creativity, and that the most worthwhile and enduring forms of communication occurred against the seeming handicap of physical distance.

Gould was not shy in the conspicuously uneasy way that, say, John Ogdon was; his often exasperated friends and colleagues tended to see him more as neurotic, single-minded or stubborn. But he did have that classic shy sense of feeling stymied by normal social codes and conventions, and having to look – in his case, with magnificent ingenuity – for alternative ways of reaching other people. And he had an extreme variety of that weird over-confidence that can afflict shy people, that they are escaping the cant and evasions of social life in pursuit of some deeper and purer connection with the rest of humanity.

Given Gould's hatred of live performance, and his faith in

the creative potential of keeping your distance from others, it is fitting that his work should invite the most delayed and distant audience response of all. His recording of the Prelude and Fugue in C from the second book of Bach's *The Well-Tempered Clavier* formed part of the 'golden record', that mix tape of music, natural earth sounds and greetings to aliens that was affixed to the outside of Voyager I and II, the spacecraft launched hopefully into the nothingness of space in 1977. No extraterrestrial audience – even assuming they ever work out, from the pictorial instructions etched into the disc itself, how to spin the record and put the stylus in the groove – is likely to hear Gould's piano-playing for at least another 185,000 years, when these spacecraft may at last enter the orbit of a star with a habitable earth.

§

At half-past four one morning in 1967 or 1968, in his bedroom in the family home in Tanworth-in-Arden, another stage-frit voice committed itself to tape. Unlike Gould's night-time recordings, this one was never meant to be preserved, still less sent into space; it seems to have been made for no one's ears in particular. But the recording survives. The voice's owner has just returned, drunk, from a party and is speaking into the mic of a Ferrograph mono recorder. His family had been capturing each other's voices since the early 1950s, when his father, an engineer, brought home one of the first reel-to-reels. 'I think there's something extraordinarily nice about seeing the dawn up before one goes to bed,' this deeply middle-class voice is saying. 'I shall probably stop talking here, because if I don't I shall start soon relating the life histories of things, which will be frightfully tedious ...'

Our voices are such markers of our identities, with signatures as distinctive as fingerprints, that anxiety will always find its way into our vocal cords. A voice is just an exhaled breath, a series of vibrations of air produced by different parts of the body from the abdomen to the lips, and a confident voice resonates with the breath of life itself. A screaming baby does not need to worry if its voice will carry; it is just a breathing body, making itself heard. But the shy and ill-at-ease generally fade into muttering monotone, whether they like it or not. Agatha Christie's voice may have found a renewed assurance alone with a tape recorder, but this Tanworth bedroom voice is classically shy: half-hearted and wavering, with a falling inflection on each phrase. It betrays those familiar bad habits, such as breathing shallowly and slouching so the voice's journey up from the diaphragm is blocked, that the shy acquire when they are unsure if others want to hear what they have to say. It is the only surviving record of Nick Drake speaking.

The back cover photograph on his first album, *Five Leaves Left*, has Drake in focus, leaning against the brick wall of a Battersea factory, while a blurred man, late for the bus, runs past him. The image captures the general aura Drake gave off of being on the edges, looking in. The writer and musician Brian Cullman recalled going for a curry with a group of friends and not even noticing that Drake was there, the spectre at the feast, until they paid the bill. Brian Wells, a Cambridge contemporary, said that Drake would often just get up while they were playing records and smoking pot in someone's room, and leave. It gave him an air of mystery, as if he had an unknown parallel life, even though he was probably just going back to his room. Wells went on to be a psychiatrist and referred to Drake in professional terms as 'defended' – compartmentalising his life, policing his boundaries, letting others in only on his terms.

It was when he moved to London to make records that Drake's natural introversion congealed into something darker. Increased shyness is a known side effect of excessive pot-smoking, as the initially disinhibiting influence of the drug can give way to anxiety and agoraphobia. The dreamy, listless haze induced by 'Mary Jane' infuses many of Drake's songs, as does the attendant sense of observing from the wings and being too timorous to join in. His producer Joe Boyd said that Drake answered the phone in this period with a muffled 'Uh, hello?' as if he had never heard it ring before. He began wandering the streets of the city, ending up in friends' houses, mutely accepting a mattress for the night and leaving the next morning without a goodbye.

Where would Drake have been without the electric microphone? When this first came along in the 1920s, it allowed singers to personalise their delivery and make a closer connection with audiences. Relieved of the need to project over the orchestra, they no longer had to sound like generic tenors or sopranos, but could sing in *mezza voce* and sound like themselves. Performers like Drake, who sang at the same volume as he spoke, even found the microphone improved their tone and brought out harmonics unheard by the unaided ear. When the first multi-track tape machines arrived in the early 1960s, soft singers could have their voices turned up high on the mix so the instruments did not drown them out.

At the Sound Techniques studios, just off Chelsea's King's Road, where Drake recorded his albums, the brilliant engineer John Wood was pioneering multi-track recording and mic'ing up voices as if they were another instrument, creating a vocal line that was clear and alluring without sounding too amplified. After experimenting with several microphones for Drake, he chose a Neumann U67, which allowed him to sing very close to the mic without it creating popping sounds out of the plosive blasts of air the mouth expels. Drake's breathy, mumbling voice now sounded haunted and beautiful. At the top of his fairly narrow register it was soft and melodic, if slightly flat; lower down it was more of a purr, and on the lowest notes almost a growl.

Drake had first hitch-hiked to France during the summer of 1965 while he was still at school, and he returned often over the next few years. In 1967 he spent four months at the University of Aix-en-Provence studying French and writing songs. Here he immersed himself in the *chanson* tradition, which began with the Provençal troubadours and their northern counterparts, the *trouvères*, and came to maturity in the informal setting of Parisian cafés and night-clubs. Declaiming the words matters more than the melody in the *chanson*, and when the electric microphone arrived it became the perfect means for *chansonniers* to exploit the rhythms and inflections of the French language. *Chansons* typically have intimate vocals with a simple accompaniment, so every syllable is audible, and, as the *chansonnier* Georges Moustaki put it, 'there is no need to sing above the level of your heart'.

Many of Drake's songs are like English *chansons*, lyric and melody working together to produce a string of vivid observations. They do not have a chorus and an eight-bar bridge like conventional songs, just a loose series of verses linked by a refrain. His voice drifts away from the guitar rhythm, each vocal line beginning just after the beat, so his phrasing seems hesitant but natural, as if he is fighting his shyness to get something said.

Although at first listen he sounds like the sensitive singer-songwriter baring his soul, Drake's songs are actually quite cagey. They might well be scenes from his life, with hints of missed opportunities ('One of These Things First'), unfulfilment ('Day is Done'), the inadequacy of words ('Time Has Told Me') and urban loneliness ('The Chime of a City Clock'). But they mostly avoid the first person, addressing instead an indeterminate 'you' or 'they'. This is typical of the *chanson*, a form that allows someone to sing their heart out while hiding behind different guises. Georges Brassens, a renowned *chansonnier* of the post-war years and certainly someone Drake would have listened to in Aix, sang bourgeois-baiting songs about sexual conquests, cuckoldry and venereal disease, complete with satirical vignettes of the police, judges and priests. But he performed them quietly and rather nervously, sat on a straight-backed chair with just his guitar, a pipe and glass of water to hand.

Françoise Hardy was another shy *chansonnière* with whom Drake felt an affinity, and who also suffered from stage fright. In May 1968 she was half-way through a show at the Savoy, and, as overawed by the place as Agatha Christie had been, she forgot the words to a new song. While a more confident performer might have brushed this off, Hardy retired from live performing later that year, and had nightmares about it for the next forty years. In the summer of 1970 Joe Boyd arranged a meeting between Drake and Hardy in her apartment on the Île St-Louis in Paris, during which Drake simply stared into his tea and did not speak. Despite this unpromising start, Drake agreed to write songs for Hardy and they had other monosyllabic meetings over the next few years. An urban legend says that he once stopped off in Paris, rang her doorbell, discovered she was out and left without even leaving a message with her maid. Since the only authoritative source for this tale would be the timid doorbell-ringer himself, it probably never happened, but the story has stuck. It sounds just like something Nick Drake would have done.

§

Nowadays, a snatch of video on YouTube of music made in his bedroom might have been all Drake needed to build a following. In those days the options for a shy performer were more limited, especially since Chris Blackwell of Island Records, Drake's parent record company, was reluctant to advertise music directly via a separate marketing department. British radio played mostly chart music, and so live shows were the only way for an artist like Drake to build an audience – forcing him to face down his stage fright.

His first big concert came in September 1969, a few weeks after *Five Leaves Left* was released, supporting Fairport Convention at the Royal Festival Hall. It was about the worst place for a nervous performer to do his first major gig. Its monster auditorium is like a giant hangar, 3,000 seats sweeping uninterrupted down to the front, with no separating pillars between performer and audience. If you are playing solo, it seems like a very long way from the wings to the centre of the massive stage. The hall's famous Egg in a Box design, in which the curved auditorium floats on stilts above the foyers, was supposed to cut out external noise, but in fact made it hard to hear at the back and sides. Drake's feathery voice barely carried. He had only brought one guitar and, because each song required bespoke retuning, he needed long gaps between songs to twiddle the machine heads, during which time he completely ignored the audience. His only admission of their presence came as he walked off and waved his guitar vaguely in their direction. According to David Sandison, Island's press officer, he could have been a roadie doing a sound check.

Smaller gigs were worse, as Drake's ethereal sound fought a losing battle against the clinking glasses and low conversational drone in pubs and bars. He wasn't bold enough to tell people to shush. The sound equipment in these venues was invariably poor, with just one mic for his voice and one for his much louder guitar, and no fold-back monitoring to allow him to hear himself. The mic picked up the sound of his chair squeaking and his jacket buttons hitting the guitar, but his voice sounded dampened and distant, not helped by him turning his head away from the mic as if he had changed his mind about being heard. Half-way through songs he would lose his nerve and start again.

The nadir arrived when he was booked for the Guest, Keen and Nettlefolds Nuts and Bolts Apprentices' Annual Dance in Smethwick at the end of 1969. About fifteen people gathered in front of the stage as he began, but most of his audience were still cleaning up after the meal and stacking chairs to make way for the disco. There is nothing lonelier-looking than a musician playing for a crowd that isn't listening. Drake's sister Gabrielle said later that he had 'a skin too few' for a creative artist, because 'you have to be able to bare your soul in your work while someone goes off and makes coffee in the middle of your performance'.

But nor was he good at coping with attention. If someone praised his music, he would shrug and walk away. When Jerry Gilbert interviewed him for *Sounds* magazine, he just stirred his tea and started the odd sentence that trailed off into silence. He barely mentioned to his sister Gabrielle that he was making his first album, and then one day in the summer of 1969, came into her bedroom, threw the LP on her bed and said, 'There you are'. It was the classic, self-defeating act of the shy: investing in something that you hope will change people's idea of you, and then announcing it with a throwaway gesture that fails to convey how much it means to you. He recorded his last album, *Pink Moon* – which consisted of just his voice, guitar and a single piano overdub – without telling anyone except John Wood, the studio engineer, and then handed in the master tapes at the Island Records reception desk in a plastic bag.

By then Drake was back home living with his parents. At some point late in each afternoon he would leave his bedroom without a word, get into his car and drive fast into the night, a ritual that seemed to offer him self-obliterating relief. A few hours later, unable to face buying petrol, which in those days meant talking to a petrol-pump attendant, his tank would be empty, and from a call box he would ring his father, who patiently drove for miles to siphon fuel into his car. On 1 August 1974, three months before Drake died of an overdose of antidepressants, his father's diary recorded a hopeful sign that he might be turning a corner. After several failed attempts, he had managed to fill up at the Tanworth garage.

In our self-service, automated world, we forget that until half a century ago, shy people had the unavoidable daily ordeal of talking to service staff: shop assistants, floorwalkers, doormen, petrol-pump attendants. Just the thought of entering a shop made the historian Thomas Carlyle unhappy, and, according to Josiah Morse, 'the idea of ordering a suit or buying gloves prostrated him'. Agatha Christie dreaded stepping off the pavement into a shop, anxious that the assistants would not understand her order. One of Elizabeth Taylor's characters similarly rehearses giving the order to the shop assistant in her head, worried she will mishear her and bring Bisto instead of Rinso, and fretting over 'how to seem off-hand enough'.

These anxieties were diminished, or at least displaced, after the arrival of the supermarket, with its invitation to browse through aisles of produce, silent and incognito. Nowadays the shy can scan their own items at the checkouts or, better still, fill their virtual shopping baskets online and click to buy; sliding doors and lifts have made doormen and porters almost extinct; and the latched-nozzle petrol pump with automatic cut-off has turned all petrol stations into lonely atolls of self-service. Perhaps this was all that Drake needed, and Glenn Gould was right: we reveal our better selves to each other when the impersonal charity of the machine serves as both barrier and intercessor. Or perhaps this would have only, as psychotherapists say, 'enabled' and set up a 'maintenance cycle' for Drake's shyness, giving him permission to retreat ever more into himself.

⁂

Some time in 1970 Joe Boyd had tried to turn Drake into a song-writing partnership with his label mate, a young woman called Vashti Bunyan. 'It wasn't a very productive afternoon,' she said later, with sweet English understatement. The last time she saw Drake was in the offices of their record company, as they were both waiting to see Boyd. He stood facing the wall and said nothing.

Bunyan's shyness was less life-hampering than Drake's, but she too – like the biblical Queen Vashti, after whom she was named, who refused to show off her beauty at a banquet as her king demanded – had a habit of going missing. It first revealed itself in her brief time at the Ruskin School of Drawing in Oxford, when she stopped going to classes and tried to present her absenteeism as an art work. She was discovered by Andrew Loog Oldham, the Rolling Stones' producer-manager, who thought he had found the new Marianne Faithfull, and in June 1965 she released her first single, Jagger and Richards's 'Some Things Just Stick in Your Mind'. But when she sang it on TV, she hid her face behind her Françoise Hardy hair and struggled to find something to do with her hands. Like Drake, she was a nervy performer, with the same problem of being unable to make her gossamer voice carry on primitive 1960s sound systems, and she was liable to break down in tears and flee the stage in the middle of gigs. The single flopped.

She went to live in a tent under a rhododendron bush at the back of Ravensbourne Art College, near Chislehurst, where her boyfriend, Robert Lewis, was studying. In May 1968 they set off in a horse-drawn gypsy caravan for the tiny islets of Isay, Mingay and Clett off the Isle of Skye, which their friend, the folk-pop singer Donovan, had just bought, intending to set up an artists' commune. On the way there she wrote songs about homecoming fishermen, the smell of peat, the sound of seabirds, Hebridean sunsets – not songs with conventional narrative lines but a series of images burning briefly like flares. They were written almost as charms or incantations, ways of blocking out the unbucolic nature of their actual journey, much of it on the busy A5, during which they were spat at by people in passing cars who thought they were gypsies. Having reached the Hebrides after a year and a half to find the artists' commune long dispersed, Bunyan returned to London at the end of 1969 and, at Joe Boyd's request, recorded an album of her songs at Sound Techniques over just a few days.

All her life Bunyan had wanted to be a disembodied voice. As a child she had been obsessed with a recording, among her father's collection of 78s, of the choirboy Ernest Lough singing 'O for the Wings of a Dove' – one of the most loved of early gramophone records, capturing a beautiful treble voice at its peak. It was made in 1927 in the Temple Church, Fleet Street, in the early days of electrically amplified recording, with Lough standing on two bibles to reach the solitary mic of HMV's new mobile recording unit. 'I am quite sure that no boy's voice has ever been recorded nearly as well as this,' wrote Compton Mackenzie in the *Gramophone*, 'and I am equally sure that I have never heard such a beautiful voice.' Bunyan played the record over and over until her dad told her off for scratching the shellac and blunting the needle.

Little was known about Lough except that he had an exquisite voice and (at time of recording) a cherubic choirboy face, which appeared on the cover of new pressings of the record long after his treble had turned to baritone. The dearth of information inspired strange rumours: he had burst a blood vessel while singing the line 'and remain there forever at rest' and dropped down dead, or had fallen and smashed his skull while playing football, or been abducted by a rival choirmaster, or died of consumption, or been killed in a car crash. Bunyan's first ambition was to *be* Ernest Lough – not the real boy to whom these strange things were said to have happened (and who actually lived into his eighties), but his acoustic effigy. The gramophone record, she felt, allowed a person to vanish and have their voice retained in wax.

Bunyan's upper notes had something of the chorister's treble about them, especially when, as in the intro to 'Window over the Bay', her voice was allowed to float unaccompanied, or, as on 'Diamond Day', she simply lala-ed as if it were another musical instrument. Boyd's production is immaculate, with the sound of each breath and string given just the right weight in the mix. Bunyan's voice, which could easily have been smothered by over-instrumentation, comes beautifully through Robert Kirby's delicate arrangements for recorder, dulcichord and strings.

But it was Bunyan's bad luck that, by the time she started making records, having an exquisite voice was no longer enough; the public needed to know who its owner was. Her album *Just Another Diamond Day* was not released until the end of 1970, by which time she'd had a baby son, who cried whenever she picked up a guitar, and she could not have toured even if she'd wanted to. The album 'just edged its way out, blushed and shuffled off into oblivion', as she put it, selling only a few hundred copies. She learned, as Drake had done, that for the shy performer being ignored feels worse than hostility.

She moved back to Scotland to raise her family, only picking up a guitar again to teach her son to play. Her three children, finding a tape of the album in the house, had to listen to it in secret in the car, because their mother could no longer bear to hear her own voice. In the lovely coinage she used as the title of her long-delayed second album, she now spent her life 'lookaftering'. Like many other hesitant women performers, child-rearing and maintaining a home gave her a pretext not to perform, to subsume her creative self into daily routine.

Bunyan was not the only shy woman musician from this era to leave behind a thin body of work and then vanish. In 1971 the Scottish folk singer Shelagh McDonald, having made two albums, went back up north and ended up living a nomadic, hand-to-mouth life, sleeping in tents around Scotland. Christina 'Licorice' McKechnie of the Incredible String Band drifted to California, where she was rumoured to have lived rough before, in 1990, writing a farewell letter to her sister from Sacramento and disappearing into the desert. The band's other female member, Rose Simpson, also vanished, before re-emerging in 1994 as the lady mayoress of Aberystwyth.

The Nottinghamshire folk singer Anne Briggs spent most of the 1960s singing starkly beautiful arrangements of English folk songs unaccompanied in pubs, driving around Ireland in a horse and cart, living in a caravan on a Suffolk heath and sleeping in woods. In 1971 she was coaxed into the studios to record two albums, having to listen to her own voice and hating it. She performed at the Royal Festival Hall that May but hated that as well, having no stage patter, finding it too formal after pub singing and, worst of all, having to perform sober because she was pregnant. Leaving her third album unreleased, she moved up to a remote village in Sutherland with her husband and two young children, where being miles from anywhere and without babysitters put an end to her career. She was persuaded to do some gigs in the early 1990s, but she was jittery walking round cities and negotiating London's tube system after a gap of twenty years and her singing on stage was shackled by nerves. She retired again, this time to live self-sufficiently on the Inner Hebridean island of Kerrera, with no neighbours within a 2-mile radius.

These musicians had vanished in an analogue world where it was easy to walk off the map and never be heard of again. Now, in the word-of-mouth cults and unlikely fan bases of the early-era internet, they were ripe for rediscovery. This is what happened to Sixto Rodriguez, a Mexican-American folk singer who began performing in the smoke-filled clubs of Detroit in the late 1960s and who had a reputation for shyness because he always played with his back to the audience – although he said this was because the rooms were small and he was trying to avoid getting feedback from his amp. Unbeknown to him, he became a bootleg star in apartheid South Africa, and in 1997 his daughter Eva found a website set up by a Cape Town record store owner, Stephen Segerman, dedicated to finding out information about him. To Segerman's amazement, for Rodriguez was rumoured to have set fire to or shot himself on stage, Eva was able to tell him that he was hiding in plain sight, renovating buildings in Detroit and living in the same tumbledown house he had occupied for forty years.

In the same year, Vashti Bunyan bought her first computer and uncertainly dialled up, with its accompanying bleeps and staticky feedback, the pre-broadband internet. With two forefingers she typed her own name into a search engine, and the first thing she read was an email from Sacramento on a message board asking if anyone knew what had become of Vashti Bunyan. She discovered that so-called crate-diggers, rare vinyl collectors, were searching for records by these lost singer-songwriters of the late 1960s and early 1970s, a genre they dubbed 'loner folk'. *Just Another Diamond Day* was now a cult album, selling for hundreds of pounds. Emboldened, Bunyan persuaded a small label to re-release it, began digging out the old acetate demos she had left in her brother's shed and, most momentously, started singing again.

She felt, she said, as if her voice had been 'in a coma for 30 years', and was unsure if any sound would come out when she stood in front of a mic. But her voice sounded exactly the same, almost as if it had been preserved in a peat bog of obscurity and neglect. In April 2003 she performed at the Royal Festival Hall, on the stage that had eaten up and spat out Nick Drake and Anne Briggs. Even singing close to the mic, her voice was wavering and whispery, reluctant to disturb the surrounding air. Listening to her relinquish old songs such as 'Diamond Day' and 'Winter is Blue' was faintly nerve-jangling, since her voice, made shakier by stage fright, felt like it would break or she would run out of breath before the end of the line. The audience found itself leaning forward and willing her to make each note.

Bunyan discovered that the new recording technologies were ideal for the stage-frit. With digital audio software such as Pro Tools and Logic she could make music on her own. She found she sang louder and more freely if no one was around. An uncertain piano player, she could record left and right hand separately, playing them both right-handed, and use the software to merge them. It made her aware of her affinity with a certain kind of middle-class woman of her own and her mother's generation who did not perform except in that English parlour tradition of accompanying themselves on the piano. On one of her new songs, 'Mother', she recalled as a girl seeing her mother, through a door slightly ajar, dancing and playing the piano, believing herself to be alone.

According to the Italian historian Carla Casagrande, it was in western Europe, from about the twelfth century onwards, that male clerics started to promote shyness as a trait that women should cultivate, in order to counter their innate tendency to gossip, whine, nag and flirt, and as a 'providential instrument' to protect their virtue. They cited the nonpareil of chaste womanly silence, the Virgin Mary, and the authority of Saint Paul, who forbade women from preaching or teaching, allowing them only, if they needed specific information, to question their spouses behind closed doors. A woman keen to talk and perform in public was too engaged with the outside world and capable of promiscuity. On the rare occasions they had to speak, women were meant to do so quietly within their own house, church or convent walls, according to the Benedictine code of *taciturnitas*. It was perhaps a residue of these centuries-old habits of mind, which had discouraged women from appearing and speaking in public, that led women of Vashti Bunyan and her mother's generation to feel so exposed on stage.

Excepting a brief turn on All Radio India during the war, Nick Drake's mother, Molly, only performed in the music room at home for her family and a few friends. She wrote and sang her own songs, in the musical theatre tradition of Noël Coward or

Ivor Novello, but darker and less melodic, a sort of middle-English blues, with strange chord shapings that clearly influenced her son's eccentric tunings. Her singing sounded tentative and apologetic. It was never meant to be heard beyond her immediate circle, and never would have been had it not been captured on the same Ferrograph tape recorder her son had used for his drunken post-party ramblings. In 2013, twenty years after her death, a tiny New York label released an album of her songs.

Like Nick Drake and Vashti Bunyan, the writer and musician Charlotte Greig grew up in the 1950s and 1960s in a family in which women sang and played the piano simply 'as a domestic skill, like arranging a vase of flowers or laying a table'. When she heard Molly's album, Greig recognised a voice that came out of a particular context – that traditional unwillingness of nice middle-class women to show off, intensified in Molly's case by a peripatetic colonial upbringing lacking the solidity and sense of entitlement one's social position might imply. Greig too was reluctant to tour and promote her work, because she was a busy mother and because she had that same aversion to self-display, the same insecurities emerging out of a rootless childhood as a naval officer's daughter. She preferred music that betrayed this kind of self-doubt, by artists like Shirley Collins and Vashti Bunyan, who sounded like they were singing to themselves. It was a quality Molly Drake seemed to have passed on to her son, who half-whispered his songs, hoping his audience would happen to overhear.

※

Just as shyness often has no logic, impinging randomly on parts of your life and leaving others untouched, so stage fright ebbs and flows in erratic ways. Even the chronically nervous Nick Drake seems to have had little trouble busking in Aix-en-Provence or performing at Cambridge May balls and student clubs, and he was word- and finger-perfect in what many musicians find the most intimidating setting of all: a recording studio, surrounded by hard-bitten, nit-picking session musicians.

But then shy people are often surprisingly good performers, or at least can be drawn to the idea of performance. This is not as illogical as it at first seems. After all, the shy know as well as anyone that life is a perpetual performance, that when they step on stage all they are doing is substituting one role for another. The psychoanalyst Donald Kaplan once suggested that stage fright's most terrifying aspect was the actor's sense of 'a complete deprivation of his everyday poise-retaining mannerisms, which are about to be supplanted by the gestures of the performance'. The terror came, Kaplan thought, from facing others without those near-invisible gestures and postures that, in the course of our daily lives, make us feel like ourselves.

Perhaps shy people are drawn to the stage because they do not have this everyday poise, so they are looking to strike another pose that might work better for them. For the shy a crisis can be easier, or at least no more difficult, than the challenges of daily life. When the lights go down and the audience falls silent, they might be just as fearful as anyone else. And yet, in the same way that shy police officers or bus conductors are said to be buoyed up by wearing a uniform, they know they have been given another chance to impersonate a fully working human being.

I have long felt more at ease speaking in public than talking to a stranger. I am reassured by clarity and structure, by physical props and affordances that tell me how I should behave. When I am behind a lectern with a microphone, my script in front of me, a glass of water to my left and a clicker in my hand, I know I am meant to speak uninterrupted, and have been given permission to do so. In a world where we have to pretend that most of our performances are natural, a performance that does not hide its status as such feels like a deliverance. Naturally, the fear returns if there is a Q&A session at the end, when I have to come out of role and will surely be *found out* by that left-field question from the audience which will induce brain freeze and a calamitous attempt to answer that ties itself up in tortured syntax before dissolving into terrifying silence. (This has happened only rarely to me in real life, but just often enough to fuel my catastrophising imagination.) That moment when the trickle of applause dies down and the chair asks for questions marks the transition between two types of performance: one feels comfortingly fake, the other scarily real.

But until that moment comes and my cover is blown, I somehow manage not to be stage-frit. As well as having an excellent word for stage fright, it turns out that the Germans have an equally excellent one for this opposite feeling. It is *Maskenfreiheit*: the freedom that comes from wearing masks. Heinrich Heine used this portmanteau term in his *Letters from Berlin* (1822) when he wrote that we feel most liberated and most fully human at a masked ball, 'where the waxen mask hides our usual mask of flesh, where a simple *Du* [the familiar form of address in German] restores the primordial sociality of familiarity, where a Venetian cloak (*Domino*) covers all pretensions and brings about the most beautiful equality and the most beautiful freedom'.

Of course, standing in front of a lectern is not quite the same as wearing an actual mask and claiming the traditional licence to party in anonymity without anyone removing it. But on stage you are still making up a version of yourself that you feel more comfortable with, real-but-not-real, a naturalness you have amplified and enlarged. Your shy self may have thrown up in the dressing-room bucket, but that other self somehow summons up the resolve not to flee from the stage in fear.

6

SHY ART

In March 1910 a man in a long overcoat, his hat pulled down over his ears, began walking round the red-brick terraced streets of Manchester. He was 6 foot 2 and ungainly, his flat feet heading in slightly different directions. In poor areas such as Longsight and Hulme, barefoot children followed him as if he were the pied piper, name-calling and mimicking his lurching step, while he dropped the odd penny for them and they fought for it on the cobbles. He was famous round these parts only as the rent man for the Pall Mall Property Company. He saw himself as an artist, but sold barely enough paintings to cover the cost of materials to paint more of them.

Although he had his first solo show in London in 1939, he was still little known to the wider public in 1952, when, at the age of sixty-five and now Pall Mall's chief cashier, he retired from the firm on a full pension. He had been known as Mr Lowry all his forty-odd-year working life, even to long-standing colleagues. He said he was too shy to use first names, as was now common. On his last day he announced flatly that he wouldn't be in tomorrow. Only after his retirement did he become famous, as he was filmed for TV and photographed against the landscapes of his paintings, without anyone knowing that these were the same streets on which he had collected rent. Afraid of being thought a mere Sunday painter, he kept his day job a secret even after giving it up.

His hair was now white, but he still had the same lolloping walk and aura of oddness, and still dropped spare coppers for chasing children. His friend, the art critic Edwin Mullins, said he looked 'like Jacques Tati impersonating General de Gaulle'. The painting of Lowry on Swinton Moss by his friend Harold Riley, of the old man's back as he stomps off in his mac and trilby, head down and hands behind him clutching his glasses, gets him just right: looking and moving away, always out of reach.

The people in his crowd scenes are the same, hurrying along on the balls of their feet, hunched forward, lost in thought. Their faces are splodges, sometimes with even the two dots for eyes missing. Those huddled in groups do not talk to each other but stand at right angles, their arms limp, as if they have frozen in a game of musical statues. 'All those people in my pictures, they are all alone you know,' he said. 'Crowds are the most lonely thing of all. Everyone is a stranger to everyone else.' In Lowry's paintings parents face away from their children, courting couples look across at each other from straight-backed chairs and patients in doctors' waiting rooms gaze ahead with thousand-yard stares.

In the 1950s the crowds in his paintings dispersed, and he began to paint solitary figures, often tramps or men shunned in the street because of their palsies or prostheses. The titles of these paintings reflect the way that people on their own, without the anchor of human relationships, are reduced to going through the motions of mundane life. *Man Eating a Sandwich*. *Man Drinking from a Fountain*. *Man Looking in the Waste Paper Bin*. *Man in a Doorway*. *Man Looking through a Hole in the Fence*. It is odd that Lowry's paintings have become the kitsch scenery for gift-shop fridge magnets and tea towels, because they are so far from being sentimental or consoling; they pulse with fear and loneliness.

In the summer of 1963 Lowry went with a friend, the young artist Sheila Fell, to London's new Mayfair Theatre, to see a revival of Luigi Pirandello's *Six Characters in Search of an Author*, with Ralph Richardson. It was a tiny, 300-seat auditorium under the Mayfair Hotel, with the seats raked up in a single tier. On a bare stage with exposed wings and simple spot lighting, the size of the space allowing for *sotto voce* acting, the gap between audience and performers seemed to dissolve, and Lowry found himself entranced. When the six characters, dressed in black Victorian clothes and gazing straight ahead, moved together slowly to front of stage, they looked like the uncommunicative, impassive people in his paintings. Lowry went twice more with Fell to see the play, and another six times alone. Pirandello's message is that we are all spiritual solipsists and that the language and social rituals that seem to link us cannot cross the chasm of comprehension between separate minds. We are, as the father in the play says, 'trapped in the commerce of ordinary words, in the slavery of social rules'.

After he had moved to the village of Mottram in Longdendale in 1948, Lowry had become still more reclusive. He had seventeen clocks in the house, his dead mother's collection, primed to ting at different times so it felt as if the house were peopled. His telephone, which he only installed after a burglary, could only make outgoing calls. The best way to contact him was to send a telegram or phone a neighbour to leave a message. The front door had no knocker. He piled up letters, unopened, in a porcelain bowl. His accountant opened the pecuniary-looking ones every six weeks, and when the rest turned brown, Lowry burned them unread. Friends knew to write their name in large letters on the envelope. Once Alick Leggat, treasurer of Lancashire County Cricket Club, opened this neglected mail with him, and extracted cheques worth £1,600.

One day in 1960 Lowry went to Sunderland, stopping for lunch at the Seaburn Hotel on the seafront. For the next fifteen years he came regularly to this hotel to stay in the same first-floor room, number 104, sometimes for weeks at a time. He often went there on impulse, travelling the 135 miles from Mottram by taxi – once while still in his slippers. As the hotel was separated from Whitburn sands only by a road and the promenade, he could look out at the North Sea from the dining room, where he always sat at the same table eating the same meal: roast beef, chips and gravy, followed by sliced bananas and cream.

In these years he painted a series of seascapes in which the mist-enveloped land, sea and sky merged into a single, Turneresque agglomeration of paint. In some of these paintings pillars stand upright and isolated in the water, waiting for the waves to batter them down. He called them self-portraits. 'Had I not been lonely,' he told Edwin Mullins one evening as his friend was driving him home, 'none of my work would have happened.'

§

No one is sure why, around 40,000 years ago, *homo sapiens* went deep into caves many thousands of miles apart – in southern France and Spain, the Indonesian island of Sulawesi, the Arnhem Land plateau in northern Australia – and began to paint bison, mammoths and deer, or to trace their hands in finger flutings on the walls. Whether the motive was shamanistic, ceremonial or homage-giving to the animals they hunted, this huge cognitive leap in human history, known as 'the creative explosion', seems to have involved retreating from the social world, for the paintings are found in remote parts of caves that no one could have lived in.

Humans have tended to see themselves as the supremely social animals, the apex communicators, elevated above the beasts by their ability to talk. But whales, dolphins and other animals have sophisticated languages that might seem even more so if we could only decipher them. Birds, it has recently emerged, have communication networks almost as fast-growing as viral internet memes. In the beech trees of Wytham Woods, near Oxford, where the university's scientists have been studying great tits since 1947, researchers discovered how these birds learned something they had been doing for almost a century – pecking the silver foil off milk bottles left on doorsteps and drinking the cream at the top. By setting the Wytham Woods tits a similar task, sliding the door of a box open to win a mealworm, scientists found that the birds passed on these skills to each other with astonishing rapidity, because they had a dense social network that encouraged imitation. It seems that our uniqueness as animals lies not in our ability to communicate at all, but in our ability to sublimate, to turn our communicative instincts into abstract and ancillary forms. We are the only living things to leave marks that can be read or seen when we are not there, conveying meaning to others independently of our presence, even the span of our lives.

The autistic scientist and writer Temple Grandin has her own hunch about why this happened: the introverts among our ancestors got tired of 'the yacketyyaks', the alpha males sat round the tribal fire sharpening their flints and boasting to each other about their bison-killing count, and went off on their own to produce the earliest human art. She imagines these art works being created, along with groundbreaking inventions such as the stone spear and the wheel, by 'some Asperger sitting in the back of a cave'.

Grandin's own life and work demonstrate how an autistic strain in the mind can be a spur to creativity. As an introverted and disturbed teenager, she longed to experience the pressure stimulation of being hugged but shrank from human contact. She visited her aunt's Arizona ranch, where she saw cattle being put in a squeeze chute: a pen with compressing metal sides, which kept them still and calm while they were inoculated, branded or castrated. Inspired, she devised a human 'squeeze machine'. It had two slanting wooden boards, upholstered with thick padding and joined by hinges to make a V-shaped trough. When she kneeled inside it and turned on an air compressor, the boards applied gentle pressure, as if they were hugging her. For Grandin, this was a useful half-way stage on the way to allowing others to touch her.

To the autistic person, neurotypical people seem to be

operating by weird social rules they have acquired mysteriously – a much more severe version, perhaps, of how the shy view the socially confident. Grandin had to learn everyday etiquette by rote, and compute what others meant by scrupulously assembling clues. Tone-deaf to rhythm and cadence, her voice sounded unmodulated, like those railway station PA systems that rise and fall and accentuate randomly. When she first started lecturing, she would stand with her back to the audience, but she soon developed a flair for it, perhaps because her normal way of talking seemed much like a performance anyway.

The first person to suggest that autism might add creativity to the human mix was Hans Asperger, a paediatrician at the University Children's Hospital in Vienna. In 1943, a year after his fellow Austrian Leo Kanner had listed the characteristics of autism, Asperger identified a similar tendency to withdrawal in some of his child patients. Unlike Kanner, he suggested it might live alongside special talents.

The astounding ability of some autistic people to solve jigsaw puzzles, memorise books or orientate themselves around towns seems to be partly a visual skill, a knack at recognising repetitive patterns and taxonomies. Autistic people have what is called 'weak central coherence', a focus on individual components at the expense of the larger picture. An autistic artist might start from a single detail – the precise topography of a knobbly kneecap, say, or a single brick on a house – building up their drawing out of its constituent parts rather than the more common method of starting with an outline and then filling it in. Some autistic artists, such as the London-based Stephen Wiltshire or the Malaysian Ping Lian Yeak, can paint massive vistas of city skylines from memory, with complex architectural features rendered perfectly. Others conjure up their own intricate worlds – such as the French artist Gilles Tréhin's 'Urville', an imaginary island city off the Côte d'Azur populated with meticulously drawn high-rises and Lowry-like stick people.

Lowry was similarly absorbed by minutiae. His paintings

were composites, accretions of detail. He would walk round the streets of Salford, Stockport or Ashton under Lyne, sketching on scraps of paper he stuffed into his pockets, and then assemble these scraps into paintings. With their carless streets, chimneys billowing smoke and passers-by wearing hats and headsquares, even his later paintings seem stuck in the early part of the century. The most common explanation for this is that he felt lost in the post-war world of slum clearances and tower blocks, so his mind's eye carried on walking the same Salford streets of his childhood. But in fact he was unconcerned with how landscapes changed over time. His interest was in the natural geometry of the north's industrial scape, the blunt horizontals and verticals of its terraced rows and factory chimneys. Sheila Fell, who came from Aspatria in the Lake District, took him out one day to paint with her in front of Skiddaw. In the late afternoon she had a sneak peek at what he was painting: another industrial townscape.

If Lowry liked a particular set of steps, or a loop of the River Irwell, it would turn up in his paintings again and again. His work is made up of lines and angles, not brushwork, which is why there are no shadows and his buildings seem to have no volume. The crowds, he conceded, were there to slot into the design. 'To say the truth, I was not thinking very much about the people,' he said. 'I did not care for them the way a social reformer does. They are part of a private beauty that haunted me.'

Asperger's syndrome was unknown in the English-speaking world until 1981, when the British psychiatrist Lorna Wing published a paper on it in the journal *Psychological Medicine*. Lowry was now dead, but a number of people observed that he had the Asperger-like fixation on detail and some of the other traits of this high-functioning autism: an attachment to routine, physical awkwardness, limited facial expression and eye contact, and a veering between social withdrawal and a relentless addressing of others that made it seem as if he were talking to a pet: 'You like that picture? Do you really? How *very* interesting. I *am* pleased.'

Lorna Wing was not equating Asperger's with shyness any

more than Grandin was. But she did believe, like Grandin, that an 'autistic spectrum' existed throughout the population and that autism covered not one discrete condition but a wide range of disorders. Nature, she insisted, reusing what Winston Churchill said about the English, 'never draws a straight line without smudging it'. For Wing, autism captured in stark form the ordinary human problem of relating to others. Like Grandin, she felt that having some autistic traits might be an essential ingredient of the creative life.

Could the origins of art itself lie in this capacity for introversion, the need to make strategic retreats from social life in order to make sense of our experiences? We all have this quality in some degree. Just as our brains have to sleep and dream to recuperate, we need periods of gestation or fallowness to germinate new ideas. As Carl Jung argued in *Psychological Types* (1921), introverts take longer than extroverts to collect their thoughts and process meanings, and need solitude to curate these thoughts into meaningful shapes. Their brains are over-stimulated when they are in contact with too many other humans for too long. Amid a noisy group of people, an introvert's cerebral cortex will overload and freeze like a computer that has run out of memory.

Some autistic people never return from these interior journeys, obsessing endlessly over a few grains of salt or the friction ridges on their fingertips, unable to direct their creativity outwards into communication. The autistic artist Jessy Park's earliest paintings were of radio dials, mileage gauges and electric blanket controls, beautifully rendered but unlikely to interest anyone other than engineers. Gradually, with her mother's help, she managed to break out of this insular enthralment with the random detail of the world and create work with wider appeal: extraordinarily particularised paintings of buildings such as New York's Flatiron or London's Houses of Parliament, accurate to the last drainpipe but painted in pastel pinks and bright oranges below purple-black skies sparkling with stars in all their correct constellations. Park also came up with the perfect neologism for the inarticulate:

'speako', a slip-up in speech, derived from 'typo'. Those who learn to express the otherness of the introverted mind help us all to see the world in new ways.

※

We are used to seeing madness, depression and other illnesses as stimuli for art; perhaps we need to see shyness in the same way. We tend to associate the twentieth-century art world with the ideal of the confidently bohemian, avant-garde artist such as Picasso or Dalí. And yet it is notable how many other artists have stood, alongside Lowry, for the *aurea mediocritas*: consistent dedication to one's work within the enabling milieu of an ordinary bourgeois life. Another such man was the Bolognan painter Giorgio Morandi. Morandi told the critic Édouard Roditi, who came to visit him in 1958 when he was sixty-eight, that he had been 'fortunate enough to lead ... an uneventful life'.

Morandi rarely left Bologna and he did not leave Italy until he was sixty-six, when he attended an exhibition just over the border in Switzerland. When visitors called at his modest apartment on the via Fondazza, he would knock politely and pause before he got permission from his sisters, with whom he lived, to walk through their bedrooms to the studio, where he worked and slept, on a single bed. Roditi saw him as leading 'the same kind of restricted social life as most of the older university professors and professional men of his native city, but with an additional touch of purely personal modesty, shyness and asceticism'. Locals knew him as *il monaco*, 'the monk'. Like Lowry, he was oddly formal in manner. He used the impersonal Italian 'you', *lei*, with all but his family and a few childhood friends. His letters, even to these oldest of his friends, were eerily restrained and self-possessed, closing with generic sign-offs and his surname.

Renowned for its university, its cuisine and its communism, Bologna is known in Italy as *dotta, grassa e rossa* (learned, fat and red). Morandi's work is the opposite: unallusive, ascetic and apolitical. His working life was spent painting, in pieces all called

Natura morta ('Still Life'), endlessly permutable arrangements of the same milk tins, biscuit boxes, caffè latte bowls and Ovaltine canisters he had picked up in the weekly Piazzola bric-a-brac market. Coated with dust and with the labels removed, they are painted in earthy hues such as raw sienna and burnt umber, the pigments of cave paintings – although with an undercoat of blues and reds that warm up these muted surface colours.

Morandi's work is reminiscent of that of another shy and solitary artist, Piet Mondrian, whose factory-perfect paintings of geometric shapes and grids in primary colours feel similarly serene and ineffable. Mondrian's work is entirely non-figurative, neater and cleaner than the world, whereas Morandi's is rooted in the concrete and particular. But they are united in their absolute refusal to beguile, to ingratiate, to *épater le bourgeois*. It is hard not to see their economy with paint as emerging out of a similar economy with life. Their art feels wrung out of their shyness.

Morandi, it must be said, belonged to a nation not noted for this character trait. The word 'privacy' has no equivalent in Italian, and the Italian temperament is often thought to be exuberant and gestural. This anti-shyness seems apparent in many of its art forms: the melodrama of Italian opera, the Futurist movement's love of violence and speed, the egocentric abandon of the symbolist-decadents and the rituals of dictatorship that Mussolini stole from their leader Gabriele D'Annunzio, such as the balcony oration delivered in the chest-pounding, hectoring style that Italians call *protagonismo*.

And yet there is a shyness and resignation about so many Italian writers and artists, particularly those who worked in the shadow of fascism. One thinks of the stark, astringent poems of Eugenio Montale, with their feeling for little things such as cigar smoke rings or cuttlefish bones, and their conscious avoidance of show-off Italian intonation and dead rhetoric. Joseph Brodsky called Montale's the 'voice of a man speaking – often muttering – to himself'. The most famous modern poem among Italians is by Giuseppe Ungaretti, Montale's fellow poet of *Ermetismo*, and is two words long, a few phonic fragments embedded in the white silence of the page: 'M'illumino / d'immenso.'

A similar shyness breeds a similar suspicion of the facile and overblown in many Italian novelists of this period, such as Italo Svevo, Cesare Pavese and Giuseppe di Lampedusa. In the foreword to his masterpiece *Dialogues with Leucò* (1947) Pavese could have been thinking of Morandi when he declared: 'I have nothing in common with experimentalists, adventurers, with those who travel in strange regions. The surest, and the quickest, way for us to arouse the sense of wonder is to stare, unafraid, at a single object.' Lampedusa did not complete his first and only novel, *The Leopard*, until he was fifty-nine, and it was only published post-humously, its flawless eye for the human comedy clearly the result of a lifetime of circumspect observation. A deeply reserved Sicilian aristocrat, he proudly claimed to have an English temperament, although on his many visits to Britain he was too shy to speak the language he knew well. 'It is always a pleasure dealing with the English,' he wrote home from London in August 1927. 'They are courteous and prompt, and their apparent stupidity is merely an immense and uncontrollable shyness.'

Of course, in the Mussolini years many Italian writers had good reason to be reserved and to adopt oblique means of expression to hide their views from the censors. Some, like Pavese, preferred to remain silent rather than have their material butchered. Jews, meanwhile, were not allowed to publish a book or even have their names listed in the telephone directory. 'I have never seriously tried to analyse this shyness of mine,' the Italian-Jewish writer Primo Levi told Philip Roth, 'but no doubt Mussolini's racial laws played an important role.' Shyness has many local and particular reasons to exist, but it is a language understood by writers and artists everywhere. Whether they are censored by others or silenced by their own fears and neuroses, their work is their way of making themselves heard.

Morandi's great inspiration was not one of his compatriots but a Frenchman, Paul Cézanne. All his life Cézanne knew off by heart a passage from Stendhal's *History of Italian Painting* (1817), in which he wrote of the melancholic artist who 'gains his ends only in a roundabout manner' and 'if he enters a room, he clings to the walls. Passionate shyness is one of the clearest hallmarks of the talent of great artists.' Cézanne's shyness was certainly passionate. The prickliness of his character seemed to arise from a phobia about being touched that he acquired as a boy, when, according to his own account, another boy kicked him up the backside while he was sliding down a banister. If anyone approached him when he was painting in the fields, he quickly gathered up his paints and easel and hurried off.

Cézanne's long-suffering wife, Hortense, had to model for him often, because he was shy in front of other models and feared the disapproval of his neighbours in provincial Aix. For his paintings of nude bathers he drew mostly on El Greco, Rubens and his own imagination. The result is a series of figures that feel as inert as his still lifes are overflowing with life. His famous promise to 'astonish Paris with an apple' revealed how much he craved recognition, but on his own terms. His wavering line and unconcealed retouchings suggest hesitancy, but, as with Morandi, who also liked to blur lines and boundaries, his pursuit of excellence within a narrow range betrayed an inner core of confidence. You need a healthy ego to be as self-denying as they were, to take that all-or-nothing attitude to your life.

Morandi's self-effacement was sharp-edged. He rarely allowed buyers of his paintings to choose one, deciding for himself which to surrender. When he finished a painting, he would hang it on the wall over his bed with others in the same sequence. After a decent interval, he wrote the fortunate new owner's name on the canvas's stretcher bars, but kept it on his wall until ready to relinquish it. He undercharged for his work and gave much of it away, but he was angry if he learned that the owner of one of his paintings had disposed of it for a profit, for he saw giving up his pictures as a cutting off of part of himself. His final act of control freakery only emerged thirteen years after his death, when the *catalogue raisonné* of his work appeared. He had given the impression that he only finished about a dozen works a year, but it was now clear how prolific he had been, creating over 1,400 oil paintings and drawings too numerous to count.

Like Mr Lowry, Signor Morandi was a pedestrian in both the broader and more literal senses: a creature of habit committed to long periods of prosaic and solitary work, and someone who spent much of his time walking. His 6-foot-4-inch frame, striking in a town where most men were a foot shorter, was a familiar sight around Bologna. He was always smoking a heavy-duty Nazionali cigarette and dressed in the same charcoal grey suit and black tie. Each weekday he walked to the shops to buy coffee and fresh fish and to the city's Academy of Fine Arts, where he taught etching and engraving, preferring to impart technique rather than teach 'art'. And several times a week he walked to mass at Santa Maria dei Servi, the plain, porticoed church where the city's poor went to worship.

Writing in 1928, the critic Leo Longanesi makes Morandi's ambulatory style sound as odd as Lowry's. 'When he walks, he seems like an old schooner, viewed prow-first; his soft felt hat perched on top of his head is a perfect top-gallant sail, touching the clouds,' Longanesi wrote. 'He dawdles, brushing against the walls, dragging his feet, with the air of someone wearing long pants for the first time.' As with Lowry, Morandi's shyness bred a life of lone, observant walking, and this naturally filtered into his work. The muddied reds and ochres of his paintings are those of any Bolognan street, and their subtle chiaroscuro is of the kind seen by anyone walking through the town's endless porticoes. Umberto Eco, speaking at the Museo Morandi in Bologna in 1993, said that his work 'can truly be understood only after you have traversed the streets and the arcades of this city and have understood that an apparently uniform reddish colour can differentiate house from house and street from street'.

In the late 1950s, while Lowry and Morandi were still pounding the streets of their respective cities, another solitary artist was half-way through a longer, more methodical stint of solitary walking. He was harder to spot than them because his manor was the wildest fell country of England's Lake District, above the intake walls that separate farmland from mountainside. If any passing walkers tried to say hello, he hid behind a rock and pretended to be relieving himself. If they claimed to recognise him, he shook his head and pointed to a retreating dot in the distance saying, 'That's the man you want.' He likened himself to Lobby Lud, the pseudonymous employee of the *News Chronicle* who would visit a seaside resort and hand out £5 to any reader who spotted him from the newspaper's description – except that Alfred Wainwright never admitted who he was, and never handed out rewards. Your best bet was to spot his familiar, solid shape through a pair of binoculars.

As a young man growing up in Blackburn, Wainwright had been unrelentingly shy and ashamed of his thick red hair, which earned him the taunting nickname 'Carrots' – not helped by the fact that his mother was also ashamed of it, and hid her strange-tinted son in a drawer when neighbours called, in case they queried his paternity. Now, in middle age, his shyness was curdling into cussedness. 'Always walk with others, they say,' he wrote in his unrevealing memoir, *Fellwanderer*. 'This is excellent advice for those who lack ordinary gumption, or are plain daft; and such people, if they go on the fells at all, which they shouldn't, can be further advised to get themselves in the middle of a big party and keep themselves hemmed in by the sweating flesh of others.'

In fact, he did sometimes walk with others, as long as it was in silence and they addressed him as 'AW' or 'Mr Wainwright'. When one of these walking friends, Weaver Owen, the manager of the Kendal branch of Lloyds bank, ventured to address him in a letter as 'Alfred', the reply began, 'Dear Mr Owen (or Weaver, if you prefer it, although personally I don't ...)'. He was happy in his adoptive Cumbria, where sheep outnumbered humans four to one and the latter were markedly shy with 'offcomers', the name given to outsiders who settled in the area. As the Lakeland saying went, 'They summer you, they winter you, they summer you again, then they might say hello.' So Wainwright was not unusual in this corner of the world, particularly among the menfolk, in being what they called 'yonderly' – looking yonder into the distance with an air of inward contemplation and distraction.

Wainwright's day job, as borough treasurer at Kendal town hall, suited a man parsimonious with words. It was the sort of pre-computerised office whose main output was words and figures dispensed on memoranda and balance sheets. Meetings were rare, and there were no photocopiers or water coolers to linger and gossip over. Wainwright's main conversations were dictations to typists and secretaries. He retired in 1967, just as the town hall finance departments were doing away with the handwritten ledgers he loved. He felt so adrift in the new world of calculating machines that he never again visited the office, despite living only a mile away.

His wife, Ruth, was shy too, and their marriage was uncommunicative and mutually miserable. After they moved to Kendal, he still used to come down on the train to watch Blackburn Rovers. Being squashed into their Ewood Park ground with 30,000 other pieces of sweating flesh did not seem to bother him. Sometimes Ruth would, unbeknown to him, catch the same train, travelling in a different compartment, and go to the match, watching from another stand and leaving before the final whistle so that she was back before him.

One day in 1952 Wainwright sat down at his desk and divided Lakeland's 214 fells into seven areas. He spent the next thirteen years of weekends packing his camera, notebook and sandwiches, taking the 8.30 a.m. bus to Ambleside or Keswick and climbing the fells, and then writing about them in books that were handwritten and drawn to the last detail. He wanted his work to be reproduced exactly as he had done it, without printers messing up the layout and type. He worked in the living room of his house on Kendal Green while his wife and son sat in silence. His garden, like Lowry's, became a wilderness; his marriage, too, was strangled in thickets of shrivelling silences.

Wainwright now brought his talent for solitary work to bear on something he really cared about. His Lakeland books were a kind of double-entry bookkeeping of the fells he so loved, with the balance sheets of assets and liabilities now bursting with love and life. Wainwright would describe the terrain of each fell in beautiful wedges of script set down with a mapping pen filled with best-quality Indian ink. By pressing harder and flattening the nib, he emboldened the lettering; by slanting, he italicised it. Wrapped round the text were his maps and drawings, meticulous in outlining routes of ascent and the ridge routes to the next fell but also cleverly three-dimensional, with tarns lying flat and walls that turned corners, tufts of heather and boulders crosshatched with painstaking penwork. Like Harry Beck, the man who designed the London tube map, Wainwright abandoned strict geographical accuracy in favour of legibility, turning messy reality into something that could be instantly taken in by the pattern-making human mind. He cut up each fell and filleted it like a master butcher, distorting diagrams of ascent and changing elevation to show detail clearly, making the whole thing fathomable. He called it 'building up mountains from plain sheets of paper'.

As the series progressed and Wainwright acquired a loyal readership, he loosened up and became chattier. Rather as a medieval monk-scribe might jot down remarks and doodles at the edges of an illuminated manuscript if he felt bored or mischievous, Wainwright let his guard down with teasing marginalia. A speech bubble would suddenly sprout from the mouth of a talking sheep, or he would riff on the fellwalker's crucial asset of 'a tough and rubbery bottom', which during descent was 'a valuable agent of friction, a sheet anchor with superb resistance to the pull of gravity'.

But Wainwright now also made less effort to disguise his misanthropy and misogyny and began to complain more shrilly of the 'slovenly layabouts, of both sexes' who infested the Lakes at weekends. The summits of popular fells, he claimed, were being flattened by the shoes of Sunday afternoon motorists and pock-marked by women's high heels. On beauty spots such as Little Hell Gate or Rossett Gill the walkers were not only verbally noisy, 'a common characteristic of the inefficient', but they also had noisy boots that uprooted sods and displaced stones. The good walkers, by contrast, moved softly and left no trace, improving the path by treading its existing contours into place with their quiet boots.

❧

Wainwright always claimed that his books were begun for his own amusement, as a love letter to the Cumbrian hills written 'after many years of inarticulate worshipping at their shrines', and meant only for him to read by the fireside when he was too old and feeble for fellwalking. He gave himself exactly thirteen years to finish the seven volumes in the series. After climbing his final fell, Starling Dodd, in September 1965, one week ahead of schedule – just before the end of the summer bus timetable put the fells out of reach – he retired to his desk to complete the finishing touches to the last book, *The Western Fells*.

His obsession with the look of his hand-drawn pages, right down to never breaking a word with a hyphen at the end of the line, does seem to share some of the self-motivations of autistic-spectrum art. It was a form of inner pedantry, meant to satisfy his own intuitive sense of rightness and completeness. After eight months of work on the first book, *The Eastern Fells*, he binned the hundred-odd pages he had finished and started again, because he did not like the fact that he had not justified the text on the right-hand margin.

But the look of a page also mattered to Wainwright for the same reason that sticking to footpaths did: a concern with fonts and typefaces showed that you cared how your actions affected others in incommunicable ways. Perhaps no one would have noticed that his text was right-justified, but on some unconscious level the extra neatness might have added to their aesthetic pleasure. Wainwright believed that the time-worn protocols of communication mattered, that they were part of a slowly accruing, shared culture just like the fell footpaths.

'Why *does* a man climb mountains?' he wondered aloud in book four, *The Southern Fells*. 'More and more people are turning to the hills; they find something in these wild places that can be found nowhere else.' This something was, he felt, an 'escape from the clamour and tumult of everyday existence … a balm for jangled nerves in the solitude and silence of the peaks'. Not everyone had found the Lake District as friendly and welcoming as Wainwright did. In his *Tour through the Whole Island of Great Britain* (1722) Daniel Defoe thought the Cumberland and Westmorland hills 'high and formidable', with 'a kind of unhospitable terror in them'. Even Wordsworth, who loved the fells, wrote in *The Prelude* of 'huge and mighty forms, that do not live'. To Defoe and Wordsworth the fells were sublime in the sense employed by philosophers such as Immanuel Kant and Edmund Burke: in their unwelcoming beauty, they combined aesthetic awe with a sense of dread.

The shy are often drawn to the natural world because it seems easier to relate to than people. But at some point they must confront its obstinate otherness, its lack of interest in and refusal to give anything back to them. 'Heartless, witless nature, / Will neither care nor know,' as the shy and prickly A. E. Housman put it in his poem 'Tell Me Not Here, It Needs Not Saying'. The fact that nature seeks no relationship with us is both consoling to shy people and not consoling enough, because it will not lessen their loneliness.

Wainwright insisted the hills were 'amiable giants', and that he was happiest when in mute communion with them. But I wonder if he protested too much. There are hints and tip-offs in the books that he really did care what others thought, and that his lonely journeys above the intake walls were undertaken so that he could come back and tell others about them. On the less glamorous northern fells he saw only three people during months of walking, making him feel like he was 'preparing a book which would have no readers at all, a script that would have no players and no public'. Here Wainwright sounds like any normally neurotic author, fretting over whether all his solitary labour would be rewarded with an audience.

Even when he was walking alone on the fells, Wainwright was interested in them not as the product of immutable geological processes but as the collective creation of humanity. He dedicated his books to those unsung individuals, such as 'the Men of the Ordnance Survey' or 'the Men who Built the Stone Walls', who made the enjoyment of the fells possible. He reserved his deepest scorn for cairn-wreckers, who desecrated these improvised summit shrines instead of adding the traditional stone to the pile, and walkers who veered from the paths, those communal works of art created by nameless feet innumerable. His books were love letters not just to the fells, but to the people who worked them, and to his readers, albeit on condition that they were a reticent and mostly male fellowship, high heels strictly forbidden. In the books, Wainwright teased them with a slow drip-drip of personal details – about his dog Cindy, or his own resemblance to an old stag – and in each volume he included one picture of himself as 'a special treat for readers'. He is usually sat on a rock looking at a view, his face obscured, with a pipe in his mouth and a cap on to hide himself still more.

He devised other ways of connecting with readers. In the last Lakeland fells book he announced that he had left a two-shilling piece under a flat stone near the Ordnance column on the summit of Lank Rigg, 'in an uncharacteristic mood of magnanimity which he has since regretted'. It was a gauge of the growing cult of Wainwright that a reader found it the day after the book was published. At the end of his 1968 *Pennine Way Companion* he promised a free pint at the Border Hotel, Kirk Yetholm, the official end of the walk, to anyone who mentioned his name to the landlord (shades of Lobby Lud). The landlord sent him the bill periodically, and by the time he died he had paid out £15,000.

Wainwright was drawing on a long tradition of indirect communication within the diasporic society of ramblers and walkers. In 1854 a Dartmoor guide, James Perrott, built a small cairn at the remote Cranmere Pool, and placed a glass pickle jar there with his visiting card inside it. Walkers who found Perrott's card added their own, and by 1888 the jar had been upgraded to a large tin box. In 1905 two walkers added a visitors' book. Others enclosed stamped and self-addressed postcards to be sent on by the next visitor, a custom with its roots in the ancient practice of leaving letters at specific points on country paths for other walkers to carry them on to the next point. This practice of 'letter-boxing' spread across the world, and on Dartmoor alone there are now several thousand letter boxes, from stone structures marked on Ordnance Survey maps to tupperware containers. The letter box, a land-locked message in a bottle with slightly more chance of being discovered than a seafaring one, was the sort of virtual relationship Wainwright liked: an uncoercive, diffident form of greeting which demanded nothing more than the acknowledgement of receipt.

After the first Lakeland fells book appeared, letters from readers arrived, first in a trickle and soon in their thousands. Some were from bedridden invalids or servicemen overseas who thanked him for vividly evoking the fells they could not see for themselves. On his desk he would build up a pile of unanswered mail and, when it collapsed, reply to a few and then build up the pile again. Unlike Lowry, he answered every one, often beginning a correspondence lasting years. Even these private letters he would write out twice, so the sent version was clean, with no crossings out.

Wainwright's kindness was all the more touching because it was clearly given with no expectation of reward and was well hidden behind the persona of a first-rate grump. 'Yes I am antisocial and getting worse as I get older,' he told Sue Lawley on BBC Radio 4's *Desert Island Discs*, before she had asked him whether he was. 'It started as shyness. It isn't shyness now. I can face anybody now and not feel inferior to them. But I'd much rather be alone.' He had found it hard to choose eight records to take with him to a desert island, he said, because he preferred silence.

When he at last agreed to appear on television in the 1980s, walking round the fells with his interviewer, Eric Robson, he refused point-blank to join in with that necessary broadcasting subterfuge of answering questions to which both interviewer and interviewee already know the answer. The crew feared they would have nothing filmable. Then, towards the end of the shoot, he became more talkative and repeated his famous wish to have his ashes scattered on his favourite hill, Haystacks. Several readers had written to him to say that, following his example, their ashes would also be scattered there. 'So I shall be in company,' he said softly. In death, he seemed not to mind sharing the fells with others.

§

Wainwright was the archetypal northern English male, seemingly self-sufficient and happy in his reticence. He was a poor interviewee not just because he was shy but also because he was a literalist who considered those who were searching for a subtext to be misguided at best and impertinent at worst. He wrote books, he insisted, for his own diversion. He walked alone because he liked his own company. He said little because he had little to say. Move along, his every answer implied, nothing to see here.

He would have had little time for that master decoder of subtext, Sigmund Freud, who saw art and writing as compensations for the failure to communicate in more direct ways and to act on our desires. For Freud, writing was 'in its origin the voice of an absent person'. By allowing us to make premeditated marks on a page that could stand in for our bodily selves, it let us transcend the imperfections of spur-of-the-moment speech. But writing was always, for Freud, an inferior substitute for such spontaneous communication. When he remarked on the magical power of words to 'make another blissfully happy or drive him to despair', he meant the spoken word – the precious coinage that the teacher uses to impart knowledge or that the orator deploys to enthral an audience.

It is unsurprising, perhaps, that a discipline founded on the 'talking cure' tended to value talk and pathologise those who were bad at it. Strict Freudians saw shyness as displaced aggression or narcissism, a retreat into an initially consoling but ultimately unfulfilling internal life as compensation for the pain of dealing with others. 'The shy individual seems to behave like an impotent child, longing to be admitted to the group of potent adults (fathers) being at the same time afraid of being too inferior and fearing to be snubbed for his presumptuous wishes,' wrote Hilde Lewinsky in the *British Journal of Psychology* in 1941. 'This fear of being snubbed represents in a figurative sense castration fear.' The shy had suppressed their vital instincts, Freudians thought, and were too afraid of the hostility of others to be fully realised human beings.

So when, on 4 September 1958, in a tiny consulting room at the Maudsley Psychiatric Hospital in Denmark Hill, London, the agonisingly shy New Zealand writer Janet Frame had her first appointment with Dr Robert Cawley, she was right to be wary. Freudianism now dominated post-war psychiatry, with its belief that intimate attachments with others were vital to mental health and that shyness, which stopped us achieving this, derived from egotism and insecurity.

The meeting had been hastily arranged after Frame had rung the hospital from a phone box near Waterloo Bridge and told them she was going to jump into the river. Frame's first impressions of Cawley – clipped English accent, forbidding black-rimmed glasses, beautifully pressed suit, polished shoes – were not reassuring. Here, she thought, was another of the cold, confident, professional men ready to box her off as crazy. But she was soon won over by his mild manner and self-protective smile, and she began to see that he was shy like her – 'a clever, uncertain man whose sole triumph in our interviews was the accuracy of his recording the content'. She answered his questions, in a just audible voice, with gently mocking scepticism and evasiveness. She liked to play language games and enjoyed the sound and shape of words regardless of their meaning, which Cawley diagnosed as a conflicted desire and disinclination to talk. Slowly he pieced together her story.

As a child, Frame's natural shyness had been aggravated by her embarrassment at her wild frizz of red hair and teeth that were so rotten that she covered her mouth when talking. In 1943, aged nineteen, she entered teacher training college at Dunedin on New Zealand's South Island, lodging with her Aunt Isy, whose husband George was slowly dying in an upstairs room. Too shy to sit with her aunt at the dinner table, Frame told her she would prefer to have a snack on the scullery sink-bench because she had little appetite and liked to study while she ate. This meant she was permanently ravenous, assuaging her hunger by eating shilling-a-bar Caramello chocolate in her room and filching gristly bits of boiled beef from her aunt's dirty plate when she wasn't looking.

In the women's toilets at college she was too embarrassed to walk from the cubicles across the echoing tiles to the incinerator for used sanitary towels. So, for a whole two years, she carried her soiled towels home to put them in the dustbin when her aunt was out, or hide them among the tombstones in the nearby cemetery. She later learned of other young women of her generation driven similarly mad by timidity, making detours into the town's surrounding bushland to dispose of their used towels. She heard of another of her peers who spent her first week in a student hostel in the dark because she was too shy to ask for the light bulb to be replaced.

At the end of her two years' training an inspector came to observe a class she was teaching and, speechless with fear, she walked out, never to return. Soon after this she tried to kill herself by overdosing on aspirin, and her enigmatic manner with doctors led to her being diagnosed as schizophrenic. She spent seven years in psychiatric institutions, undergoing 200 sessions of electro-convulsive therapy with no anaesthetic. She would have had a prefrontal lobotomy, had a doctor not found out that she had won a prize for her first book, *The Lagoon*, and cancelled her appointment. She escaped to Ibiza and then London, where a Maudsley psychiatrist told her she was not schizophrenic after all. She felt bereft without the condition that had come to define her, and it was shortly after this that she threatened to throw herself into the Thames.

Ever since a teacher had identified her to the rest of the class as shy, she had seized on it as a glamour-giving quality, the special preserve of artists and poets. She began to invest everything in her writing, retreating into a parallel world she called the 'Mirror City', which came to seem as if it had more purchase than the real world that she floated through like a silent, timorous ghost. She was loath to spend the only currency of hers that might have any worth in this real world – talking about her life in the Mirror City – for fear its magic would be disenchanted. On the boat to England she would not even divulge the titles of her books to a stranger, because of what she called her 'primitive shyness' about her writing and her 'reluctance to reduce or drain into speech the power supply of the named'.

§

All writers have this sense of a split between their literary and real selves; for Frame the contrast defined her life. 'In conversation I am bedevilled,' she wrote in 1955. 'In written expression an angel will visit.' Her muteness or inarticulacy in the flesh meant that many took her for an imbecile. She had channelled all the intelligent, lucid elements of her character into the self that sat alone at a writing desk waiting for an angel to appear. It is common enough for writers to use a pseudonym, but Frame took the rarer step of publishing under her own name and living pseudonymously. In May 1958, a few months before she met Cawley, she changed her name by deed poll to Janet Clutha (after Dunedin's river) and carried on writing as Janet Frame.

If he had been a strict Freudian, Cawley would have found rich pickings there. But he wasn't, and he instead arrived at a highly unusual diagnosis. All her life Frame had been urged to come out of her shell and meet more people. Cawley's course of treatment was that she should live alone and write. As her first dose of medicine, he suggested that she write about her time in mental hospitals. Frame did what the doctor ordered and produced her novel *Faces in the Water*. It tells the story of the withdrawn and lonely Istina, misdiagnosed as mad and forced into institutions where, almost as punishment for her shyness, daily life is humiliatingly public. Patients have to use doorless lavatories under the stern supervision of a nurse, are made to dress up in party clothes and have scarves tied in bows round their heads to cover their shaven, lobotomised skulls. Frame delivered the manuscript to Cawley, like a baby, nine months after he discharged her. 'It's not brilliant,' he told her, 'but it will do.'

When Cawley suggested that Frame should simply learn to live with her shyness, he was flouting the psychiatric consensus and taking a risk with a suicidal patient. His maverick thinking evolved naturally out of his personality, at which Frame had already guessed. When they met, he was thirty-four, like her, but still only a trainee. A bout of near-fatal anaemia and other serious illnesses in adolescence had set him back years in his education, and the ensuing indignities – such as standing naked in front of several doctors with whisky breath who staggered round him passing him unfit for National Service – had eaten up his confidence. When he first met Frame, he was recovering from a partial gastrectomy and feeling fragile. In Jane Campion's film of Frame's life, *An Angel at My Table*, the actor playing Cawley channelled him as a Laingian existential psychiatrist, with a hipster beard, a rug wrapped over his shoulders and an insouciant manner. But R. D. Laing's anti-psychiatry movement was some years away, and Cawley was no subversive. All he had was that stubborn streak which is surprisingly common in the shy.

The psychiatrist Anthony Storr identified a typical profile of a therapist into which Cawley fits: the 'watchful, over-anxious child' who becomes 'a listener to whom others turn, but who does not make reciprocal relationships on equal terms of mutual self-revelation'. A shy therapist and a shy patient could find the analytical relationship especially fruitful because the consulting room gave them a space and a structure to talk to and listen to each other.

Storr, like Cawley a shy, friendless child plagued by near-fatal illnesses (asthma and septicaemia), also matched the description. Growing up at Westminster Abbey, where his father was sub-dean, he had found consolation in music, taking his gramophone at night up to the organ loft so that his favourite Bach and Handel would ring out around the nave. Like Cawley, Storr came to feel that solitariness had its uses and that salvation did not always lie in others. Unlike Freud, who thought that the creative arts were a second-best substitute for the sex drive, Storr came to believe that an imaginative life was part of our evolutionary inheritance. The naturally solitary could find meaning in their lives by embracing this inheritance rather than, as Freud advocated, trying to cure make-believe with cold reason.

Cawley's sessions with Frame helped him see that we could never know someone else entirely and that complete cures were often elusive. Although Freud aspired to turn psychoanalysis into an exact science, for Cawley it was about following leads and hunches, a way of listening to and telling stories that helped people to make some sense of their lives. He wrote later that Frame had taught him about 'the evanescent nature of the arbitrary boundaries between knowledge and imagination, and art and science'. She remained similarly grateful to him all her life, believing he had saved her just as surely as the psychiatrist who had cancelled her lobotomy.

⁂

One Friday in February 1963 – in the worst month of the worst English winter of the century, the one that proved the final straw for Sylvia Plath, left virtually housebound in Primrose Hill – Frame arrived at a large Victorian semi-detached house in Heaton Moor, a suburb of Stockport, near Manchester. She had been invited to stay for the weekend by the *Guardian* writer Geoffrey Moorhouse, who lived there with his New Zealand wife and their two small children. A few months earlier Frame had given Moorhouse her first press interview, an experience that she found distressing and, over the remaining forty-one years of her life, repeated rarely. Moorhouse described her as 'a shortish woman with a great halo of frizzy, gingery hair, very quietly spoken, and she smiled a lot to fill in pauses between speech, which could be quite disconcerting'.

Frame's novel *Towards Another Summer*, not published until after her death but written immediately after this weekend, throws the slenderest veil of fiction over it. Grace Cleave, an excruciatingly shy writer with brittle mental health and a mass of untameable hair, has rashly accepted Philip Thirkettle's invitation to stay for the weekend in Winchley with his wife, Anne, and their two small children. Grace finds the weekend torture. While Philip is a solicitous host, she is disconcerted by the keenness of his questions and the way he pounces on her answers. As he pauses and waits for her to speak, she buckles under the weight of expectation and her words 'scuttle to the sheltering foliage of incoherence'.

Grace finds it impossible to make logical sentences out of subjects and predicates while anyone else is within earshot. So instead she rehearses platitudinous lines in her head – 'I do like cheese on toast', 'I've so enjoyed your cooking', 'Yes, I like Winchley' – and sometimes manages to say them. Answers to questions that she knows she will be asked, such as whether she intends to return to New Zealand, she lifts 'from an uncomplicated store of samples set aside for the purpose'. She feels under house arrest, fleeing to her freezing bedroom as soon as she can and crying herself to sleep. She longs to sit in her London bedsit at her Olivetti typewriter, with the warm light of the Anglepoise shining over the keys, 'sending out noisy signals to herself'.

Frame loved her typewriter, feeling as orphaned without it as today's teenagers when unglued from their smartphones. It was the prosthetic limb that connected her with the world. 'I have so little confidence … in the area beyond my desk and my typewriter,' she wrote to an agent. Being allowed use of her typewriter in New Zealand mental hospitals was a hard-won concession that earned her a reputation for being high-maintenance. She loved the sensuality of typing: that click of the ratchet as you fed the paper in, the ping of the carriage return bell, the final whoosh as you pulled the paper out.

There was nothing timid about Frame's two-fingered typing. The New Zealand writer Frank Sargeson, who lent her his garden hut to write in and overheard her typewriter's keys yattering away like a Kalashnikov, called it 'typing for dear life'. It gave her a sense of industry, as if she were actually *making* writing, as tangibly as someone weaving cloth. Bashing out a draft of *Towards Another Summer* in the spring of 1963, she wrote to a friend that 'my typewriter is wearing out; the keys have become quite vicious – they are biting into the paper ... I have tiny stencilled o's and a's and n's lying on my table.'

The tongue-tied are always eloquent in their daydreams. In *Towards Another Summer* Grace imagines a Mirror City in her head in which her hosts 'flush with pleasure' at her free-flowing sentences and sparkling aperçus. But her rich interior life never finds an outlet. In one *tour-de-force* passage Philip and Grace take a trip into town and he points out the Winchley Viaduct, presumably meant to be the Stockport Viaduct, that megalith of the railway age, made from ten million bricks, which so fascinated Lowry and which appears often in his paintings. As Grace clears her throat for Philip's benefit and stares meaningfully at the viaduct as if taking in the effect, she goes off on a long thought-riff about buildings as 'outcrops of human flesh and spirit, corns, cancers, stone prayers ... sighs, statements, denials', and marvels at the bravery of mortals who, buffeted by time and the elements, can still create these edifices which are more than walls and a roof. But what comes out of her mouth is, 'Yes. I see what you mean, that it is best in this light.'

The French philosopher Jacques Derrida has argued that the entire tradition of Western thought, all the way back to Plato's *Republic*, suffers from an intellectual bias which he calls 'phonocentrism' – the idea that speech, which we learn instinctively, is a more natural form of expression than writing, which we learn tortuously. Frame's fictional alter egos are shy, inarticulate people stuck in such a phonocentric world. It is a world that insists on seeing writing as the poor, impure relation of speech, when they all believe the opposite, that the babble and prattle of the spoken word can never equal the depth and nuance of writing. In Frame's 1963 novel *Scented Gardens for the Blind* Vera Glace has a daughter, Erlene, who has willed herself mute and sits alone in silence and darkness. 'What is the use of speech?' Erlene reflects. 'On and on, saying nothing, the tattered bargain-price words, the great red-flagged sale of trivialities, the shutdown sellout of the mind?' People dread her silence, she thinks, because 'it is transparent; like clear water, which reveals every obstacle … the cast-off words and thoughts dropped in to obscure its clear stream'.

Ever since she was a little girl, Frame had loved lighthouses. Her father would drive them south in their Lizzie Ford to the beach at Waipapa Point, and while he got out his fishing rod, the rest of the family would picnic in sight of the lighthouse. In *Scented Gardens for the Blind* the young Vera Glace also holidays with her family at Waipapa, where the lighthouse keeper lives alone, and in the winter the boat that supplies him with fuel and food is often delayed for weeks, so the only contact he has with the world is the odd flashing signal from a passing ship. One day Vera is picnicking on the beach when she spots a small boat being rowed away from the lighthouse. Two men are holding down the screaming keeper, who has gone mad.

In Frame's novel the lighthouse and its keeper stand for the fragility of all human attempts to connect with others. Like a beam sweeping the horizon for the benefit of passing ships, we must reach out to others even when the language meant to link us together is so elusive and inadequate to the task. 'Nothing must be allowed to silence our voices,' Vera reflects. 'We must call out to one another … across seas and deserts flashing words instead of mirrors and lights.' Erlene agrees that words are like lighthouses, 'with their beacons roaming the seas to rescue the thoughts or warn them against perilous tides, cross-currents, approaching storms'. But, as we learn at the novel's end, Erlene does not exist except in the mind of Vera, a sixty-year-old spinster who has not spoken for thirty years. She is as remote and unreachable as the Waipapa lighthouse keeper.

When her autobiography brought her a new level of fame in the 1980s, Frame began appearing unwillingly at New Zealand arts festivals. Everyone who saw her said the same thing: she was, despite her obvious unease, her small stature and ordinary appearance – her teeth now straight and false, her hair white and becalmed – an electric presence. When she gave a reading at the Wellington International Festival of the Arts in March 1986, every place in the 2,000-seater venue was taken, and seatless latecomers lined the walls and aisles. Oddly, for someone who had spent her life being tongue-tied, it was her voice that captivated: child-like and bell-clear, somehow conveying both strength and helplessness. She seemed sincerely mystified by the standing ovation she received.

After this brief sortie into superstardom Frame retired from public life with the aid of a new piece of technology she was uncharacteristically effusive about: the answerphone. Her attempts to shut out reality became more zealous. She moved house often to escape other people's noise, driven mad by the sound of revving motorcycles, weekend DIY fanatics and the 'penis-motormowers' of suburban Dunedin. She draped her windows with blankets to dampen the noise. Although she now received visitors vanishingly rarely, the New Zealand dance artist Douglas Wright did manage to befriend her in the late 1980s. Her frequent house moves made him think of her as 'the star witness in a never-ending criminal trial whose testimony is so valuable and damning she must be moved from refuge to refuge under complete protection'. She spoke in a series of short little whispering gasps, but with 'the ringing clarity of a great diva who is resting her voice'. She listened intently, with tiny murmurs of encouragement, a rare gift for attentiveness which he felt could only have been acquired by someone who knew what it felt like to be entirely ignored.

As ever, her keyboard was her flimsy connection to the world. She continued to write her books on her trusty typewriter, being used to the feel of the keys. But for the last years of her life she became an early adopter of all the latest laptops, her face radiant in the monitor glare as she browsed the embryonic internet and sent some of the earliest emails to the thousands of people who still wanted to call this unsociable woman their friend.

§

Perhaps there is something about lighthouses that appeals to introverts, who need to make regular withdrawals from the social world but still retain a link with it. For lighthouses are a concrete expression of our common humanity. Their beacons turn and blink eternally because we accept that people we may never meet, whom we may do no more than flash our lights at in the dark, are also our concern. The Finnish writer and artist Tove Jansson was as fascinated as Janet Frame by this facet of lighthouses. In her work they become a symbol for the solitary artist, isolated by choice from individual people but grabbing hold of that slender thread that links us to unknown others.

In the summer of 1947, aged thirty-three, she built a log cabin on Bredskär, one of the Pellinki islands off the Gulf of Finland, where she and her family had summered since she was a girl. Although she built it on the farthest rocks out to sea, it was still too near civilisation for her. She hatched another plan to emigrate with her brother Lasse to the Polynesian island of Tonga, and yet another to found an artists' colony in Guipúzcoa in the Basque country or in an empty villa with hanging gardens near Tangier. In 1964 she simply moved further out to sea, building a hut on Klovharun, a tiny, barren island in the Pellinki archipelago where she lived with her partner, the artist Tuulikki Pietilä, for half the year. And still it was not far-flung enough. She longed to live on Kummelskär, a rocky landmass in the outermost chain of skerries with no harbour or fresh water.

As a young girl she had been fascinated by the two small

lighthouses on Kummelskär, and her dream had been to build a giant lighthouse there that would cast its beam over the whole of the Gulf. But as an adult she found she couldn't live on the island without timber to build a hut, and she couldn't buy timber without a building licence, which the local Fishermen's Guild vetoed because they feared her presence there would disturb the fish. It was only late in life, when she was getting too frail to stay even on Klovharun, that she gave up on Kummelskär.

Jansson's dream of being on an out-of-the-way island looking after the lighthouse inspired the most sombre of her Moomin books, *Moominpappa at Sea*. Suffering from an inexplicable *Weltschmerz*, Moominpappa takes his family on a sea journey to a lighthouse on a skerry so small and remote that it looks like a speck of dirt on the map. On arrival, they find it desolate and occupied only by a catatonic fisherman who responds to their questions with grunts. The Moomins retreat into themselves. Moominpappa sulks and hides himself in the fog. Moominmamma works out her longing for Moominvalley by painting its flora on the white walls of the lighthouse. Their son, Moomintroll, longs to commune with the mute sea horses. The silent fisherman turns out to be the ex-lighthouse keeper driven mad by loneliness.

Jansson was a great admirer of the psychoanalyst Karen Horney's book *Neurosis and Human Growth: The Struggle toward Self-Realisation*, translated into Swedish in 1953. According to Horney, there are three kinds of neurotic 'solution' to feeling unsafe or unloved: the expansive, the resigned and the self-effacing. The expansive neurotics pursue mastery over others; the resigned strive for independence and self-sufficiency; and the self-effacing are conflict-phobic, criticising themselves before others have the chance.

The Moomin books are full of self-effacing neurotics who rely on others to shore up their own feelings of inadequacy, but who retain a sort of perverted pride in their self-contempt. With only the thinnest line of ink – a tiny widening of the eye pupil, perhaps, a downturned eyebrow or the sole of a foot treading charily through snow – Jansson conveys their shyness and fear. Her scraperboard illustrations scratch her characters out of a background of black India ink as if they are emerging warily out of the gloom. They hug themselves self-protectively, look wide-eyed with fright or sideways with unease. Shrewish characters hide under sinks or tables or wander round the world in search of the horizon, never saying a word. A little girl is frightened into invisibility by the woman who looked after her and becomes slowly visible again under the care of the Moomins, her face finally appearing when she sinks her teeth into Moominpappa's tail. You cannot truly exist, Jansson warns, until you let others know you exist.

Jansson said she had once had a letter from a small boy who said he felt unnoticed by others and fearful of everything. In reply she wrote *Who Will Comfort Toffle?* (1960), about a shy, scared little troll who feels alone until he finds a frightened girl, Miffle, who needs consoling. Child psychotherapists often use this book as a teaching aid to encourage shy children to make friends. 'If my stories are addressed to any particular kind of reader,' Jansson told an interviewer, 'then it's probably a Miffle. I mean those who have trouble fitting in anywhere, those who are on the outside, on the margins.' She received many letters from Miffles, she said, children who were 'timid, anxious and lonely'.

But if this makes Jansson sound like a touchier-feelier version of Dr Seuss, nothing could be less true. Her work is tough-minded and bracingly averse to sentiment. The Moomins, whose forebears lived behind stoves, are deep introverts, fond of wandering aimlessly in the forest on their own, enjoying its silence and stillness, disturbed only by the distant sound of an echoing axe blow or the odd lump of snow thudding down from the branch of a tree. They love hibernating in winter, feeling safe as they burrow into warm, private spaces. And in the last Moomin book, *Moominvalley in November*, they move away without saying a word to anyone, leaving their needy and neurotic hangers-on – the orphan Toft, the obsessive-compulsive Fillyjonk, the anal-retentive Hemulen – to pine after them.

Jansson's lesson is not that shy people should come out of their shells; it is that they should learn to become non-neurotic introverts. For Moomins may sulk and skulk fleetingly, but most of the time they are neither needy nor neurotic. Their response to a problem is to think deeply and then make something – a hut, a painting, a poem, a boat carved out of bark – as a way of whittling meaning out of a terrifying world.

※

Jansson had taught herself, in Horney's classification, to be a resigned neurotic, channelling her talent for solitude into creative work. But all her life she remained shy in the company of other artists, lacking confidence about her paintings since her writing had taken over. And she was an ingrained introvert, liable to take to bed with psychosomatic stomach pains at the thought of having to speak in public. Her need to retreat regularly to Klovharun before re-entering the world was classic introvert's behaviour. Islands, she wrote, are 'a symbol of constructive solitude … Sometimes one has to escape so as to be able to return out of pleasure and not out of compulsion.' She became more stubbornly solitary as she got older, saying she'd had enough of the Moomins and wanted to shut herself away and paint still lifes. 'I could vomit over Moomintroll,' she wrote.

Jansson's later stories, written for adults, have this same sense that all communication is finally destined to fail and that solitude can be joyous and life-affirming. In 'Travelling Light' the unnamed narrator gives up his life and boards a ship, feeling relieved when the ship has moved too far from the quay for anyone to call out to him. He wants to be alone and to ignore 'any disposition to encourage in the slightest degree the surrounding world's irresistible need to start talking about its troubles'. In 'The Squirrel' a woman lives alone on an island, her only human contact being listening on her walkie-talkie to the conversations between passing ships. She develops a strange, wordless rapport with a squirrel, which eventually sails away in the woman's boat, leaving her happily alone again.

In 'The Listener' Aunt Gerda is a diligent letter-writer and rememberer of birthdays with a reputation for being a great listener, partly because she finds it hard to express herself. She listens 'with her whole large, flat face, unmoving, leaning slightly forward', and is in essence 'not much more than silence'. Then she suddenly becomes tardy with her letters, which grow imper sonal. She forgets names and faces and stops listening to people altogether, listening only to the rain or the sound of the elevator in her apartment block going up and down. She now devotes her life to making a map of the people she knows and the links between them – romantic liaisons in pink, divorces in violet, hate in crimson – creating and destroying relationships with a few strokes of her pen. But the task is impossible: the relationships keep changing, and even the largest piece of shelf paper is not big enough to accommodate all the revisions. If this story is a parable, its lesson is unclear. Is it that relationships cannot simply subsist on paper, but must thrive in the messiness of real life? Or that these real-life relationships can be more enervating than nourishing, and someone who listens too well may be crushed under the weight of others' needs?

What is clear, however, is that in all these stories Jansson was writing out her own wish to keep the world at halter's length. In her Helsinki studio she sorted her mail into piles on the stairs, under categories such as 'wants something', 'begs an answer' and 'can wait'. She reserved a special loathing for letters that signed off presumptuously: 'Thanks in advance.' She collated some of this clingy, semi-hostile correspondence in her late piece, 'Messages'. *My cat's died. Write at once. We look forward to your valued reply soonest concerning Moomin motifs on toilet paper in pastel shades. I will come and sit at your feet to understand.*

She proposed an authors' law similar to the laws protecting nesting birds, a closed season in which they would be left alone. After a schoolteacher got her entire class of forty pupils to write to her, Jansson told an interviewer: 'I do hate those children, and I wish I could strangle them with a rubber band.' In fact, she was a dutiful correspondent and answered her thousands of letters without resort to secretaries, often peppering the margins with elegant drawings. She did, though, learn to finesse how to bring a cloying correspondence to an end, by signing off her last letter 'with worried greetings'.

≋

It seems apt that so many of these shy writers and artists spent their last years piling up unread mail and answering it with varying degrees of diligence. The shy person who sends art or writing out into the world is, after all, consenting to embark on a similar exercise in asymmetrical communication, with no guarantee they will ever receive an answer. One of the impulses underlying art is our sense that other kinds of dialogue have failed, and that we need to absent ourselves and communicate at one remove if we are to communicate at all. Art and shyness both draw on *l'esprit de l'escalier*, that conversation we carry on in our heads after the other person has gone.

This form of communication is a gamble. It may require years of self-imposed solitude, so that something intended as a cure or coping mechanism for shyness only ends up aggravating it. Shy artists, unable to bear the risk of potentially awkward communication in the present, take an even bigger risk, betting the farm on a vicarious exchange that might, if they are lucky, pay off in some long-deferred future. Even if they succeed they can end up like Lowry, walking alone on Whitburn sands, drawing on the beach with his stick and looking out at the sea, wondering if spending his life in the solitary service of art had been a life well lived, or just a way, as he put it, of 'getting rid of the days'.

But if it were easy to make ourselves understood, if we could commune like Saint Augustine's angels or *Star Trek*'s mind-melding Vulcans and simply tip the contents of our brains into other people's brains, there would be no need to paint pictures, make music or write words. Some of the most triumphant human associations are those achieved at a distance when all other attempts have miscarried. We are most touchingly human when we have failed to get something across and we have to reach someone else by stealth or subterfuge instead. The shy artist knows how to make use of these failures to connect – the doubts and hesitations we all feel in the presence of others.

7

THE WAR AGAINST SHYNESS

On 22 January 1959 a twenty-one-year-old footballer, Bobby Charlton, appeared on ITV's quiz show, *Double Your Money*. The show's format was that contestants began on a £1 question and doubled or quit until, if they kept answering correctly, they won £1,000. With its showbiz feel and its smarmy host, Hughie Green, it was an odd programme for the introverted Charlton to be appearing on. In a studio only 300 yards away from the Wembley pitch where he had played nervelessly for England he was petrified, and became more so as he kept answering questions correctly over the next two shows. He started shaking as soon as he entered the soundproof booth where he had to answer the questions, barely able to put on his earphones.

But he was good at quizzes, and got every question right until he reached the £500 mark. Now, needing just one more correct answer for the jackpot, he lost his nerve and refused to enter the soundproof booth. His claustrophobia had worsened after being in a plane crash a year earlier at Munich airport, when twenty-three passengers, including eight of his teammates, had died. After some panic, the producers bent the rules to let Charlton stay on the stage to answer the question, and he won the jackpot. With the money he bought his father, a Northumberland miner often on short time, an Austin car.

When he had arrived at Manchester United as a fifteen-year-old apprentice in 1953, Charlton's innate shyness marinated in his homesickness and the locals' failure to decipher his Northumbrian accent. Around the time of his *Double Your Money* appearance, the journalist Arthur Hopcraft interviewed him on the doorstep of his lodgings, with the blushing interviewee holding on to the door handle, trying to answer the questions amiably enough but leaving sentences unfinished and words hanging in the air. Munich had deepened his natural reserve. Before it, he had been known to croon Frank Sinatra songs on the training ground; after it, never.

In July 1961 another talented teenage footballer arrived at United, from Belfast's protestant, working-class Cregagh estate. George Best was also crippled by shyness, the kind that meant he would never challenge a shopkeeper who short-changed him. When Hopcraft interviewed him as an eighteen-year-old, Best's voice was shaky and barely broken, and he bit his lower lip and looked at his interviewer's breast pocket or over his head. When he got the bus from his landlady's house in Chorlton to the training ground, he made sure he had the exact change, because he had the same problem as Charlton: the conductors couldn't fathom his accent.

Once the United manager, Matt Busby, who lived near by, pulled up at Best's bus stop in his Jaguar and offered him a lift. Busby was a charismatic boss, mostly kind and fatherly but able to invest a mere sigh or stare with a glint of steel. Arthur Hopcraft asked him if he thought his players were shy of him, and he conceded, apparently unaware of his own magnetism, that the apprentices were 'often nervous and speechless when they first joined the club'. Best was so tongue-tied in Busby's car that from then on he would hide in the bus queue if he saw it coming. Busby noted his discomfiture and contrived not to see him.

As soon as they crossed over the white-lime line that marked the edge of a football pitch, though, Charlton and Best left their shyness behind, gloriously fulfilling Busby's ideal of football as a game of both passion and grace. Charlton said later that the younger players were so shy of their manager that they could only speak to him indirectly, on the pitch. 'His presence seemed to electrify all of us,' he recalled. 'We would tear into the game like lions. It was the only way, in a sense, that we could communicate with him.' Charlton marauded through the midfield, thundering in shots from thirty yards out. Best was a matador, tormenting lolloping centre halves with his vast repertoire of shimmies and swerves. His boyhood hero had been Zorro, the Spanish nobleman who discombobulated his opponents while hiding his identity behind a black sackcloth mask. Best would beckon defenders towards him, daring them to tackle him, once even taking off a boot and passing with his besocked foot. Back in the dressing room, he took off his Zorro mask and was mild-mannered and mumbling again.

§

There was a strain in working-class British culture that tolerated, even esteemed, shyness in its men. In the early twentieth century, the historian Deborah Cohen has argued, the respectable working classes began to prize a trait that had been associated with the Victorian middle class – reticence – as a way of dissociating themselves from the brashness and bolshiness of those below them in the social scale. This soft spot for shyness accounts partly for the popularity of music-hall characters such as George Formby Sr's innocent, hen-pecked 'Silly John Willie', and Jack Pleasants, whose billing announced him as 'The Bashful Limit' and whose signature song was 'I'm Shy, Mary Ellen, I'm Shy'. In his films George Formby Jr essentially reprised his father's character, that of a gauche Lancashire lad with a nervous laugh who bashfully woos an upper-class heroine and sings songs like 'I'm Shy' and 'Why Don't Women Like Me?' Shy working-class men found solace in solitary hobbies such as pigeon-fancying, fishing, allotment-keeping and pottering around in sheds.

The non-verbal rituals of ballroom dancing, and rowdier communal dances like the Lambeth Walk and the hokey-cokey, which did not even require individuals to request the pleasure of a dance, were popular, according to Mass Observation, because they broke down the barriers of 'shyness and stranger-feeling'. Studying the protocol in a Bolton dance hall filled mostly with young mill workers in 1938, Tom Harrisson, Mass Observation's co-founder, noticed that a young man would ask a woman for a dance simply by touching her on the elbow and waiting for her to fall into his arms. A couple thus created might dance the whole night saying nothing to each other and then go their separate ways, without the man even escorting the woman off the dance floor. At the end of the night the sexes would reform into their original separate groups around the door. Just to make double-sure that these inhibitions remained, no dance hall was licensed to sell alcohol, and kissing was often banned. Harrisson noted that, for those who found even these settings too daunting, the dancing schools had 'developed a special secondary role, as shelters for shy, quiet, clumsy, crowd-hating or inferior-feeling people, who are able, as perpetual learners, to contact the opposite sex and dance, without the selective scramble or public display of the full-size dance-hall'.

A decade and a war later, in May 1948, in a report titled 'Awkward Moments', Mass Observation relayed the responses to a question it had asked its panel of volunteers: 'What are the main things that embarrass you?' It received a wide range of answers: visiting a strange house and not being able to make the toilet flush at first pull; someone reciting poetry a few feet away; being caught looking at your face in a mirror; discovering your flies were undone; being told you had 'had a bad shave this morning'; being seen going in or out of a public toilet; people saying 'Aaah!' when a dog came on the screen at the pictures; your companion talking too loudly on the bus; overhearing dirty jokes; other people saying 'cheerio', 'chin-chin' or 'wizard'. The enforced communality of wartime seemed to have done little to break down shyness and stranger-feeling; awkwardness still extended deep into British social life.

Benjamin Seebohm Rowntree and G. R. Lavers, conducting a sociological survey of the nation's cultural and spiritual life in 1947 and 1948, found some heartbreaking examples of shyness. Mr R., a nineteen-year-old office clerk, had hardly ever spoken to a girl except at Christmas parties. He liked watching football but had never played it as his parents thought that boys who did were common, and he went to the pictures only because he 'enjoys the darkness of a cinema because people cannot look at him'. Mrs F., a fifty-year-old widow, did many small kindly acts for neighbours, but as soon as they were done 'scuttles away again to her lonely dwelling', and she had stopped going to church because she could not bear being seen by so many people. Mr R., a forty-year-old bachelor, had been engaged twice but both his fiancées had broken it off, 'being repelled by a shyness which they mistook for coldness'. In Rowntree and Lavers's account, infused with a large measure of the former's late Victorian puritanism, innate English reserve had found a new haven in the pagan, solitary anaesthetics of gambling, drink, cinema and the football pools.

The playwright Alan Bennett, a teenager in the late 1940s, had inherited from his mother a sense that shyness stood for sensitivity and refinement. For her, it was a burdensome virtue which you might prefer not to have but which did at least save you from being 'common', an antithetical state to shyness with 'a degree of groundless pushing yourself forward'. Bennett's family had just upgraded from boarding houses to hotels for their holidays, although they found them 'theatres of humiliation' and eating in public 'every bit as fraught with risk and shame as taking your clothes off'. This instilled in Bennett a sense of life as a quagmire of social awkwardness which turned him later on into a keen student of Erving Goffman.

In fact Bennett was intrigued to discover that, just as he was first navigating hotels as a teenager, Goffman's theories of social embarrassment were being incubated in a very similar kind of establishment, the tourist hotel in Baltasound, Unst, where he worked in the scullery as second dishwasher while conducting his doctoral fieldwork. The need to keep up a genteel pretence with guests from beyond the island turned the Baltasound hotel into a stage set. The maids would watch new arrivals through the kitchen window, differences in light intensity allowing them to be unseen, rather like actors peeking through the stage curtain at the audience assembling. In the hotel kitchen, mould would be scraped off the soup, pats of half-used butter retouched and recycled, and dirty glasses given just a quick wipe.

Goffman's time at the Baltasound hotel inspired his first book, *The Presentation of Self in Everyday Life* (1959), in which he divided social life into two areas. In front regions people kept up a constant act, while in back regions those who knew each other well took off their social make-up and 'lapsed into an associable mood of sullen, silent irritability'. For Bennett's family, hotels were front regions that demanded pitch-perfect performances not just from the people who worked there but from guests as well. After his father had awkwardly tipped the porter, they breathed a sigh of relief at having their hotel room to themselves, as if they had bluffed their way into the enemy camp.

※

In his 1955 book *Exploring English Character* the anthropologist Geoffrey Gorer argued, in a suspiciously confident generalisation, that 'most English people are shy and afraid of strangers, and consequently very lonely'. Just over half of them, in Gorer's survey, thought themselves 'exceptionally shy'. But, perhaps in a sign of shifting attitudes, only a quarter thought their shyness to be a good thing, and four-fifths thought themselves less shy than they used to be. This is the story Britons began to tell themselves in the post-war years and especially as the 1960s wore on. Class distinctions were blurring, people were less cowed in the presence of their betters, the worst types of social stuffiness were dissolving and the icy exterior of English reserve was melting away.

By the mid-1960s the personality gulf between George Best and Bobby Charlton, born just nine years apart, seemed to signify this shift. As he became a senior pro at United, Charlton's teammates came to construe his shyness as aloofness, few of them noticing that, as he puffed on his half-time cigarette, his hands were shaking. Best went the opposite way. With his slim-fit suits, pointed shoes and collar-length hair, he was English football's first pop idol. His face endorsed Fore aftershave, Spanish oranges, Stylo football boots and Playtex bras. He liked seeing his name in the papers and was endlessly obliging, happy to stand on his head if a photographer requested it. In 1966 he opened his first fashion boutique in Manchester, calling it the 'mod shop for the extrovert male'.

The stars who were the new models of working-class masculinity in the 1960s – such as Terence Stamp, Michael Caine, David Bailey, George Best and the Beatles – were likely lads, chancers, men about town. The 1960s cult of youthful *chutzpah* had little time for the circumlocutions and periphrases of English reserve. As Jonathan Aitken put it in his 1967 book about swinging youth, *The Young Meteors*, 'publicity has become the modern *vice anglais*'.

In fact, although he seemed to have shaken off his shyness to become the most famous Lothario of his era, George Best now relied on what psychologists call 'liquid extroversion'. When sober, he was still so shy he couldn't ring up a restaurant to book a table and would cross the road rather than pass a bus-stop queue. He developed a habit of skipping training or a big match and catching a plane to anywhere. Once he missed the train to a match against Chelsea and was discovered by the media holed up in the Islington flat of the actor Sinéad Cusack; another time he simply refused to come out of the bedroom of his house in Bramhall. In May 1972 he failed to report for the Northern Ireland squad and decamped to a Marbella hotel, where he told a reporter that he had retired from football. He did play on and off for United and other clubs again, but the same pattern of no-shows repeated itself. The problem was not just drink; it was whatever the drink was meant to drown out. Years later, in his autobiography, Best wrote, 'I've never really got over my shyness.'

Shyness turned out to be as resilient as all the other things the swinging 1960s were supposed to have swept away, such as class snobbery, sexual hypocrisy and middle-aged complacency. The playwright Terence Rattigan had built a whole career out of exploring English reticence, lonely stoicism and well-meant evasion. But by the 1970s he had spent two decades in a theatrical climate that embraced emotional intensity and social indignation and found his interest in formality and repression passé. Even on the other side of the 1960s, though, he had not changed his mind about the nature of the English problem, whatever Jonathan Aitken and his young meteors might have thought. 'Do you know what "le vice anglais" – the English vice – really is?' asks Sebastian Cruttwell in his 1973 play *In Praise of Love*. 'Not flagellation, not pederasty – whatever the French believe it to be. It's our refusal to admit our emotions.'

In a BBC documentary he made about the Crown Hotel in Harrogate in 1988, Alan Bennett also reflected on the strange non-death of English diffidence. He certainly found less of the awkwardnesses of his youth in the new world of the business away-day and the mini-break, a world transformed by American consumer openness and the Thatcherite free market's aversion to old snobbery. 'Class isn't what it was; or nowadays perhaps people's embarrassments are differently located,' he reflected to camera. And yet Bennett's writing, like Philip Larkin's poem about sexual intercourse beginning in 1963, betrays a nagging sense that, while the world has changed, human nature is constant. His parents thought that social ease was got by the education they didn't have, but they didn't see, Bennett said, that 'what disqualified them was temperament, just as, though educated up to the hilt, it disqualifies me. What keeps us in our place is embarrassment.'

Bennett's own fear of embarrassment meant that he passed up the chance to have dinner with Jackie Kennedy and Adlai

Stevenson with the rest of the cast of *Beyond the Fringe* in New York in 1963, and to have lunch with his hero Cyril Connolly, after he pretended not to have got the card inviting him. 'I clung far too long to the notion that shyness was a virtue,' he wrote forty years later, 'and not, as I came too late to see, a bore.'

Shyness persists as well for Bennett's characters, whether they are, like Graham Whittaker in *A Chip in the Sugar*, a lonely middle-aged bachelor still living with his mother, or, like the young Andy in *Getting On*, a virginal teenager whose father mistakenly believes he is living in a 'haze of pot and cheap fellowship'. Life, impatient of their fears and hesitancies, is leaving them behind. Not only had the death of shyness been exaggerated, but its sufferers were living in a new era in which it was no longer the ambiguous virtue it had been to Bennett's mother, nor the immutable condition the Victorians called 'constitutional shyness'. It was now a disability it was your duty to overcome.

※

The first real skirmish in the war against shyness took place in a New York brownstone a block and a half from Central Park. In 1965 the psychiatrist Albert Ellis began a free Friday evening workshop there, at his newly established Institute for Rational Living. In each session, dispensing dramatically with the tradition of the silent psychoanalyst talking to the couch-lying patient, he would publicly analyse two or three volunteers using a kind of therapy he called 'disputing'. In front of an audience, Ellis told his patients in a loud, nasal voice to stop being so irrational. Freud's ideas, he told them, were 'horseshit from start to finish', and most people were 'out of their fucking minds'.

As a young man growing up in the Bronx, Ellis had been achingly shy – and had tried to cure his affliction during daily visits to the Botanical Gardens, by setting himself the task of talking to the women who sat alone on the stone benches eating their packed lunches. After a month he declared this exercise a success because, although out of the 130 women he had approached thirty walked off without speaking and the one woman he arranged a date with never showed up, 'nobody vomited and ran away'. He had discovered that social rejection, the great fear of the shy, was bearable.

Ellis began prescribing 'shame-attacking exercises' for his patients, which resembled the strategies of the ancient Stoic and Cynic philosophers he had read while growing up, who tried to shame their pupils and then convince them they had no reason to be ashamed. A shame-attacking exercise was a piece of outlandish behaviour that was embarrassing to yourself but harmless to others, such as loudly announcing the time in a department store ('10.30 a.m. and all's well!'), stopping a stranger in the street and saying, 'I just got out of the loony bin, what month is it?', walking a banana on a leash along a busy street, or buying several packs of condoms in a pharmacy and asking for a bulk discount. The lesson of Ellis's work, which formed the basis of cognitive behavioural therapy, was that we have negative reactions not to events but to our beliefs about them. If we stopped nurturing our shyness by avoiding social situations, we would realise that our anxieties are misplaced.

Like Ellis, Philip Zimbardo grew up in the Bronx, the eldest child in a large Sicilian family. In 1939, aged five, he caught double pneumonia and whooping cough and, in those days before widespread drug and antibiotic treatments, had to spend six months in the children's ward of the Willard Parker Hospital for infectious diseases. In a bleak, grey ward with a vast sea of iron bedsteads and hardwood floors smelling of disinfectant, the children were not allowed to touch or kiss anyone else for fear of contagion. The young Philip watched many of his fellow patients die. In the middle of this hellish experience he learned to charm the nurses to get a bit of extra butter or sugar from them and led fun games with the other children, such as imagining that their beds were rafts on the Hudson. He was teaching himself the power of social ease.

Zimbardo had a younger brother, George, who developed chronic shyness as a toddler after wearing leg braces to correct his infantile paralysis. Whenever someone knocked at the door of their home, he would count to see if all the family were present. If they were, he would run to one of two hiding places: under his bed or behind the locked bathroom door. He cried constantly on his first day at school, clinging to his mother's dress in fear. Mrs Zimbardo then had the idea that it might help if he pretended to be a masked man like his hero, the Lone Ranger. They made a hooded mask out of a brown paper bag, cutting out spaces for the eyes, nose and mouth and colouring it in, and the teacher told the class that they were not to unmask the new boy. He wore the mask until the end of the year, by which time he was no longer shy. It was a redemptive American story: shyness could be conquered through perseverance, creativity and a mother's love.

In 1971, as a young psychology professor, Zimbardo conducted the notorious Stanford prison experiment. Student volunteers acted as prisoners and guards in a pretend prison in the basement of the Stanford University psychology building. The guards began treating the prisoners brutally, and many inmates internalised their subordinate positions and began sheepishly obeying their tormentors. It became so gruesome that the study had to be stopped a week early. The following year, discussing the prison study in a psychology class, it occurred to Zimbardo that shy people might be incarcerating themselves in a silent prison, in which they acted as their own guards, setting self-imposed constraints on their speech and behaviour which nonetheless felt involuntary. He set up the Stanford Shyness Survey, starting with his own students and going on to interview thousands of people. Eighty per cent of those interviewed said they had been shy at some point in their lives, 40 per cent said they were currently shy, and 4 per cent said they were shy all the time with almost everyone. By making it a matter of self-definition, Zimbardo enlarged the meaning of shyness and showed that it waxed and waned in different situations and could afflict even the most assured social performers.

Brought up in a tight-knit Bronx neighbourhood with a lively street culture, Zimbardo began to think of shyness as a particularly modern problem. He was saddened by the Saturday shopping-mall children he saw in California who, while their mothers shopped, sat bored round fountains eating Big Macs or pizza to the sound of piped-in lounge music, before being driven home to their suburban subdivisions. In 1977 he set up the Stanford shyness clinic, a free facility for adolescents and adults. It was, some felt, fortuitously placed in Silicon Valley, where among male computer scientists there might be a high proportion of techno-recluses conversing in computer code in rooms lit only by the glow of their VDUs.

§

Meanwhile a second front had opened up in the war against shyness, at Oxford University. Michael Argyle traced his interest in social psychology, which he pioneered in the UK, back to his concern for a school friend whose shyness had made him miserable. When he started his research in the Applied Psychology Unit at Cambridge in 1950, it was full of people studying motor skills, and he began to wonder if social skills might be similar to motor skills in that they both depended on feedback, whether it was interacting with a machine or listening to and looking at other people. It occurred to him that social skills might be taught and become second nature, like striking a golf ball or shifting gears on a car.

Argyle began researching the unspoken rules of human interaction, what he called 'non-verbal communication'. His Social Skills Research Group at the Institute of Experimental Psychology at Oxford, formed in 1963, began devising experiments to examine the minutiae of eye movements and head nods. A young researcher, Adam Kendon, who later became a leading authority on gesture, was an amateur cinematographer and started filming conversations between experimental volunteers at the Institute. Captured on film, two people talking could clearly be seen to synchronise their non-verbal cues in a sort of gestural waltz.

In his much-cited 1965 article 'Eye-contact, distance and affiliation' Argyle argued that there was an equilibrium level of physical closeness, eye contact and other signs of intimacy. If one of these aspects changed, the others changed to compensate. So the closer two people stood together, the less eye contact they would make, and a person would even stand closer to a second person if their eyes were shut. Eye contact was so crucial that wearing a mask or even dark glasses was enough to derail a conversation – although if both parties were invisible it wasn't a problem, perhaps because the telephone had habituated people to this scenario. In another study Argyle and his team put hostile, friendly and neutral verbal messages in different combinations with hostile, friendly and neutral non-verbal ways of delivering them to see what effect they had on the listener. They arrived at an arresting statistic: non-verbal communication was twelve-and-a-half times more powerful than language in conveying meaning.

In 1966 the *British Journal of Social and Clinical Psychology*, which Argyle had co-founded, published an article that was reported widely in the British press. In a field study of couples sat in coffee shops in different cities, Sidney Jourard, a professor of psychology at the University of Florida, had found that in the Puerto Rican capital, San Juan, couples touched each other – by hand-holding, back-stroking, hair-caressing or knee-patting – 180 times per hour. In Paris it was 110 times per hour; in Gainesville, Florida, it was twice per hour; in London, it was never.

In another experiment Jourard gave several hundred of his students a sort of butcher's beef chart with an outline of a human figure with twenty-two numbered zones – heads, hands, buttocks and so on. Jourard asked them to mark which parts of their bodies had been seen naked and which had been touched by family and friends, and which parts of these people's bodies they had seen naked and touched. The growing use of the bikini and bathing briefs meant that the question about what had been seen naked did not produce very interesting results. A more arresting finding was that most people, unless they were lovers, touched others only briefly on the hands, arms and shoulders. In Puerto Rico, by contrast, men commonly walked arm in arm with other men, and women with women, in the street.

Jourard concluded that America and Britain were 'contactless societies'. In the US this 'touch taboo' even extended to barbers using electric scalp massagers strapped to their hands so that they did not touch their customers' heads. And yet, for Jourard, the large number of massage parlours in US and UK cities betrayed a desire for contact that was not being met in normal relationships. Many American motel rooms were equipped with 'Magic Fingers', a patented device which, on inserting a quarter, would vibrate the bed gently for fifteen minutes. Jourard concluded that 'the machine has taken over another function of man – the loving and soothing caress'.

The new therapies and encounter groups that came out of California in the late 1960s, which prescribed the open expression of emotion and generous doses of hugging and Swedish massage, sought to cure Western society of this unhealthy touchlessness. Bernard Gunther, at the Esalen Institute in Big Sur Hot Springs in California, taught full-body and finger-head massage techniques as a path to 'sensory awakening'. Some of Gunther's more *outré* methods – such as mutual hair shampooing and the 'Gunther hero sandwich' (whole groups spooning one another) – failed to catch on. But the massage therapists probably did help Britain and America to become more tactile societies – which is one reason why, by the 1980s, 'magic fingers' had largely disappeared from American motel rooms (another being that it was easy to break into the machines to steal the coins).

No one would have mistaken the clean-cut, church-going Argyle for a Californian hippie, but in a quieter way he was a product of the same expressive revolution of the 1960s. Citing Jourard's research at a meeting of the British Association for the Advancement of Science, he lamented our 'non-touching culture'. But these cultural differences reinforced his sense that social skills were learnable and teachable. Argyle's new social psychology suggested that people's personalities were not crystallised in childhood or adolescence but capable of change. His bestselling book *The Psychology of Interpersonal Behaviour* (1967) argued that many mental problems were due not to a psychopathology beginning in early childhood, as Freudians thought, but to a lack of social skills.

In 1968 Argyle set up a social skills training programme at the Littlemore Psychiatric Hospital, near Oxford, which had pioneered the use of small group meetings with patients instead of the traditional methods of strait-jacketed restraint and confinement in padded cells. Argyle wanted to carry on this enlightened tradition. He believed that a common trait in mental patients was their inability to make friends, owing to their failure to take any interest in people or see their point of view, and their consequent 'very low level of rewardingness to others'.

He set these patients exercises to improve their postures, enliven their expressions and animate their gestures. They learned to 'moodmatch' the voice tone, expression and body language of their conversational partner. If their voices were monotonous, a common failing among the shy or depressed, they were taught to vary pitch. Since a falling inflection was often the hardest thing to correct in a shy person's voice, patients were given a voice key – a sort of vocal pedometer with a counter triggered by a microphone at a certain noise level. If you got enough 'counts' for speaking loud enough, you received a reward. The hardest thing these patients had to do was to watch videos of themselves and be shown how sullen, bored or hostile they looked to others. They then had to take apart these instinctive gestures and expressions and reassemble them more agreeably, like out-of-form golfers reconstructing their swings.

Argyle's methods caught on and were rolled out into many areas of life. Schizophrenics were taught social skills in order to overcome their alienating sense of otherness. Violent prisoners were shown how to deal politely with situations that might lead to conflict. Alongside these people, whom Argyle named the 'socially inadequate', there were line managers, doctors, teachers, service workers – anyone whose job involved dealing with people or the public – who had to be schooled in social skills as well. Every work training day now seemed to have its role-play exercises and video tutorials about how to talk to other members of the human race.

Argyle became a cheerleader for Scottish country dancing, which he did every Wednesday for years and recommended as a universal cure for shyness. Just as Robert Burns took up Scottish dancing to 'give my manners a brush', Argyle felt that its careful tracing of progressive patterns to a set choreography could teach people social skills. Sequences such as 'reels of three' and 'grand chain' were mini-tutorials in the importance of taking polite turns and coordinating touch and gaze, rather as babies enjoyed matching sequences of smiles and glances with their mothers. Scottish dancing welcomed newcomers, had few conflicts or cliques and, since the rules were so clear, evoked little fear of failure or stage fright. It could also carry a hint of risk-free romance that required no words or commitment from the participants.

Like his American comrades-in-arms in the campaign against shyness, Argyle possessed the evangelism of the missionary, not the empathy of a fellow sufferer. An outgoing personality with a barking laugh, who at parties wore a revolving and flashing pink bow tie, he came to feel that extroverts were happier because they expected to get on with people, and so they did. 'The happy people are a lot less popular than they think they are,' he said. 'The depressives are a lot less unpopular. But on the whole, the depressives are generally nearer the truth.' He saw no rational reason for people to be shy and lonely, and was puzzled by the reluctance of intelligent people to learn the social skills that would make them happier. When he ran the first conference on non-verbal communication in Oxford in 1967, he was baffled by 'the amazingly inept and socially incompetent behaviour of some of the world's greatest experts on social behaviour. No satisfactory explanation was found for this despite much discussion.'

❧

Late one Saturday night in December 1978, an unemployed nineteen-year-old was not to be found in the pub or watching *Match of the Day* like most of his peers. Steven Morrissey had the kind of personality that Michael Argyle might have called 'unrewarding to others'. He was sat on his own in the living room of his parents' council house on King's Road in Stretford, near Manchester, watching the first of a new series of Alan Bennett plays on ITV. *Me, I'm Afraid of Virginia Woolf* was the story of Trevor Hopkins, a shy lecturer in English at a northern polytechnic, who on buses was never without a book, not because he liked reading but because it gave him somewhere to look, and who suffered from curate's bladder, being unable to pee in a public toilet if anyone else was at the urinal. Morrissey felt that, for the first time, his own sense of humour about what Rattigan called 'le vice Anglais' had been caught on screen.

In 1992 Morrissey, now in his early thirties, dropped a CD through the letter box of his near neighbour Alan Bennett in Gloucester Crescent, Camden Town, with a note inviting him for tea. Bennett accepted, and the two men became friends, in spite of the awkwardness Bennett felt at addressing Morrissey by his second name – ironically, in his youth it had been the transition to first-name terms that signalled a hard-won intimacy – so he ended up not calling him anything.

In his cultural tastes, Morrissey often looked beyond the popular culture of his formative years of the 1960s and 1970s, referring back to older role models to help him cultivate a personal mythology of shyness and silence. He loved the then unfashionable A.E. Housman, who published short poems about unstated and unreturned love at decades-long intervals. He dreamed of being Dirk Bogarde, living alone in a Chelsea mansion flat and hiding himself under a cloth cap in the street so he never had to speak to anyone. He had a soft spot for George Formby, especially the song 'Why Don't Women Like Me?', which he played as interval music at Smiths concerts. And he developed a special fascination with Jimmy Clitheroe, a radio comedian who lived as a recluse in Blackpool before, in 1973, overdosing on barbiturates on the day of his mother's funeral.

Morrissey's shyness was shaped by a tough Secondary Modern where the PE teacher made his class run round the gym while he took pot shots at them with a medicine ball. One school contemporary recalled Morrissey just walking round, looking at things intently, as though 'he had a shield round him'. At least some of the time he wore glasses, which he hated. They were the standard-issue 524 Contours, with the thick black plastic frames, millions of pairs of which had been perched on British noses since the founding of the National Health Service in 1948. By 1972, when the thirteen-year-old Morrissey was forced to wear glasses, most people were paying for commercial frames to go with their NHS lenses, and wearing 524 Contours meant both that you were a 'speccy four-eyes' and that your family was too poor to afford anything else. After leaving school in 1975 with no qualifications, he enrolled for a year-long O-Level cram at Stretford Technical College, where he stopped wearing his glasses. Without them he couldn't see beyond a couple of feet, so he gained a reputation for snubbing people, which aggravated his shyness. For the next few years he became, in his own phrase, a 'back-bedroom casualty'.

The period of our lives when we experience what Janet Frame called 'the adolescent homelessness of self' is when we are most naturally disposed to shyness. The teenage years are ones of uncertainty about our futures, failed experiments with identity, hormonal mood swings and physical and social ungainliness. Teenagers will often hug themselves (not coincidentally, perhaps, this became one of Morrissey's distinctive moves on stage) because they feel deprived of physical affection and unsure how to obtain it. They are drawn to displaced forms of communication – texting, letters to pen pals, diaries with locks and keys, badly emoted poetry scrawled in exercise books – as a way of bypassing their blushing, grunting selves.

But the shy, solitary teenager is also a modern invention, a product of the post-war rise in youthful disposable income and the changing layout of houses. It is only quite recently that most young people have had the privacy of their own bedroom, and so in the late 1950s the first British teenagers began retreating from the family TV room to their own rooms to play 45 rpm singles on their portable Dansette record players or tune into Radio Luxembourg on their transistor radios. The signal from the Radio Luxembourg transmitter could only be received satisfactorily after dark, when it was able to defeat the curvature of the earth by striking the ionosphere and bouncing back down to Britain. As it played late into the night, teenagers would listen with their radios under their pillows, enhancing a sense of the new youth culture as something to be experienced intimately and clandestinely.

The history of British pop music is tied up with this emergence of the teenage bedroom as a place where young people could smoulder away and nurse their private crushes, protected by the 'Keep Out' sign on the door. Morrissey was simply an extreme example of such a withdrawal, which in his case lasted for years, into his early twenties. In his tiny box bedroom he painted his window glass black, closed the curtains and shut out the world, longing only for 'those tiny crackles that are about to introduce that record'. He often did not leave the house for a month at a time.

He did sometimes go out to buy his favourite stationery from Ryman's and to post letters, for he had begun a caustic correspondence with the music press, assuming a persona quite at odds with his real-life self. 'Go and see them first and then you may have the audacity to contradict me, you stupid sluts,' he wrote to the *New Musical Express* after it was insufficiently approving of the Buzzcocks. 'If these rock classics don't give you thrills to the joy of living,' he scolded a *Sounds* critic foolish enough not to share his love of the New York Dolls, 'then I suggest you stick with the Sex Pistols whose infantile approach and nondescript music will no doubt match your intelligence.'

In this pre-internet age Morrissey relied, like many other shy British teenagers, on the organisational marvel of the Royal Mail, and the cheapness of its second-class postage, to keep in touch with his fellow humans from a distance. The most intense crisis of his adolescence, he later said with his trademark blend of flippancy and dead seriousness, was when the price of stamps rose by a penny. The Smiths song 'Ask', which seems to be coaxing someone, perhaps Morrissey's younger self, out of his shyness, recalls this teenage letter-writing life. When he began writing the odd concert review for *Record Mirror*, Morrissey assumed the *nom de plume* of Sheridan Whiteside, after the character, inspired by the critic Alexander Woollcott and played by Monty Woolley, who dispenses scathing wit from a wheelchair in *The Man Who Came to Dinner*. It was a well-fitting mask for an awkward adolescent with fantasies of influence and revenge. This mingling of shyness and savagery was to become his calling card.

§

When Morrissey was twenty-three, a young musician called Johnny Marr knocked on the door of his house in Stretford and asked him if he wanted to form a band. Marr was the perfect liberator of a shy person: cool, garrulous and utterly un-shy, he was nonetheless well disposed to cults of melancholy and outsiderdom. The Smiths' rhythm section was less indulgent. The bass player, Andy Rourke, lived near Morrissey, and they shared the bus home from band practice in silence. 'You started counting the lampposts,' Rourke recalled. He and the band's drummer, Mike Joyce, agreed that their new lead singer was singularly unsuited to stardom.

But Morrissey was fortunate in the time he chose to become a star. In 1980 a small group of independent labels had launched the indie chart, published every week in the *NME*. Indie bands tended to see conventional kinds of promotion as 'selling out', choosing to build up their following instead through avant-garde fanzines, small gigs and a then thriving and articulate music press. In reaction to the power suits, shoulder pads, designer labels and pumped-up bodies of mainstream 1980s fashion, the indie dress code was Oxfam granddad chic, with collarless shirts and cardigans hanging off underfed-looking, pale bodies.

Indie bands were rarely pictured on their own album covers,

and they posed unsmilingly for press shots, the glassy-eyed pout being the approved expression of earnest commitment. Their publicity shyness came with a side order of surliness. It was normal for bands to barely speak above a mumble when interviewed on radio or TV, and to have next to no stage patter. Paul Haig, the lead singer of the Scottish post-punk band Josef K, would tape introductions to songs to play over the PA system at gigs rather than talk to the audience.

Of course, young men ostracised at school as misfits had long formed bands as a way to circumvent their shyness, nursing dreams of stardom to avenge their feelings of inadequacy. But indie culture was something more: shyness as a personal and political philosophy, a response to what it saw as the coarsening of British life in the Thatcher years. The clichéd *mise en scènes* of the decade – city boys shouting across trading floors, red-braced yuppies mouthing off in wine bars about house prices, PR executives yelling down brick-sized mobile phones – seemed to the decade's refuseniks to be symptomatic of a new braggadocio afflicting national life. Thatcherism, opposition to which was *de rigueur* in indie culture, championed what the Conservative thinker Shirley Robin Letwin called the 'vigorous virtues' of energy, ambition and independence over the 'softer virtues' of humility, modesty or reticence. It set itself against that very English culture of diffident disdain that saw it as unmannerly to be too eager or thrusting.

Shyness was a concept that, like humour, Margaret Thatcher simply did not compute. Almost everything about her, from her one-note volubility to her decisive way of walking, with her handbag clutched in front of her like a steering wheel, suggested someone with little time for English reserve. In Jung's famous typology she was a classic extrovert: 'All self-communings give [them] the creeps. Dangers lurk there which are better drowned out by noise.' She was suspicious of waverers and shilly-shalliers, people who talked with a nuance and subtlety that she saw as mere fudging and evasion. One of these unfortunates was her chancellor and foreign secretary Geoffrey Howe, whose owlish reserve she at first tolerated and by the end found irritating. Another was Oliver Knox, the Bletchley Park code-breaker for whom Elizabeth Taylor had been governess in the early 1930s, and who now worked at the free-market think tank the Centre for Policy Studies. Thatcher, who liked her advisers to be as bluff with her as she was with them, did not care for his hedging manner and christened him 'Mr Erm'.

Of course, the shy people Thatcher really resented were the work-shy. This is not just a play on words: in the 1980s the high and seemingly intractable unemployment figures meant that, along with the millions of unwillingly jobless people, a small subculture developed of diffident, daydreaming artists and musicians who saw signing on as a badge of authenticity with bittersweet appeal. For all Thatcher's rhetoric in favour of the workers over the shirkers, it was not until after she left power that the government began seriously to cut and target benefits. And so the unemployment figures during her premiership led to something of a burgeoning of creative endeavour as emerging bands survived on the dole and housing benefit while hoping for their break. Jarvis Cocker, a shy teenager who formed the band Pulp in the hope that fame would cure his feelings of social ineptitude, but who spent most of the 1980s signing on, called it, when he at last became famous in 1994, 'the golden age of dole culture'.

Indie labels were headed by their fair share of exuberant characters, such as Tony Wilson of Factory Records and Alan McGee of Creation. But some were run by hardcore introverts – such as the monkish, softly spoken Geoff Travis of Rough Trade and Ivo Watts-Russell of 4AD, so shy that his own publicity shots were of the back of his head. Watts-Russell was drawn to unearthly, darkwave musicians like the Cocteau Twins, Bauhaus and Pale Saints. Brendan Perry, of 4AD band Dead Can Dance, said that he 'attracted that kind of energy, of quite shy people, like he was looking for musicians hidden under stones, making this fragile music'.

The longed-for breakthrough in an indie band's career was the landing of a session on John Peel's radio show. Peel eschewed the unremittingly upbeat waffling of his Radio 1 colleagues from this era, hiding his shyness behind a laconic surface. In his musical tastes he upheld the cause of English irony and understatement against what he saw as the slick, soulless Americanism of MTV culture and the big stadium bands. He preferred under-the-radar acts, losing interest somewhat if they did anything too in-your-face, like signing to a major label or having a hit.

The crucial aspect of indie music was that it was amenable to solitary, introspective listening. When the Smiths were in the recording studio, Johnny Marr always asked himself how the music would sound in their fans' bedrooms. The 1980s was the last great age of the vinyl record and its sensual rituals: carefully removing it from its sleeve and holding it with the thumb in the central hole, placing the stylus delicately on the record and hearing that crackle and pop as it traced the groove and then, while listening to the music, poring over the liner notes and lyrics on the back. Like most indie bands, the Smiths hated the shiny blankness of the compact disc. Morrissey's rearguard action in defence of vinyl was to address his fans teasingly through cryptic messages etched into the run-out grooves of Smiths records: *Are you loathsome tonight? Would you risk it for a biscuit? I don't know anyone that's happy, do you?*

In June 1984 the Smiths performed 'Heaven Knows I'm Miserable Now' on *Top of the Pops*. As he sang, Morrissey looked into the high distance as if dissociating himself from the surrounding tackiness – the customary balloons, glitter balls and disco lights in the studio being woefully mismatched with the song – before turning away from the audience at the end and bowing to no one in particular. He was wearing a hearing aid he didn't need and, instead of his usual contact lenses, the NHS Contours he had rejected as a teenager. NHS glasses had come to symbolise the state's support for both the optically weak and the poor: a year after this Smiths' *Top of the Pops* appearance they were abolished and replaced by a voucher system. Now that thick throwback frames are part of skinny-suit geek chic, it would be easy to miss the symbolic significance of these first stirrings of the cult of nerddom. 'Morrissey, the lead singer of The Smiths, is what American high school students would call a nurd [*sic*],' wrote one of the *Guardian*'s music critics. 'A nurd is a large, gangling being, good at his studies but awkward in all social situations and doomed to romantic failure.'

In an English tradition stretching back to early twentieth-century aesthetes such as Ronald Firbank and Stephen Tennant, Morrissey had turned his shyness into a persona in which reality and artifice were indistinguishable. He was the reverse of that style of indie pop termed 'shoegazing', in which bands would stare through their overgrown curtain fringes at the stage floor during gigs, because they were either too timorous to face a crowd or too busy concentrating on the FX pedals at their feet. Instead, as he stepped forward from what he called 'the huddled shyness of my life', he became, to the astonishment of the Smiths' rhythm section, a showman.

As Marr's strong melodic lines and licks turned his awkward-scanning words into stirring music, Morrissey would offset the limited range of his voice with wild falsetto yodelling while rotating gladioli above his head, waving his hands or clasping them together in exhortation, throwing confetti in the air, stripping to his waist and writhing on the floor. Smiths concerts turned into revivalist events for fans who had experienced their music in solitude and now wanted to share this strangely joyous miserabi-lism with others. Morrissey would help them through the bouncer cordon on to the stage and into his arms, as if laying on hands and curing them of their shyness.

※

In 1986 I started sixth-form college in Rusholme, a dishevelled area of inner-city Manchester immortalised in the Smiths' song 'Rusholme Ruffians', just as the band split up, to the lamentation of many of my new classmates. Post-industrial Manchester was some years away from what was not yet called urban regeneration, and its soot-sodden warehouses and bricked-up terraces, when seen through a steamed-up bus window dotted with Mancunian drizzle, seemed soaked in melancholia. I began to see that Morrissey, who posed for pictures in these settings with his band mates, was turning the landscape of his youth into one big pathetic fallacy, a mirror for existential loneliness.

The college had its share of male Morrissey clones, wearing cast-off Crombie overcoats, walking round in a bubble of solitude and, one imagined, writing sixth-form poetry in their bedrooms and waiting to be rescued by a knock on the door from a mouthy lead guitarist. Every week in the lonely hearts ads in *City Life*, the Mancunian version of *Time Out*, pale and interesting young men quoted freely from Morrissey's lyrics to hint that they were as intriguingly shy as him.

The kinds of epistolary relationships that had sustained Morrissey now began to form around him. His teenage acolytes put together fanzines in their box bedrooms with scissors, glue stick and Letraset sheets, and like-minded souls sent letters with coins sticky-taped to them to make up the cover price. These fanzines, with names like Smiths Indeed and This Charming Man, spawned lively letters pages and pen pal networks. The Royal Mail, in the era before email and the blogosphere began to take over such functions, was coming to the rescue of the shy and speechless for one last time.

Morrissey gave timid people a way of dramatising the thwarted or inconclusive encounters of their lives. 'Sitting on an Intercity train from Leeds to London last autumn, an attractive woman of 40ish caught my eye and smiled warmly,' wrote one young man in his contribution to a book made up of Smiths fans' reflections. '"Jeane" was playing on my walkman at the time. Instantly, she became Jeane and it was as if I was singing the song to her in my head. Sadly, she got off at the next stop (Doncaster) and we didn't speak.' The hyper-rational Albert Ellis, who thought shyness and romantic love very similar in the forms of neurotic fantasy life they inspired, would have despaired at all these Morrissey fans self-mythologising their unrequited feelings.

In the mid-1960s Dorothy Tennov, a psychology professor at the University of Bridgeport in Connecticut, became interested in why unrequited love was such an affliction of the shy. She had first noticed the phenomenon when normally conscientious students, distracted and late with their assignments, broke down in tears in her office and turned out to be nurturing unspoken passions for fellow students or tutors. After conducting many interviews with sufferers, she devised her own word, limerence, as a better term for something we would normally call infatuation or being in love. Limerence was an involuntary state suffered equally by men and women, across cultures and personality types, involving 'intrusive and obsessive thoughts, feelings and behaviors from euphoria to despair'. Demurring from Freud's famous claim that being in love was caused merely by the blocking of our sexual urges, Tennov noted that sex was fairly tangential to limerence, which had more to do with the acute sensitivity of humans to signs of approval or rejection from others.

Limerence, Tennov argued, could produce a 'sometimes incapacitating but always unsettling shyness' in the presence of the love object, and even around other people as well. Its symptoms were similar to deep embarrassment: heart palpitations, trembling, flushing, a churning stomach, awkwardness, stuttering and, more rarely, fainting. The all-consuming anxiety of limerents was whether their feelings would be reciprocated; inconveniently, the fear that they might not be was both painful and enhanced their desire for the loved one. Limerents took a lot of convincing before they accepted that their love would never be returned, especially if, frozen with shyness, they had not made their feelings known to the love object – thus failing to avail themselves of what Diana Athill calls the quickest and most reliable cure for a broken heart: the killing of all hope.

The association of lovesickness with torpefying shyness is evident in some of the earliest surviving fragments of poetry. In one of Sappho's verses, written around 600 BCE, she lists her symptoms when she looks at the woman she loves: 'O Brocheo, I see you / And speech fails me, / The tongue shatters, / My skin runs with delicate / Flame ...' The link between love and shyness was consolidated in the ideal of 'courtly love', emerging in the courts of twelfth-century Provence, captured in the writings of Chrétien de Troyes and Andreas Capellanus and carried into the French countryside by troubadours. This ideal was based on Catharism, a neo-Manichean heresy which saw the realms of spirit and matter as opposed, and the human spirit as imprisoned in the dark desires of the flesh. 'Every lover grows pale at the sight of the beloved,' wrote Capellanus in his *Art of Courtly Love* (*c.*1184–6). 'A lover is always timorous.'

Courtly love was in love with the idea of love, preferring desire that was unfulfilled and unarticulated to the consummated kind. Its sweet, self-ennobling longings came to dominate the Western idea of romance. According to Sir Philip Sidney in *Astrophil and Stella* (1691), lovers are always tongue-tied, 'dumb swans, not chattering pies'. In his essay *On Love* (1822) Stendhal writes of the lover reproaching himself for 'lack of wit or boldness' in the presence of the loved one, when in fact 'the only way to show courage would be to love her less'.

The natural mode for the shy lover was the lyric poem: as emotion recollected in tranquillity, at a safe distance from the beloved, it eternalised one's embarrassment within a classic literary form. In his book *Keats and Embarrassment* Christopher Ricks argues that one of the great consolations of poetry, with its public articulation of intensely private feelings, is that it helps us to express embarrassment and put it to creative use, making us feel less lonely and estranged in the process. Keats, he argues, was a poet particularly attuned to, and insightful about, embarrassment. He felt embarrassed by his lack of formal education, his relatively lowly apprenticeship as an apothecary, his poetry's poor critical reception, his height (only just over 5 feet tall) and his sometimes unrequited and excessive love for Fanny Brawne. His ecstatic communions with nature arose out of a realisation that, according to Ricks, 'among the sane, fortifying, and consolatory powers [nature] has is the power to free us from embarrassment, to make embarrassment unthinkable'.

Keats's willingness to face the subject of embarrassment directly in his poems and other writings allowed him, Ricks argues, to turn awkwardness into 'a human victory'. He was brave enough to be gauche, to identify with that period of life, adolescence, when we are most shy and embarrassed but also most open to the insights inspired by such feelings. In Keats, youthful naivety and immaturity are 'not just excusable errors, but vantage-points'. Ricks contrasts him with Byron, who dismissed Keats's work as 'mental masturbation' and who offered up a different model of nonchalant pretence 'as a *cordon sanitaire* against contagious embarrassment'.

Morrissey was clearly Keatsian in this Ricksian sense of being open to his own awkwardness. Many of his songs, such as 'Half a Person' and 'Never Had No One Ever', are about loneliness and unrequited feeling, climbing into empty beds, feeling ugly and unwanted. But he could channel Byron as well when he felt like it, seeming to offer up his heart and 'launch my diary to music', as he put it, and then pulling back before things got too embarrassing. His lyrics veered between the first and second person, a teasing mix of earnestness and evasiveness, and their mordant sense of humour let him skirt nimbly round a point without over-literalising it.

The same paradox was clear on the frequent occasions he spoke to journalists – for he was the most talked-to and talked-about shy person of his age. Here he would stray into potentially uncomfortable areas like his clinical depression, his celibacy and his association of love with non-reciprocation and pain, but he covered it all with a protective patina of waspish wit and wryness, his words carefully chosen and his sentences elegantly built. As a boy from a school that had stamped on every sign of intellectualism and pretension, he had taught himself the art of rhetoric, but in a way that was slightly skew-whiff, over-fond of arcane words and piled-up adjectives, as if he were flicking through

Roget's Thesaurus in his head: 'The suggestion irks me constantly … Against my better judgement I'm affixed to *EastEnders* … I have a dramatic, unswayable, unavoidable obsession with death.'

The Byronic veneer with which Morrissey coated his Keatsian embarrassment was necessary for an age that was becoming uneasy about unrequited feeling. In her book *Why Love Hurts* the sociologist Eva Illouz argues that unrequited love, idealised in poetry since the Provençal troubadours as a sign of profundity and sensitivity, has itself become an embarrassment in contemporary culture. Modern love is meant to be the coming together of enlightened self-interest, with partners offering intimacy and commitment in return for the same. When love hurts, according to this ethos, it is simply a mistake made by two people who are incompatible. In an age that values emotional mutuality, unrequited love signals immaturity and low self-esteem. A new word emerged to describe this unenviable state, a word that had once meant destitute and deserving, but now meant clingy and insecure: needy.

※

Morrissey was the ideal pop idol for this new age, which prized emotional literacy but was wary of neediness. Despite the occasional glimpse of it in his song lyrics, he mostly avoided that self-hating timidity that is the other side of abandoning your heart to another. The source of his personal allure was that he seemed able to bare his soul without becoming a social casualty, crowning himself the king of the losers but addressing his people from a place of strength. While the shyer and shoegazey types from other indie bands lost career momentum because the attention did not sit well with them, Morrissey revelled in it. It was unusual to encounter someone so secure in his misanthropy – someone who, in an age that made the search for intimacy and empathy its chief preoccupations, refused them both. He was a fittingly paradoxical figure to emerge at the end of a long but inconclusive war against shyness. For Morrissey showed that it was still OK to be shy, that shyness could even acquire an inverted glamour as long as you could make it look like a form of cultural dissidence, a sort of quiet defiance against the square world.

After the Smiths broke up, Morrissey's *taedium vitae* became such a confidently delivered shtick that it swerved into self-parody. He told one interviewer that he lived above 'the slimy, unstoppable urges'. The great thing about music, he told another, was that it was 'communication with people without the *extreme* inconvenience of actually phoning anybody up'. For those messages not conveyable in song, he conversed by fax. Appearing on *Desert Island Discs*, he said he couldn't wait to be a castaway. His chosen luxury was a bed because 'going to bed is the highlight of my day … I like to be hidden and I like to sink … it's the brother of death.'

But people like Morrissey, who put their shyness to work in the service of a pitch-perfect persona that walks a tonal tightrope act between self-pity and self-confidence, are rare indeed. He thrived as an isolate and malcontent; most of us do not. Someone so coolly and effortlessly above the fray is a seductive role model for a shy person, one that stops you having to confront your own 'low level of rewardingness to others'. Eventually most of us come to see that our feelings of unbelonging are unexceptional, and that the truly heroic act is to carry on trying to connect with others, even if it can be dispiriting to keep doing something you are not very good at.

There are no accolades for reaching this kind of accommodation with the world, for being mediocre at being ordinary. Other people never applaud you for not seeming shy, probably because they are more worried about fooling you with the same trick. No one hails Bobby Charlton for doggedly wrestling with shyness all his life. Even now he prefers to give interviews over the phone and dreads public speaking, despite being able to talk very well without notes and often with feeling. Not for him the defiant stance of the self-confidently shy – just an admirable getting on with life and living, which is its own form of gallantry. He never talks about his shyness, and has written two books of autobiography that ignore it completely. He will only admit to wishing he had worked harder at school, 'so today I would be able to explain myself better'.

THE NEW ICE AGE

In 1990 a newly qualified psychiatrist, Saitō Tamaki, began working in the outpatient programme in Sofukai Sasaki Hospital in Funabashi, just outside Tokyo. He soon noticed that many parents were coming to him with one very similar problem. Their teenage or young adult children, usually the eldest or only son, had stopped going to school or work. They had locked themselves in their bedrooms, taped the windows shut and refused to come out, except to go to the toilet or to collect the meals that their mothers left on trays outside their doors. They often slept through the day and then spent the night watching TV, listening to CDs, playing computer games and self-medicating on *shochu*, Japanese vodka.

The retreat of these young men could last for years, well into their twenties or even thirties, in what Saitō called an 'adolescence without end'. Parents often felt responsible for and ashamed of what had happened to their children, so the problem went under-reported and the numbers were hard to gauge. This is, of course, the methodological bind when measuring any form of shyness:

by its nature it is more likely to be unspoken and invisible, and absence of evidence is not evidence of absence. But on the grounds that he came across as many of these cases as schizophrenics, of which there were about a million sufferers in Japan, Saitō boldly estimated that there were a million such young recluses as well. Using a word that had been floating around since the 1980s, meaning to withdraw or shut oneself in, he named these young people *hikikomori*.

In 2001 the Japanese Ministry of Health, Labour and Welfare officially named the *hikikomori* as a social problem, defining them as young people who refused to leave their homes for six months or more. Outreach workers, called *rentaru oneesan* or 'rental big sisters', were employed to visit them. In a country with a high proportion of only children, these surrogate siblings tried to coax the *hikikomori* out of their homes to live in halfway-house dormitories where they could learn to interact with their peers over a game of cards or volleyball.

The *hikikomori* were, it seemed, the other end of the 1980s Japanese problem of *karoshi*, death by overwork. They too looked like casualties of Japan's single-track educational and career escalator, which had become even more brutal with the bursting of the Asian economic bubble in the early 1990s. Fewer young people could now rely on the jobs-for-life system of *shushoku katsudo*, the mass hiring of new graduates by the big firms, and had to enter a precarious new world of low-wage, dead-end work. But for those young people, such as the *hikikomori*, who felt alienated or left behind by this new social contract, their families were usually affluent enough, in this still prosperous nation, to feed and shelter them even if they brought no money into the household. In a country with high rents and cramped living space, twenty-something Japanese often still lived with their parents anyway. The sociologist Masahiro Yamada, in a pithy but pitiless phrase, called them 'parasite singles'.

Many believed the *hikikomori* could only have emerged in Japan, within the unique collective mentality of the *Shimaguni*, or 'island nation'. Some traced it back to the Samurai warrior tradition of training in solitude so that others could not see one's weaknesses. Others linked it to the elaborate and anxiety-inducing politeness that rules daily life in Japan, where people whisper when speaking into phones in the street, public toilets are fitted with a 'Sound Princess' which drowns out the noise of peeing with the fake effect of a lavatory flushing, and the pervasive habit of bowing even extends to the vending machines, which bob deferentially as they deliver your drink. The Japanese for 'shy', *hitomishiri*, literally means 'coming to know people' and refers specifically to the moment a baby learns to tell its mother apart from a stranger and cries when held by the latter. It is seen as a healthy stage in the child's development, and shyness, by extension, is often kindly viewed.

The high-functioning cousins of the *hikikomori* were the *otaku*, the young nerds who fuelled Japan's market for computer games and comic books and who were often found in the maid cafés of Akihabara, Tokyo's electronics district. Here waitresses dressed up as French maids, an image fetishised in *anime* and *manga*, and played Connect 4 or *jan-ken* (rock-scissors-paper) with them, kneeling by the table to stir milk and sugar into their coffee, even spoon-feeding them while addressing them as 'master'. The bestselling success of the 2004 novel *Densha Otoko* ('Train Man'), about a shy computer programmer who meets a beautiful sophisticate on a train when he stands up to a drunk harassing her, was clearly fed by the same kind of wish-fulfilling fantasies.

The work of the Japanese writer Haruki Murakami has often explored these themes of withdrawal and loneliness among his young compatriots. His novel *After Dark* is set near one of Tokyo's night-time districts (probably Shinjuku's Kabukichō, the 'Sleepless Town') on a single night from midnight to 7 a.m. Its subjects are those who, after the last train to the suburbs has gone, withdraw to the secluded booths of all-night diners and karaoke bars. At the novel's centre are two *hikikomori*-like young women, Eri and Mari, who are sisters but do not talk to each other. Eri has been sleeping for two months, doing the minimum she needs to keep alive without intravenous feeding, eating the meals left on her desk and going to the toilet when no one is around. Mari was bullied at school, which made her throw up her food and gave her crippling stomach aches, so in her mid-teens she stopped going. She is now recovered but still lives largely at night and is drawn towards the Alphaville Love Hotel. Here couples stay by the hour, choosing their windowless room from large photos and numbered buttons on display in the foyer.

Like many of Murakami's novels, *After Dark* is both typically Japanese and more widely suggestive of the existential anomie of any modern capitalist city, with its fraying of community, weak social links and itinerant living. The discreet Japanese love hotel, where the bill is settled via automated cash machine or passing money to a hand poking out from behind frosted glass, is not so very different from the global non-place of the budget chain hotel, a smart-card, chip-and-pin world that allows us to complete our transactions without speaking to a soul. These are the kinds of anaesthetised, anonymous places that shy people often find consoling because they are so benignly indifferent to us. They allow us to be in public and private at once, like semi-gregarious ghosts, ignored and invisible but with humanity all around us.

Saitō Tamaki certainly did not think the *hikikomori* were the result of a purely Japanese pathology. He saw them instead as part of a problem faced by all post-industrial societies ruled by free-market economics, where young people had to cope with casualised work and an uncertain future. The contrast was in how and where their alienation showed itself. In the West, confining teenagers to their homes – 'grounding' them, as Americans say – is, in a culture that values mobility, a punishment. But in Japan children are taught from an early age the distinction between the safe, intimate space of *uchi* ('inside') and the intimidatingly formal world of *soto* ('outside'), the routine of taking one's shoes off on entering a home underlining this sense of transition into another realm. Saitō claimed that *hikikomori* were also emerging in South

Korea and in parts of Europe such as Italy and Spain where many young people still lived with their parents. In Britain and the US, alienated youths were more likely to be on the streets.

For Saitō, the *hikikomori* were simply a local symptom of something more general: a modern life that isolated us from each other. Bernardo Carducci, director of the Shyness Research Institute at Indiana University Southeast, pointed to a similar phenomenon in America that he called 'cynical shyness'. The most likely sufferers were friendless young men who, finding it hard to form relationships, responded by retreating into a fantasy life and dehumanising the people who had rejected them. Such a sensibility infected the so-called 'trench coat mafia' of Littleton, Colorado, a group of disaffected young men at Columbine High School from whose number Eric Harris and Dylan Klebold emerged to shoot their teacher and twelve of their classmates dead. In 2007 Carducci told a meeting of the American Psychological Association that those responsible for the eight deadly high school shootings in the last decade had all been cynically shy. *Time* magazine reported Carducci's findings under the headline 'When shyness turns deadly'.

※

A commonly diagnosed phobia in Japan is *taijin kyofusho*: fear of interpersonal relations. Those suffering from *taijin kyofusho* worry that their presence upsets others, either through excessive eye contact, blushing, body odour or breaking wind. It is especially common among young men, the group most likely to become *hikikomori*.

Phobias are real feelings, but they are also ways we think and talk about those feelings. They allow us to cut up the rich tapestry of human misery into patchwork pieces that can be given a name and a set of symptoms. Similar kinds of phobia recur in different historical times and places, but subtly altered and going by different names. *Taijin kyofusho* has been diagnosed in Japan for over a century, but it was only in 1980 that the American

Psychiatric Association's Diagnostic and Statistical Manual of Mental Disorders added the somewhat similar 'social phobia' to its third edition (*DSM-III*).

A young South African psychiatrist, Isaac Marks, had first diagnosed social phobia in the mid-1960s, while working at London's Institute of Psychiatry and the Maudsley Hospital. In a review of the Maudsley's phobic caseload he observed that roughly 8 per cent of the patients were anxious about social situations and would tremble when they became the focus of attention. Their symptoms did not quite fit the then most common diagnosis, agoraphobia. Agoraphobics worried about being in crowds, but theirs was more a fear of being crushed or enclosed by a mass of people rather than, as with the social phobics, a fear of the judgemental gaze. Agoraphobia was suffered mostly by women, but social phobia did not discriminate by gender and had its own unique symptoms, such as the fear of eating, drinking, vomiting, blushing, speaking and writing in front of others. Marks's findings, however, were meant to be tentative, and he had mixed feelings about them leading eventually to the inclusion of social phobia in the *DSM*.

The *DSM* had long been influential in America, where your health insurance will only pay to treat your mental illness if you have a diagnosis with a *DSM* code. But *DSM-III*'s aim was to bring global uniformity to psychiatry. It succeeded brilliantly, being translated into many languages and becoming the standard reference work for mental disorders across the world. Shyness began to enter the clinical nomenclature, with official means of measuring it such as the Cheek and Buss Shyness Scale, the Social Reticence Scale and the McCroskey Shyness Scale. Each had its itemised checklists and scores, giving an ill-defined and vague set of feelings, shyness, the gloss of measurability. Those judged on the McCroskey scale, for instance, were invited to agree or disagree with statements such as 'I don't talk much', 'Other people think I am very quiet' and 'I am a shy person'.

In his book *Shyness: How Normal Behavior Became a Sickness*

Christopher Lane suggests that the publication of *DSM-III* was the key moment in a biomedical turn in psychiatry which saw mental illnesses mainly as disorders to be treated with drugs. The Freudians had been losing clout since the 1960s because their treatments seemed long, labour-intensive and only erratically effective. In 1993 a drug initially intended as an antidepressant, Paxil, was marketed in the US as alleviating what the *DSM* now referred to as 'social anxiety disorder'. 'You know what it's like to be allergic to cats, or dust, or pollen. You sneeze, you itch, you're physically ill,' one advert said. 'Now, imagine that you felt allergic to people.'

Drugs designed for other purposes were soon redeployed and pressed into service. Prozac and Zoloft, better known as antidepressants, were also found to alleviate social anxiety. So were Oxytocin, the 'cuddle hormone' meant to increase bonding between parent and child, and Quetiapine, used initially for schizophrenia. Within the pharmaceutical industry this rematching of drugs to diseases was known as 'condition branding'. Critics called it 'disease mongering' – part of an ominous aspiration to free society of the overly awkward, introverted or Eeyorish. The war against shyness, it seemed, had opened up a new front in the huge hinterland of the unhappy.

§

The historian of science Ian Hacking has argued that what he calls 'transient mental illnesses' – those, such as social phobia, that seem to bubble up only at particular moments in history – are partly a product of the discourses that allow them to be named, described and observed. In a kind of looping effect, doctors create these disorders by their diagnoses and treatments, and patients unconsciously define themselves in the light of these prescriptions. But this does not mean that transient mental illnesses are simply a result of voguish taxonomies; they are also real, felt afflictions. Mental illnesses are transient not just because we find new names for the same feelings, but also because certain feelings find 'an ecological niche' – a hospitable habitat in which to thrive at that particular moment. The symptoms shift as the opportunity to manifest them shifts. For instance, many of the fears that Marks's 1960s social phobics had about writing in public – secretaries scared they would be unable to take shorthand, others afraid to enter a bank in case their hands shook while writing a cheque – have since been overtaken by technology.

'What is become of all the Shyness in the World?' wrote Jane Austen, anticipating this idea, in a letter of 1807 to her sister Cassandra. 'Moral as well as Natural Diseases disappear in the progress of time, & new ones take their place. Shyness & the Sweating Sickness have given way to Confidence & Paralytic complaints.' A century or so ago the mentally distressed suffered fainting fits, convulsions or dissociative fugues; now they suffer from clinical depression, eating disorders or social phobia. In each age the symptoms are real enough, and so presumably is the misery.

All forms of mental illness exist on a continuum with what we need, for our own sanity, to see as normality. There have been times in my life when I have avoided queues and crowds, locked myself in my office and ignored the knocking door, or failed to answer the ringing telephone. But when does something tip over invisibly from being merely sadness-inducing to being pathological? I have so often seen the symptoms in others – young people unable to walk beyond the threshold of their own front doors for weeks at a time, hyperventilating at the idea of entering a packed room, floored by the thought of eating or drinking in a public place – that it has crossed my mind that modern life might indeed be an enabling niche for the anxious and shy.

In his keynote address to the first international conference on shyness, organised in Cardiff in 1997 by the British Psychological Society, Philip Zimbardo argued that shyness was becoming an epidemic. Noting that the number identifying as shy in his Stanford Shyness Survey had risen to 60 per cent, he feared the arrival of 'a new ice age' of non-communication. He blamed the illusion of contact offered by email, the internet and mobile phones, even the replacement of cashiers by ATMs, all of which loosened the 'social glue' of casual contact. By the year 2000, he predicted, it would be easy to go a whole day without talking to anyone else.

This decline of associational life is a familiar refrain in the work of other American social theorists such as Robert Putnam, John Cacioppo and Sherry Turkle. They suggest that loneliness is the virus of modern existence, cultivated amid our customised consumer lifestyles, which isolate us from one another and then sell us cheap techno-fixes to ease the pain. We rely ever more on what Turkle calls 'sociable robots' that displace flesh-and-blood intimates – such as Siri, the Apple iPhone digital assistant, or Paro, the cuddly baby harp seal used in elderly care in Japan, which makes eye contact and responds to being stroked. We are becoming a culture of semi-absent citizens, 'alone together', since even in public our faces are buried in cellphones and tablets, head-phones cushioning us from other people's noise and our glances turned downwards to converse with friends elsewhere via those dancing thumbs on our touchscreens. This new machine age allows us to relate to each other in amounts we can control like a saline drip.

§

And yet there is a curious thing about this new ice age created by technology. The free market may indeed be turning us into atomised consumers who buy, read, listen and talk to each other virtually, or make our way silently through the aisles of produce and insert our PINs at the android checkouts with their satnav voices. But the market also wants to know all about us. It insists that nothing get in the way of the free flow of information, that we live out our private lives in an electronic public square where everyone is naked and unashamed. Facebook calls this form of online self-disclosure, which handily links our identities to our purchase histories and makes us easier to target by advertisers, 'radical transparency'.

The rise of social networking and the smartphone has made it normal for people to lay bare their private lives, posting photos of themselves in states of inebriation or updating the world on their changing relationship status in ways that would have seemed bizarre to all of us a few years ago, and that still seem bizarre to me. Like the *Big Brother* housemates who really do appear to forget that the cameras are there, these social networkers have lost any sense that there is a different type of language and behaviour suitable for public as opposed to private life. Their default mode is that of a free-flowing, private conversation, albeit one that strangers can overhear.

I have spent much of my adult life artfully avoiding looking in mirrors or at my reflection in shop windows. I feel like a Martian dropped into this new world of selfie sticks, digital avatars and that unnerving little talking-head rectangle of yourself in the corner of the screen on Skype. Are there really citizens of this brave new world who will happily upload photos of themselves to dating apps that allow strangers to select 'like' or 'nope' to their pictures, swiping away rejected suitors as if they were swatting flies? It feels as if we have sleepwalked into something strange, become inured in a mere historical blink to this major reboot of the limits of personal intimacy.

I comfort myself with this thought: it is the conceit of every era to think it has changed everything utterly. After about 150,000 years of evolution the human personality must surely be resistant to short-range effects. New technologies do not change our natures; they mould themselves around them. While many people online seem unaware that they are in public, others craft a bulletproof cyber-identity that is never punctured by their offline life. There are now anti-Facebook apps that allow you to send anonymous messages to your whole address book or that self-destruct after being read, just like on *Mission: Impossible*. One of the lessons of the internet is that the desire for privacy and anonymity is very resilient, even if fulfilling that desire online does not always make us kinder or more considerate. There will always be a pull between our social instincts and our desire to creep away from the tribal campfire and be alone with our thoughts. In all of us that tension is differently strung, but surely it was ever thus, since the first hunter-gatherer went to the back of the cave for a sulk.

In *DSM-III* social phobia had merited just a few paragraphs. But in *DSM-5*, published in 2013, it stretched across seven pages. While stressing that 'normative shyness' was 'not by itself pathological' – hardly a reassuring caveat – it listed a wide range of symptoms for social anxiety disorder. The sufferer was concerned that 'he or she will be judged as anxious, weak, crazy, stupid, boring, intimidating, dirty, or unlikable'. Variants included paruresis, or 'shy bladder syndrome', the inability to urinate in a public toilet with others present, and 'selective mutism', a particular anxiety about speaking in social settings.

It is striking that it is especially the shy and anxious that we now diagnose in this way. I wonder if this is because, just as depressives respond better to therapy than psychopaths, it is somewhat easier to make the overly timid more confident than it is to make the overly confident more timid – partly because the timid are more likely to be self-questioning and open to treatment in the first place. If the drug companies ever did decide to expend their energies on the much trickier task of developing medication to induce an appropriate level of shyness in the insufferably bumptious, I can think of a few people I would like to nominate for the clinical trials.

I now realise why, although I once thought about asking a doctor to prescribe me Seroxat – the British name for Paxil, available on the National Health Service – I never went ahead with it. The sadness caused by shyness is real, and helping others to take the edge off that sadness is a noble aim. But taking a drug for social anxiety – for feeling stupid, boring or unlikeable – feels like shouting at the wind, arguing with the rain. It feels like trying to find a cure for being alive.

※

In the late 1960s the neuroscientist Oliver Sacks was working with patients at the Beth Abraham Hospital, a 'home for incurables' in the Bronx, who had fallen victim to the *encephalitis lethar-gica* or 'sleepy sickness' epidemic in the 1920s and had been in semi-conscious limbo for over forty years. When Sacks treated them with the drug L-dopa, normally prescribed for Parkinson's disease, they emerged dramatically from their catatonic states. Sacks became fascinated by people such as this, who underwent dramatic personality changes owing to brain damage, drugs or surgery. The long-buried effects of neurosyphilis led one of his patients, a shy ninety-year-old woman, Natasha K, to shake off her inhibitions and flirt with young men. A brain carcinoma turned another patient, a reserved research chemist, Mrs B., into a facetious joker. These cases seemed to suggest that our person-alities were fragile things, because they were contained entirely within that delicate and damageable object, the brain.

And yet a recurring motif in Sacks's work is that people are abnormal after their own fashion, and diseases adjust to our uniqueness. People with crippling conditions such as lethargica or catatonia are still indubitably themselves. The idea that the imma-terial personality could be housed wholly within the material brain is a shocking thought that for most of human history was inconceivable and even sacrilegious. And yet equally shocking in its own way is Sacks's central discovery: that this three-and-a-half pound lump of jellified fats and protein between our ears manages to sustain a coherent human personality that lasts, for most of us, all our lives.

Sacks himself was proof of this. He suffered from childhood with unshakeable shyness, his loneliness relieved by some of the usual shy stratagems (chronic letter-writing, workaholism, Dutch courage) and some less usual ones. As a young man in England in the 1950s he loved motorbikes, because they offered – just as they did for T. E. Lawrence, another victim of English reserve who liked to ride at speed on powerful Brough Superiors on bad roads – an escape from self-consciousness in their sensual union of body and machine. Sacks also found the biker community welcoming; motorcycles seemed 'even in stiff England, to bypass the barriers, to open a sort of social ease and good nature in everyone'. In the early 1960s, living near Santa Monica's Muscle Beach, he over-compensated for his timidity, rather like the 7-stone weakling of the Charles Atlas bodybuilding adverts, with a brief but fanatical career as a weightlifter. In later life he sought sweet self-forgetting in water, spending hours each day swimming alone in Long Island Sound.

Sacks's writings are littered with autobiographical fragments that reveal how his life was blighted by his shyness. His first book, on the involuntary twitching known as myoclonus, was never published because he gave his only copy of the manuscript to an expert in the field who shortly afterwards committed suicide, and Sacks was too shy to ask his widow for it back. He compared his passivity in relationships to his encephalitic patients, who never initiated contact but who could catch a ball thrown by someone else. When he tried to learn sign language, he found his forefingers repeatedly forming the crossed-swords symbol for 'but'. Along with other shy physicians such as W. H. R. Rivers and Robert Cawley, however, he found the structured nature of the clinical relationship a liberation from social unease and was able to form close relationships with his patients.

As a neuroscientist he called his shyness a 'disease' and was inclined to posit clinical causes, such as his lifelong prosopag-nosia or 'face blindness', which meant that he could not recognise people, even his own reflection, and learned to identify others from their silhouettes. He avoided parties, knowing they would lead to embarrassing situations, such as failing to greet friends or greeting strangers as friends. No doubt this would worsen anyone's shyness, since human faces are unlike those of other animals in being very unlike each other, and recognising faces, which most of us do brilliantly, is one of the basic building blocks of social life. But Sacks conceded that the root causes of his own shyness were as much psychological as neurological. Ever since he had been bullied by a psychopathic prep school teacher, part of him, he said, felt 'forbidden to exist'.

Sacks had the further predicament of wanting to be known and recognised but being unsure that this was allowed. When his first book, on migraine, was reviewed in the British press, his father, also a doctor, was appalled to find his son in the newspapers, for at the time one could be struck off the medical register for advertising. Sacks half-agreed with him, and for years misread the word 'publish' as 'punish'. This base-level reserve in his personality stayed constant, even after some fairly reckless encounters with psychoactive drugs in 1960s California. On reaching old age, he declared himself 'sorry to be as agonizingly shy at 80 as I was at 20'. Diagnosed with ocular cancer, he would close the door and cry, but found that even on his own he was too shy to scream.

⁂

Personal growth is the growth industry of our age. Its guiding principle is that personality is plastic and pliable, a skill set you can learn and change. Dale Carnegie's children populate the mind-body-spirit shelves of bookshops: *How to Talk to Anyone, Goodbye to Shy, Make Yourself Unforgettable, How to Light Up a Room and Make People Like You.* They trade in stories of recovering shy people who have transformed themselves from depressed solitaries into social butterflies, the psychological equivalent of those slimmers of the year who pose delightedly inside their old and now outsized pair of trousers. The shyness institutes use phrases like 'social fitness classes', which make working on your personality sound like going to the gym. In this positive-thinking mode, shyness always has to be 'busted' or 'conquered'.

But if I have learned one thing from exploring the lives of shy people, it is that our personalities do not do these kinds of handbrake turns. All the people I have written about in this book were as shy at the end of their lives as at the start of them. They found ways to hide it, channel it, finesse it or work round it, but it never went away. And I suspect that, if I make it to my ninth decade as Sacks did, I too will simply have found more ways to adapt to my shyness, just as a stammerer learns to avoid certain words.

In her 1959 book *The Day's End* the nurse Pamela Bright wrote about working on Middlesex Hospital cancer ward. She noted that her patients died in the same manner in which they had lived – 'aggressive, shy, fussy, humorous, grateful, weary, talkative and assertive, they all had their word to say and then departed'. The egocentric were high-maintenance to the end, the theatrical orated their last words *con brio*, and the unassertive expired quietly in the small hours, not wishing to cause bother, 'slipping out of life as wild animals creep away into solitary places'. Of course, it makes no sense to cling to your shyness when your life is nearly over and what anyone thinks of you is immaterial. Why be self-conscious when your consciousness is about to end? But then, since when did shyness make any rational sense? If you were rational, you'd have cured your shyness earlier, when it might have done you some good.

I have come to think of my own shyness as an unyielding reality, rather as Sacks's patients' personalities were never entirely erased even by lesions and carcinomas in their brains. The best strategy, I have realised, is Zen acceptance. If I just accede to my shyness as an obdurate fact, like having sticky-out ears or crooked teeth, I can live with it. I have decided, as the software developers say, that being shy is a feature, not a bug. I now just assume that after any conversation with a stranger I will come away feeling slightly defeated. In the manner of those passive-aggressive signs they used to have in shops warning people off asking for credit, I should probably wear a badge that says, 'Please do not expect sparkling conversation, as its failure to materialise may offend.'

If I stop berating myself, the symptoms are relieved and I can start paying more attention to the world and to others. Shyness feeds on itself, so if you don't think about it, it may not get better but it doesn't get worse. I do my best to struggle against it while learning to live with it, to be neither ashamed of it nor secretly proud of it. And so the war against my own shyness has ended in an uneasy truce.

As hostilities are suspended, at least I can say that I managed to body-swerve the fate of the *hikikomori*. No one needs to leave my meals on a tray by my door or hire a surrogate sibling to coax me out of the house. I no longer think of myself as giving off some invisible, people-repelling pheromone. I am occasionally seen walking round in public spaces in daylight, and in the evenings I can be taken to parties and left on my own without anyone fearing I will do a tearful flit. If someone knocks on my office door, I answer it (most of the time); if the phone rings, I pick it up (usually).

In other words, I can rustle up a passable impression of a normal person because I know it is part of the deal, the levy we pay on being alive, even if it sometimes feels I have to scrape together every penny of emotional effort to pay it. And, like a reformed smoker, I long to leave the pub or restaurant table with the nicotine addicts and nip outside for a few furtive drags of the precious drug of solitude. I once attended a fire safety awareness lecture at work in which we were told that on entering any building we should take note of the emergency exits, so we knew how to leave in a hurry when the alarm sounded. That's me, I thought: always with one eye on the door, my escape route planned.

§

'Do you not think that shyness can be a gift to us?' a friend said to me. 'I mean, by giving us a slanted outlook, a special way of seeing the world?' I demurred then, but I am coming round to her way of thinking. Shyness is an unwanted gift most of the time. But a gift it still is, its attendant feelings of apartness granting us hard-won insights we cannot now imagine living without.

In a beautiful essay, 'On Being Ill', Virginia Woolf writes about how the experience of illness can shatter 'that illusion of a world so shaped that it echoes every groan, of human beings so tied together by common needs and fears that a twitch at one wrist jerks another'. When we are ill, we become deserters from 'the army of the upright' and look on that army as fighting a brave but futile cause, while it in turn shuns or forgets about us. The otherness of being ill, its enforcement of stillness and isolation, makes us see that we are all, finally, on our own in this world. In our normally healthy state we keep up the genial pretence and try 'to communicate, to civilize, to share'. But in illness 'this make-believe ceases'.

And yet illness, Woolf suggests, also opens up 'undiscovered countries', new fields of awareness that can be as creative as they are chastening. They remind us that our lives are built on sand and that in the end nothing matters. People trapped in the impenetrable bubble of grief often say the same thing: forced to step outside the routines of communal daily life, they see them for what they are, a collectively conjured-up chimera. Shyness offers us a low-intensity but longer-lasting version of this state of feeling lifted out of the swim of social life, looking askance at a world that seems baffling and strange.

It is true that the sense of alienation this brings, just as with illness and grief, may turn us slightly mad, like the unnamed narrator of *Rebecca*, who wonders how many people there are in the world like herself 'who suffered, and continued to suffer, because they could not break out from their own web of shyness and reserve, and in their blindness and folly built up a great distorted wall in front of them that hid the truth'. But being behind that distorted wall also lets us look at the social world from the outside in. And that *is* a gift – as long as we keep a grip on reality by scaling the wall occasionally, and joining in once again with the make-believe of the army of the upright.

⁂

We still cannot make up our minds about shyness. Some see it as a form of rudeness or conceit, others as a sign of sensitivity and sagacity in the insincere soup of social life. I have come to feel that it has little meaning other than itself. It is so dirt-common that no especially disagreeable or virtuous human attributes can be extrapolated from it. It cohabits with egotism and self-pity as readily as with modesty and thoughtfulness. Shyness is just *there*, another piece in the intricate jigsaw of human diversity, and all that studying it has taught me is what I knew already: human behaviour is endlessly rich and odd.

In her book *The Scars of Evolution* Elaine Morgan argues that many parts of the human body are merely accidental residues of the weird, purposeless process of evolution. That kink in the lumbar region of the spine that allows us to stand up, for example, is an evolutionary bodge, which means that our vertebrae are unable to take too much strain without slipping out of place. And so a choice made by a few of our ape-like ancestors about 4 million years ago, to stop moving on all fours and stand erect, accounts for today's most common reason for being off work: lower back pain. In a phenomenon that evolutionary biologists call maladaptive behaviour, traits that evolved to allow an animal to thrive in one situation may not work in another.

A common myth about evolution is that it works like clockwork, with a clear design and purpose, and that it is always looking for the ideal answer to the problems of existence. In fact, all that billions of years of evolution have done is to turn nature into a beautiful, glorious mess. Natural selection rarely alights on the perfect solution. It just eliminates the unworkable, and ends up with billions of different solutions to the problem of being alive. Perhaps that is all shyness is: just one of those billions of different solutions to this problem. No one, and certainly not me, would call it an optimal solution. But it is *a* solution, part of what the nature writer Richard Mabey nicely calls the 'redundant embroidery' of existence. Shyness is another piece of evolutionary happenstance, an unplanned derivative of our strange human capacity for thinking about ourselves. And rather like lower back pain, which eases with time but is prone to recur, it can ebb and flow, afflicting us without warning like sciatica.

Without shyness I suppose people might be happier, in the same way that they might be happier without back twinges or other random defects like acne, myopia, varicose veins and dandruff. But perhaps the world would also be a little blander, less creative and less interesting. Nature may be a mess, but it has an ingenious capacity for making the best of a bad job. Evolution's incremental tinkerings do improve things. The lower vertebrae of our backs, for instance, have grown gradually bigger over millennia to sustain better the weight they have to bear. If, as Morgan puts it, 'the first few million years of bipedalism were the worst', then the same could be said for shyness: after living with it for so long, we should have learned to rub along with and even make use of it. And just as the natural world needs unlovely things such as peat bogs and earthworm colonies to maintain its equilibrium, so perhaps the world needs the shy too – and the bold, and all shades in between – to make up the delicately balanced ecosystem of human behaviour.

Shyness is simply part of our awareness that we share the world with other living creatures and that co-existing with them is awkward but unavoidable. Even non-thinking life forms seem to have some inkling of this, as an English forestry expert called Charles Lane Poole discovered when, in the early 1920s, he undertook extensive, solitary surveys of the timber resources of Australia and Papua New Guinea, then under Australian rule. Despite a teenage shooting accident that had left him with a hook instead of a left hand, he was a brilliant and brave tree-climber, and he explored the forest canopy in a way that no scientist had done before.

When viewed from the rainforest floor, the canopy looks like a single mass of tangled vines and foliage. But Lane Poole discovered that, at its top, even in a fully stocked forest, there were gaps: the leading shoots of neighbouring trees stopped growing and left a respectful distance of a few feet between them. This occurred often among trees of the same species, as if they were looking out for their own, but it also occurred between species – and in the rainforest there could be hundreds of species per hectare. Lane Poole, a cavalier character with no trace of English reserve, came up with a sweet name for this phenomenon: crown shyness.

Although scientists have in recent years had ample opportunity to explore the rainforest canopy, on inflatable research platforms delivered by airship and resting on treetops, they have yet to solve the mystery of why crown shyness occurs. One theory is that it is caused by wind sway, which leads to the abrasion and death of the sensitive growing tips. Another is that the tips sense greater shade when they are near other leaves and stop growing in order to increase their share of sunlight. Yet another is that it is a way for trees to ward against leaf-eating caterpillars and other pests, the equivalent of refusing to shake hands for fear of catching someone's germs. But no one is sure, just as no one knows why a similar phenomenon occurs in the sea, among coral reefs.

Crown shyness is, of course, a metaphor replete with anthropomorphism. Trees and corals are not really shy of each other, any more than violets really shrink. But for Richard Mabey crown shyness is a handy metaphor. It points, he says, to a basic truth about life on earth: that it is pragmatic and collaborative, not ruled by the kill-or-be-killed logic that we are used to thinking of as the law of the jungle. More than half the earth's plant and animal species live in forest canopies, and most of them live synergistically, respecting each other's space. Life is a matter of negotiation and adjustment to conditions rather than destroying competitors in pursuit of that much misconstrued Darwinian ideal, the survival of the fittest.

I prefer to see shyness like this. Just like the tips of trees in the rainforest, we are shy because we know we are different from other living things. And because humans also carry around with us this rare cargo of self-consciousness, we are uniquely aware that, for all our need for intimacy, we face the world alone. The human brain is the most complex object in the known universe, the journey from one brain to another is the most difficult we will ever make, and every attempt at conversation is a gamble, with no guarantee we will be understood or even heard. Given these unbending realities, isn't a little shyness around each other forgivable?

I have fought all my life the sense that being shy is a personal affliction that has left me viewing life from its edges. This feeling was early acquired and now seems hard-wired, for no amount of mature reflection seems entirely to rid me of it. But at least I now see in my more lucid moments that it is an illusion. Not only is shyness essentially human, it may even be the master key that unlocks our understanding of those sociable creatures, *homo sapiens*, lumbered with this strange capacity for turning in and reflecting on themselves. Shyness isn't what alienates me from the rest of herd-loving humankind; it's the common thread that links me to them.

NOTES

In order to keep the notes to a minimum, I have not referenced quotations from ancient or out-of-copyright texts that are easily searchable online, and have only referenced direct quotations and important information. Where the latter is taken from a text I have also quoted, I indicate this after the reference to the quote with 'see also'.

1. A Tentative History

p. 1 '*shake hands … and she fled*': David Wright, *Deafness: A Personal Account* (London: Faber, 1990), p. 88.

p. 4 *The evolutionary anthropologist Robin Dunbar …*: Robin Dunbar, *Grooming, Gossip and the Evolution of Language* (London: Faber, 1996), p. 121.

p. 6 '*an unintentional breaching experiment*': Susie Scott, 'The shell, the stranger and the competent others: towards a sociology of shyness', *Sociology* 38, 1 (2004), 128.

p. 8 '*their shyness … malevolent to revenge*': Eliza Edmonston, *Sketches and Tales of the Shetland Islands* (Edinburgh: Sutherland & Knox, 1856), p. 79.

p. 8 '*by the mere … the flock*': Fridtjof Nansen, *The First Crossing of Greenland*, vol. 1, trans. Hubert Majendie Gepp (Cambridge: Cambridge University Press, 2011), p. 188.

p. 9 *The most fearful were the working* …: Helen Mahut, 'Breed differences in the dog's emotional behaviour', *Canadian Journal of Psychology* 12, 1 (1958), 37, 39.

p. 12 *'lizard cliques'*: Lesley Evans Ogden, 'Do animals have personality?', *Bioscience* 62, 6 (2012), 536. See also 533–4.

p. 12 *Jeffrey Kahn has argued* …: Jeffrey P. Kahn, *Angst: Origins of Anxiety and Depression* (New York: Oxford University Press, 2012), p. 51.

p. 14 *'Pudor rusticus'*: Reid Barbour, *Sir Thomas Browne: A Life* (Oxford: Oxford University Press, 2013), p. 114.

p. 14 *'a natural blush … free from loquacity'*: J. T. F., 'Biographical sketch of the author', in Sir Thomas Browne, *Religio Medici, A Letter to a Friend, Christian Morals, Urn-Burial and Other Papers* (Boston, MA: Ticknor and Fields, 1862), pp. xiii–xiv.

p. 14 *'that there were any … way of coition'*: 'Religio Medici', in *Thomas Browne: 21st-Century Oxford Authors*, ed. Kevin Killeen (Oxford: Oxford University Press, 2014), p. 73.

p. 14 *'most amiable sweetness … his Countenance'*: Barbour, *Sir Thomas Browne*, p. 411.

pp. 14–15 *'I am naturally bashfull … wondring eyes'*: Browne, 'Religio Medici', in *Thomas Browne*, ed. Killeen, pp. 42–3.

p. 15 *'To be knav'd out … burning burials'*: Thomas Browne, 'Hydriotaphia or Urne-Buriall', in *Thomas Browne*, ed. Killeen, p. 533.

p. 15 *'One way of tackling it … individual level'*: Theodore Zeldin, 'Personal history and the history of the emotions', *Journal of Social History* 15, 3 (1982), 345.

p. 16 *'life began in silence'*: Vicky Allan, 'It's good to talk', *Scotland on Sunday*, 22 August 1999.

p. 16 *'A doom of reticence … each other'*: W. Compton Leith, *Apologia Diffidentis* (London: Bodley Head, 1917), p. 2.

p. 17 *'surely this mead … umbrageous?'*: Thomas Kendrick, 'In the 1920s', *The British Museum Quarterly* 35, 1/4 (1971), 6.

p. 17 *'In their depths … tossing his hair'*: Compton Leith, *Apologia*, pp. 2, 73.

p. 17 *'consentient in one grace… within themselves'*: Compton Leith, *Apologia*, pp. 60, 62.

p. 18 *'through bashfulness … be sick'*: Robert Burton, *The Anatomy of Melancholy* (Philadelphia, PA: J. W. Moore, 1857), p. 235.

p. 18 *'Stoicism has qualities … altogether shun'*: Compton Leith, *Apologia*, p. 72.

p. 19 *'the seat of shame ... signum pudoris'*: Carlin A. Barton, *Roman Honor: The Fire in the Bones* (Berkeley, CA: University of California Press, 2001), pp. 224, 226.

p. 20 *'the first ancestor ... unnatural masks'*: Compton Leith, *Apologia*, pp. 62, 65, 64.

pp. 20–1 *'the savage world ... like an indiscretion'*: Compton Leith, *Apologia*, pp. 52, 55.

p. 21 *The archaeologist and television personality* ...: Glyn Daniel, *Some Small Harvest: The Memoirs of Glyn Daniel* (London: Thames & Hudson, 1986), p. 238.

p. 21 *'a very distinguished ... bird of prey'*: David Cannadine, *G. M. Trevelyan: A Life in History* (London: HarperCollins, 1992), p. 50.

p. 22 *'Good ... good'*: J. H. Plumb, *The Making of an Historian: The Collected Essays of J. H. Plumb,* vol. 1 (Brighton: Harvester Wheatsheaf, 1988), p. 5.

p. 22 *'curious ... barking shyness'*: Plumb, *Making of an Historian*, p. 7.

p. 24 *'rampageous ... cool, good soil'*: Reginald John Farrer, *Alpines and Bog-Plants* (London: Edward Arnold, 1908), p. 252.

p. 25 *'Les grands timides ... and detours'*: Robert A. Nye, *Masculinity and Male Codes of Honor in Modern France* (Berkeley, CA: University of California Press, 1998), p. 223.

2. This Odd State of Mind

p. 27 *When his eldest daughter* ...: see Randal Keynes, 'Anne Elizabeth Darwin', *Oxford Dictionary of National Biography* (online edition); and Charles Darwin, 'A biographical sketch of an infant', in Marston Bates and Philip S. Humphrey (eds), *Charles Darwin: An Anthology* (New Brunswick, NJ: Transaction, 2009), pp. 409–10.

p. 27 *'odd state of mind'*: Charles Darwin, *The Expression of the Emotions in Man and Animals* (London: John Murray, 1872), p. 330.

p. 28 *He told Darwin which microscope to buy* ...: Adrian Desmond and James Moore, *Darwin* (London: Penguin, 1992), p. 110.

p. 28 *'a curious man ... driest pump imaginable'*: Duane Isely, *One Hundred and One Botanists* (Ames, IA: Iowa State University Press, 1994), p. 133.

p. 28 *'enwrap rather than to explain ... for yourself'*: Asa Gray, 'Notice', *The American Naturalist* 8, 8 (1874), 477.

p. 29 *'I think my silicified ... Mr Brown's heart'*: Desmond and Moore, *Darwin*, p. 227.

p. 29 *'poured forth a rich … minute points'*: Charles Darwin, *Selected Letters on Evolution and Origin of Species with an Autobiographical Chapter*, ed. Francis Darwin (New York: Dover, 1958), p. 33.

p. 29 *'two dead weights … disappear entirely'*: Desmond and Moore, *Darwin*, p. 284.

pp. 29–30 *'I am shy … boring self'*: William Bryant, *The Birds of Paradise: Alfred Russel Wallace: A Life* (Lincoln, NE: iUniverse, 2006), pp. 32–3.

p. 30 *'suffering over again … constitutional shyness'*: Alfred Russel Wallace, *My Life: A Record of Events and Opinions* (London: Chapman & Hall, 1905), pp. 59, 258.

p. 30 *'the most peculiar and the most human'*: Charles Darwin, *Expression of the Emotions*, p. 310.

pp. 30–1 *'lifeless sheath … life made visible'*: G. W. F. Hegel, *The Philosophy of Fine Art*, vol. 1, trans. F. P. B. Osmaston (London: G. Bell and Sons, 1920), p. 200.

p. 31 *'beautiful and interesting … the heart'*: Thomas H. Burgess, *The Physiology or Mechanism of Blushing* (London: John Churchill, 1839), pp. 7, 173.

p. 31 *'the stimulus which excites … instinctive passions'*: Burgess, *Physiology or Mechanism of Blushing*, p. 156.

p. 31 *'an extreme state of morbid sensibility'*: Burgess, *Physiology or Mechanism of Blushing*, p. 48.

pp. 31–2 *'makes the blusher … self-attention'*: Darwin, *Expression of the Emotions*, pp. 338, 345.

p. 32 *'rarely cry, except … acutest grief'*: Darwin, *Expression of the Emotions*, p. 155.

p. 32 *'une taciturnité … pride of the Prussian'*: Paul Langford, *Englishness Identified: Manners and Character, 1650–1850* (Oxford: Oxford University Press, 2000), pp. 180, 226.

p. 33 *'une conversation … rather than conversation'*: Langford, *Englishness Identified*, pp. 188, 176. See also pp. 177, 185.

p. 33 *'separation in union … English life'*: Langford, *Englishness Identified*, p. 103. See also pp. 106, 104, 102.

pp. 33–4 *'the most noticeable … are formed'*: Edward Bulwer-Lytton, *England and the English* (New York: J. & J. Harper, 1833), pp. 28–9.

p. 34 *'made the lone places … ball rooms'*: Alexander Kinglake, *Eothen: or Traces of Travel from the East* (London: John Ollivier, 1844), p. 264.

p. 35 *'shy and indolent … and intelligent'*: Kinglake, *Eothen*, pp. 266–8.

p. 35 *'first stare … very unimportant subjects'*: Alexis de Tocqueville, *Democracy in America, Part the Second, The Social Influence of*

Democracy, trans. Henry Reeve (New York: J. & H. G. Langley, 1840), p. 178.

p. 36 *'the booted leg of Kinglake ... very proud'*: Rev. W. Tuckwell, *A.W. Kinglake: A Biographical and Literary Study* (London: George Bell and Sons, 1902), p. 21.

p. 36 *'His common talk ... in July'*: Kinglake, *Eothen*, pp. 248, 251.

p. 36 *'I (the eternal ... and I saw them'*: Kinglake, *Eothen*, p. 276.

p. 37 *'full of talent ... Oceans of Soup'*: Gerald de Gaury, *Travelling Gent: The Life of Alexander Kinglake (1809–1891)* (London: Routledge & Kegan Paul, 1972), p. 48.

p. 37 *He hated hearing his name ...*: Gaury, *Travelling Gent*, p. 129.

p. 37 *Kinglake also stopped accepting invitations ...*: Gaury, *Travelling Gent*, p. 92.

p. 38 *'for I do not wish ... hands of Hags'*: Gaury, *Travelling Gent*, p. 81.

p. 38 *'I did not say ... orders of her master'*: A. W. Kinglake, letter, *The Times*, 14 July 1860.

p. 39 *'as if they were willing ... tone of gentlemen'*: Ralph Waldo Emerson, 'English traits', in *The Portable Emerson*, ed. Mark Van Doren (London: Penguin, 1977), p. 415.

p. 39 *'honourable secrecy ... any sort'*: David Vincent, *The Culture of Secrecy: Britain, 1832–1998* (Oxford: Oxford University Press, 1998), pp. 34, 48–9.

p. 39 *'dynamic understatement ... most unfortunate'*: Michael McCarthy, *Say Goodbye to the Cuckoo* (London: John Murray, 2009), pp. 141–2.

p. 39 *'I am reluctant ... yes'*: R. A. W. Rhodes, *Everyday Life in British Government* (Oxford: Oxford University Press, 2011), pp. 198–9.

p. 40 *'There are men ... their meadows'*: Hippolyte Taine, *Notes on England*, trans. W. F. Rae (New York: Holt & Williams, 1872), pp. 66, 161.

p. 40 *'a man may conceive himself ... several feet'*: Tuckwell, *A. W. Kinglake*, p. 125.

p. 41 *'I have all my life ... conquer it'*: Gaury, *Travelling Gent*, pp. 128–9.

p. 43 *'the singularly unattractive ... Welbeck Abbey'*: Nikolaus Pevsner, *The Buildings of England: Nottinghamshire*, rev. Elizabeth Williamson (London: Penguin, 1997), p. 370.

p. 44 *'to penetrate ... subterranean depths'*: 'The Duke of Portland at Welbeck Abbey', *Derbyshire Times and Chesterfield Herald*, 13 July 1878.

p. 44 '*The sudden mood ... in the mirrors*': *Ottoline: The Early Memoirs of Lady Ottoline Morrell*, ed. Robert Gathorne-Hardy (London: Faber, 1963), p. 73.

p. 45 '*the silent but ... open grave*': 'Death of Mr. Herbert Druce', *The Times*, 15 April 1913.

p. 45 '*merely from constitutional shyness*': Duke of Portland, *Men, Women and Things: Memories of the Duke of Portland* (London: Faber, 1937), p. 32.

p. 48 *One creation myth had it that* ...: John MacKinnon, *In Search of the Red Ape* (London: Collins, 1974), p. 16.

p. 48 '*fond of retirement ... familiar to him*': 'The orang-outang at Westminster', *Dundee Courier & Argus*, 7 September 1880.

p. 49 '*sighed and looked ... motionless morosity*': Siegfried Sassoon, *The Weald of Youth* (London: Faber, 1942), p. 234.

p. 49 '*a shy and offended deerhound*': Philip Hoare, *Serious Pleasures: The Life of Stephen Tennant* (London: Hamish Hamilton, 1990), p. 91.

p. 49 '*farouche*': *Ottoline at Garsington: Memoirs of Lady Ottoline Morrell 1915–1918*, ed. Robert Gathorne-Hardy (New York: Knopf, 1975), p. 121.

p. 50 '*one more in the procession ... he was in them*': Sassoon, *Weald of Youth*, p. 230.

p. 50 '*the poor little thing ... its own futility*': Siegfried Sassoon, *Complete Memoirs of George Sherston* (London: Faber, 1972), p. 509.

p. 51 '*before he had finished ... faces of his audience*': Richard Slobodin, *W. H. R. Rivers: Pioneer Anthropologist, Psychiatrist of The Ghost Road* (Stroud: Sutton, 1997), p. 17.

p. 51 '*The half-shy look ... human integrity*': Sassoon, *Complete Memoirs of George Sherston*, pp. 533–4.

p. 52 *Sitwell had ascertained that* ...: Osbert Sitwell, 'Introduction', in Ronald Firbank, *Five Novels* (New York: New Directions, 1981), p. xii.

p. 52 '*as a gesture of politeness ... single grape*': Siegfried Sassoon, *Siegfried's Journey, 1916–1920* (London: Faber, 1945), p. 137.

p. 53 '*Where I reign ... entirely unknown ...!*': Firbank, *Five Novels*, p. 12.

p. 54 '*export the ideal ... international exhibition*': Jean Moorcroft Wilson, *Siegfried Sassoon: The Journey from the Trenches, A Biography (1918–1967)* (London: Duckworth, 2003), p. 188.

p. 55 '*backing into the limelight*': Mark Amory, *Lord Berners: The Last Eccentric* (London: Sinclair-Stevenson, 1998), p. 63.

p. 55 '*I wish I could understand ... Enoch Arden complex*': Moorcroft Wilson, *Siegfried Sassoon*, p. 115.

p. 55 '*Do not beam ... poise, not pose*': Stephen Tennant, 'Be smart, and grace will follow of its own accord', *Daily Mail*, 15 June 1928.

p. 56 '*until our eyes ... shy undertone*': Ferdinand Mount, *Cold Cream: My Early Life and Other Mistakes* (London: Bloomsbury, 2008), pp. 139–40.

p. 57 '*the emaciated face ... hydrogen bomb*': D. Felicitas Corrigan, *Siegfried Sassoon: Poet's Pilgrimage* (London: Victor Gollancz, 1973), p. 192.

p. 58 '*To Siegfried ... Siegfried Siegfried*': Corrigan, *Siegfried Sassoon*, p. 199.

p. 58 *In his latter years, his social life amounted ...*: David Foot, *Beyond Bat & Ball: Eleven Intimate Portraits* (London: Aurum, 1995), pp. 43–4.

p. 59 '*the essence of English ... deluxe samizdats*': Philip Hoare, 'Where did the joke end?', *Spectator*, 22 November 2008, 54.

p. 59 '*partly like arrangements ... drunken unpacking*': Christopher Isherwood, *The Sixties: Diaries Volume 2: 1960–1969* (London: Chatto and Windus, 2010), p. 77.

p. 60 '*an immense sympathy*': Nicholas Shakespeare, 'Standing back from life', *The Times*, 11 March 1987.

p. 60 '*something like accidia ... Middle Ages*': V. S. Naipaul, *The Enigma of Arrival* (London: Penguin, 1987), p. 53.

p. 60 '*the rawness of my colonial's nerves*': Naipaul, *Enigma of Arrival*, p. 95.

pp. 60–1 '*big things ... applauded on sight*': Naipaul, *Enigma of Arrival*, pp. 70, 191.

p. 61 '*an English eccentric's ... touching his belongings*': Sarah Checkland, 'Final glorious days of eccentric's dream house', *The Times*, 8 October 1987.

p. 62 '*idle, silly queen ... lunatics*': Paul Theroux, *Sir Vidia's Shadow: A Friendship across Five Continents* (London: Penguin, 1999), pp. 166, 165.

p. 62 '*shyness and suspicion ... frugal kindness*': Paul Theroux, *The Kingdom by the Sea* (London: Penguin, 1984), p. 126.

p. 62 '*among the more ... struggling with*': Adam Phillips, '*Mr Phillips*', in *Equals* (New York: Basic Books, 2002), p. 205.

3. How Embarrassing

p. 64 '*I once offered ... to the ground*': B. Jack Copeland, *Turing: Pioneer of the Information Age* (Oxford: Oxford University Press, 2012), p. 64.

p. 65 *According to his mother, Sara ...*: Sara Turing, *Alan M. Turing* (Cambridge: Cambridge University Press, 2012), p. 16.

p. 65 '*He appears ... at a Public School*': Andrew Hodges, *Alan Turing: The Enigma* (London: Vintage, 1992), pp. 23–4, 26.

p. 66 *'Whenever you thank … positively apprehensive'*: David Leavitt, *The Man Who Knew Too Much: Alan Turing and the Invention of the Computer* (London: Phoenix, 2007), p. 119.

p. 66 *better appreciated by another machine*: 'The mechanical brain', *The Times*, 11 June 1949.

p. 66 *'Darling Sweetheart … Yours beautifully …'*: Hodges, *Alan Turing*, p. 478.

p. 67 *Early one morning in the autumn…*: William Newman, 'Viewpoint: Alan Turing remembered', *Communications of the ACM* 55, 12 (December 2012), 40.

p. 67 *'gentle and clean'*: G. H. Hardy, *A Mathematician's Apology* (Cambridge: Cambridge University Press, 1967), p. 121.

p. 68 *'all his life … out of the ordinary'*: C. P. Snow, 'Foreword', in Hardy, *A Mathematician's Apology*, p. 16.

p. 69 *'Shetlanders take some knowing … word from them'*: W. P. Livingstone, *Shetland and the Shetlanders* (London: Thomas Nelson & Sons, 1947), pp. 79–80.

p. 70 *'afraid openly to surrender … shyness of the soul'*: Sue Prideaux, *Edvard Munch: Behind the Scream* (New Haven, CT: Yale University Press, 2005), p. 2.

p. 71 *'Ae, ae … nae sae bad'*: Erving Goffman, 'Communication Conduct in an Island Community', PhD, University of Chicago, December 1953, p. 183. See also pp. 186, 181.

p. 71 *'Good crowd … past spaekin about'*: Goffman, 'Communication Conduct', pp. 188, 194–5. See also pp. 187, 263–4.

p. 72 *'unfulfilled expectations … truly wears the leper's bell'*: Erving Goffman, *Interaction Ritual: Essays on Face-to-Face Behaviour* (London: Penguin, 1972), pp. 105, 107. See also pp. 101–2.

p. 72 *One rare biographical morsel …*: Rom Harré, *Key Thinkers in Psychology* (London: Sage, 2006), pp. 183–4.

p. 72 *Goffman seems to have felt rather at home …*: Greg Smith, *Erving Goffman* (Abingdon: Routledge, 2006), pp. 12–13.

p. 73 *'My real aim … for interviews'*: Goffman, 'Communication Conduct', pp. 2, 5.

p. 73 *'loudly applauded … completely silent'*: Darwin, *Expression of the Emotions*, p. 324.

p. 73 *The comedian Michael Bentine …*: Michael Bentine, *The Shy Person's Guide to Life* (London: Granada, 1984), p. 13.

p. 74 *'sometimes, a victim … within seconds'*: Henry J. Heimlich, 'The Heimlich maneuver', *Clinical Symposia* 31, 3 (1979), 4.

p. 74 '*That's what I get … a shield*': William Ian Miller, *Humiliation: And Other Essays on Honor, Social Discomfort, and Violence* (Ithaca, NY: Cornell University Press, 1995), p. 95. See also pp. 15–16, ix–x.

p. 75 '*In doing so he might … shame-threshold*': Norbert Elias, *The Civilizing Process: The History of Manners and State Formation and Civilization*, trans. Edmund Jephcott (Oxford: Basil Blackwell, 1994), p. 111, 493.

p. 76 '*walking decisively … sort of cruelty*': Nicola Beauman, *The Other Elizabeth Taylor* (London: Persephone Books, 2009), p. 39.

p. 78 '*A great many … succeed best*': Frank Kermode and Anita Kermode, 'Introduction', in Frank Kermode and Anita Kermode (eds), *The Oxford Book of Letters* (Oxford: Oxford University Press, 1995), pp. xxi–xxii.

p. 78 '*at which Englishwomen have excelled*': Elizabeth Taylor, 'The Letter-Writers', in *Complete Short Stories* (London: Virago, 2012), p. 182.

p. 78 '*Would you like to …?*': Robert Liddell, *Elizabeth and Ivy* (London: Peter Owen, 1985), p. 81.

p. 78 *Liddell and Taylor agreed …*: Liddell, *Elizabeth and Ivy*, p. 74.

p. 79 '*one could write letters to the dead*': Beauman, *The Other Elizabeth Taylor*, p. 224.

p. 79 '*stripping the mask … rain-quenched landscapes*': Roger Manvell, 'Britain's self-portraiture in feature films', *Geographical Magazine*, August 1953, 222.

p. 80 '*Isn't 'e ever … orf with 'er?*': Philip Hoare, *Noel Coward: A Biography* (Chicago, IL: University of Chicago Press, 1998), p. 361.

p. 80 '*profess total inability … plot hinges*': 'Germans boo British film', *Manchester Guardian*, 16 November 1946.

p. 80 '*the darkest place between two lamps*': Elizabeth Taylor, *A Game of Hide and Seek* (London: Virago, 2009), p. 243.

p. 81 '*like a trapped … beautiful owl*': Elizabeth Jane Howard, 'Introduction', in *A Game of Hide and Seek*, p. vii.

p. 81 '*I just wanted … to look at*': Geoffrey Nicholson, 'The other Elizabeth Taylor', *Sunday Times*, 22 September 1968.

p. 81 '*My hands become ice … occupational disease*': Letter, 12 February 1951, in N. H. Reeve (ed.), *Elizabeth Taylor: A Centenary Celebration* (Newcastle: Cambridge Scholars, 2012), p. 106.

p. 81 '*under-rated forms of suffering*': Elizabeth Taylor, *The Soul of Kindness* (London: Virago, 1983) p. 216.

p. 81 '*I never think … trivial emotion*': Elizabeth Taylor, 'Hester Lilly', in *Complete Short Stories*, p. 11.

p. 81 '*In the morning ... three cheers*': Elizabeth Taylor, 'The Rose, The Mauve, The White', in *Complete Short Stories*, p. 179.

p. 82 '*I do not think ... terribly embarrassed*': 'Contenders for the golden crown of British fiction', *The Times*, 22 November 1971.

p. 82 '*glad that she was alone ... strange phenomenon*': Elizabeth Taylor, 'The Blush', in *Complete Short Stories*, p. 179.

p. 82 *The anthropologist Bronislaw Malinowski* ...: Michael Young, *Malinowski: Odyssey of an Anthropologist, 1884–1920* (New Haven, CT: Yale University Press 2004), p. 403.

p. 83 '*suddenly and unwillingly ... other's nakedness*': Clifford Geertz, '"From the native's point of view": on the nature of anthropological understanding', in *Local Knowledge: Further Essays in Interpretive Anthropology* (New York: Basic Books, 1983), p. 64.

p. 83 *wowomumu*: Michael Young, *Fighting with Food* (Cambridge: Cambridge University Press, 1971), pp. 262, 51.

p. 84 *dafnu ... piso*: Sue King and Angela Clifford (eds), *Local Distinctiveness: Place, Particularity and Identity* (London: Common Ground, 1993), p. 19.

p. 85 '*an attitude of ... emotional involvement*': Herbert Hendin, *Suicide and Scandinavia: A Psychoanalytic Study of Culture and Character* (New York: Grune & Stratton 1964), p. 43.

p. 86 '*cries of despair ... long afterwards*': Åke Daun, *Swedish Mentality*, trans. Jan Teeland (University Park, PA: Pennsylvania State University Press, 1996), p. 133. See also pp. 59, 46, 44, 124.

p. 86 *Ingmar Bergman, the son of a Lutheran minister* ...: Peter Cowie, *Ingmar Bergman: A Critical Biography* (London: Secker & Warburg, 1982), p. 6.

p. 86 *according to a poll conducted* ...: Daun, *Swedish Mentality*, p. 118.

p. 86 '*reserve Danes ... Latin jollity*': Susan Sontag, 'A letter from Sweden', *Ramparts*, July 1969, 26.

p. 88 *As a young man, he was deeply self-conscious* ...: David Michaelis, *Schulz and Peanuts: A Biography* (New York: HarperCollins, 2007), pp. 173, 299.

p. 88 '*Shyness is the overtly ... any importance*': Michaelis, *Schulz and Peanuts*, p. 177.

p. 89 '*a powerful wish to be invisible*': *Desert Island Discs*, BBC Radio 4, 12 February 1995.

p. 90 '*the shepherd of ... unhappy people*': Judith Yaross Lee, *Garrison Keillor: A Voice of America* (Jackson, MI: University Press of Mississippi, 1991), p. 33.

Notes

p. 91 *'with the precision ... the victim'*: 'E. B. White', in George Plimpton (ed.), *Writers at Work: The Paris Review Interviews: Eighth Series* (New York: Viking, 1988), p. 15.

p. 91 *'nature and beauty ... the case'*: William Strunk Jr. and E. B. White, *The Elements of Style: Third Edition* (New York: Macmillan, 1979), pp. xiv, 80.

p. 91 *'both a mask ... genitals'*: *Letters of E. B. White*, ed. Dorothy Lobrano Guth, rev. Martha White (New York: Harper Perennial, 2007), p. 470.

p. 92 *'perpetually disgruntled ... against a wall'*: Garrison Keillor, *Lake Wobegon Days* (London: Faber, 1986), p. 152.

p. 92 *'To pick up a phone ... justifiable to me'*; David Usborne, 'I've got to get away from here', *Independent on Sunday*, 3 January 2010.

p. 93 *'a mild, shy, gentle ... assumed name'*: Nathaniel Hawthorne, 'Preface to *Twice-Told Tales'*, in *Tales and Sketches* (New York: Library of America, 1982), p. 1153.

p. 93 *'porcupine impossibility ... we know!'*: Richard Hardack, *Not Altogether Human: Pantheism and the Dark Nature of the Human Renaissance* (Amherst, MA: University of Massachusetts Press, 2012), p. 14.

p. 93 *'In Detroit ... regrettably, a nerd'*: *Newsweek*, 8 October 1951, 28; *OED* entry (online edition).

p. 95 *Two sociologists from the University of Tampere ...*: see Eija-Liisa Kasesniemi and Pirjo Rautianen, 'Mobile culture of children and teenagers in Finland', in James E. Katz and Mark Aakhus (eds), *Perpetual Contact: Mobile Communication, Private Talk, Public Performance* (Cambridge: Cambridge University Press, 2002), pp. 176, 183–4.

p. 95 *Other scholars of cellphone culture have shown ...*: see Bella Elwood Clayton, 'Virtual strangers: young love and texting in the Filipino archipelago of cyberspace', in Kristóf Nyíri (ed.) *Mobile Democracy: Essays on Society, Self and Politics* (Vienna: Passagen Verlag, 2003), pp. 225–35; and Gerard Goggin, *Cell Phone Culture: Mobile Technology in Everyday Life* (London: Routledge, 2006), p. 76.

p. 95 *The number of handsets had grown to 7 million ...*: Janey Gordon, 'The cell phone: an artifact of popular culture and a tool of the public sphere', in Anandam Kavoori and Noah Arceneaux (eds), *The Cell Phone Reader: Essays in Social Transformation* (New York: Peter Lang, 2006), p. 52.

4. Tongue-Tied

p. 97 '*shy, yet arrogant ... old hags*': Bronislaw Malinowski, *Argonauts of the Western Pacific* (London: Routledge & Kegan Paul, 1932), pp. 46–7.

p. 97 '*sat dully on stones ... islanders!*': Young, *Malinowski*, p. 535.

p. 98 '*whence comest thou ... uneducated classes*': Bronislaw Malinowski, 'The problem of meaning in primitive languages', in C. K. Ogden and I. A. Richards, *The Meaning of Meaning* (London: Routledge & Kegan Paul, 1923), pp. 313, 315, 314.

p. 98 '*vocal grooming*': Dunbar, *Grooming*, p. 78. See also pp. 121, 123.

p. 99 *In The Descent of Man* ...: see Charles Darwin, *The Descent of Man*, eds James Moore and Adrian Desmond (London: Penguin, 2004), p. 123; and Joseph Jordania, 'Music and emotions: humming in human prehistory', in Rusudan Tsurtsumia and Joseph Jordania (eds), *Problems of Traditional Polyphony: Materials of the Fourth International Symposium on Traditional Polyphony* (Tbilisi: Nova Science, 2010), p. 42.

p. 99 '*weighs lightly ... frasmakare*': Daun, *Swedish Mentality*, p. 119.

p. 99 '*Talking apparently ... national vice*': Sontag, 'A letter from Sweden', p. 26.

p. 100 '*the silent Finn*': Jaakko Lehtonen and Kari Sajavaara, 'The silent Finn', in Deborah Tannen and Muriel Saville-Troike (eds), *Perspectives on Silence* (Norwood, NJ: Ablex, 1985), p. 195.

p. 100 *In his autobiography, Ingmar Bergman* ...: Ingmar Bergman, *The Magic Lantern: An Autobiography*, trans. Joan Tate (New York: Viking, 1988), pp. 18, 8.

p. 101 '*Magnificent personality ... in his tones*': Vere Hodgson, *Few Eggs and No Oranges: The Diaries of Vere Hodgson 1940–45* (London: Persephone Books, 2005), p. 11.

p. 102 '*flowed like glue*': Antony Beevor and Artemis Cooper, *Paris after the Liberation, 1944–1949* (London: Penguin, 2004), p. 109.

p. 102 '*shyness and moody ... of the South*': G. K. Chesterton, 'A shy bird', in *A Handful of Authors: Essays on Books and Writers*, ed. Dorothy Collins (London: Sheed and Ward, 1953), pp. 211–12.

p. 103 '*sat in a dignified ... impossible character*': Charles Williams, *The Last Great Frenchman: A Life of General de Gaulle* (London: Wiley, 1997), p. 347.

p. 103 '*like digging ... a trowel*': Harold Nicolson, *Diaries and Letters, 1907–1964*, ed. Nigel Nicolson (London: Phoenix, 2005), p. 469.

p. 103 *Ferdinand Plessy, a fellow POW* ...: Jean Lacouture, *De Gaulle: The Rebel 1890–1944*, trans. Patrick O'Brian (London: Harvill, 1990), p. 53.

Notes

p. 103 'We people are never ... too strong': Gregor Dallas, *1945: The War That Never Ended* (London: John Murray, 2005), p. 90.

pp. 103–4 'One must speak little ... not speak': Jonathan Fenby, *The General: Charles de Gaulle and the France He Saved* (London: Simon & Schuster, 2010), p. 69.

p. 104 His son recalled that de Gaulle ...: Fenby, *The General*, pp. 69, 7.

p. 104 'Nothing could be more ... the crowd': General de Gaulle, *War Memoirs: Unity 1942–1944*, trans. Richard Howard (London: Weidenfeld & Nicolson, 1959), p. 315.

p. 105 'The advantage of ... in public': Williams, *The Last Great Frenchman*, p. 346.

p. 105 One day in Cairo in 1941 ...: Adrian Fort, *Archibald Wavell: The Life and Times of an Imperial Servant* (London: Jonathan Cape, 2009), p. 224.

p. 106 In a series of lectures ...: General Sir Archibald Wavell, *Generals and Generalship* (London: Penguin, 1941), pp. 40–42.

p. 106 'might fall in love ... silences': Diana Cooper, *Trumpets from the Steep* (London: Hart-Davis, 1960), p. 136.

p. 107 'Armies were like plants ... we listed': Nicholas Rankin, *A Genius for Deception: How Cunning Helped the British Win Two World Wars* (New York: Oxford University Press, 2009), p. 106.

p. 107 'a cover for shyness or sentiment': Rankin, *A Genius for Deception*, p. xi.

p. 107 '1916, sir ... Headquarters?': Rankin, *A Genius for Deception*, p. 183.

pp. 107–8 'Military Jeeves ... absorbent watchfulness': Rankin, *A Genius for Deception*, p. 177; Thaddeus Holt, *The Deceivers: Allied Military Deception in the Second World War* (New York: Scribner, 2004), p. 12.

p. 109 The Egyptian prime minister commended him ...: Harold E. Raugh, *Wavell in the Middle East, 1939–1941: A Study in Generalship* (Norman, OK: University of Oklahoma Press, 2013), p. 96.

p. 109 'this is not ... an important raid': Jonathan Dimbleby, *Destiny in the Desert: The Road to El Alamein – The Battle That Turned the Tide* (London: Profile, 2013), p. 32.

p. 110 Noel Annan, who worked as a military ...: Raugh, *Wavell in the Middle East*, p. 80.

p. 110 'hard to make anyone ... and character': Raugh, *Wavell in the Middle East*, p. 80.

p. 111 'too ordinary an excuse ... their children': Joan Bright Astley, *The Inner Circle: A View of War at the Top* (Boston, MA: Little, Brown, 1971), p. 73.

p. 111 '*His fine head … those qualities*': Alan Moorehead, *Don't Blame the Generals* (New York: Harper, 1943), p. 127.

p. 111 '*It may almost … a defeat*': Dimbleby, *Destiny in the Desert*, p. xiv.

p. 112 '*sinn[ing] against … the skies*': A. P. Wavell, 'Foreword', in A. P. Wavell, *Other Men's Flowers* (London: Jonathan Cape, 1944), pp. 19, 17.

p. 112 '*the oyster*': Fort, *Wavell*, p. 246.

p. 113 *On one occasion, in his twenties* …: Denis Judd, *King George VI, 1895–1952* (London: Michael Joseph, 1982), pp. 96–7.

p. 115 '*Only those who have … by pity*': John W. Wheeler-Bennett, *King George VI: His Life and Reign* (London: Macmillan, 1958), p. 27.

p. 115 '*I know of nothing … untold agony*': Mark Logue and Peter Conradi, *The King's Speech: How One Man Saved the British Monarchy* (London: Quercus, 2010), p. 44.

p. 116 '*might unwittingly … over a cliff*': Nicholas Mosley, *Time at War* (London: Weidenfeld & Nicolson, 2006), p. 6.

p. 116 '*In matters of life … you stammer*': Elizabeth Grice, 'How the King's speech therapist gave me hope', *Daily Telegraph*, 3 February 2011.

p. 117 *He told Logue of an anxiety dream* …: Logue and Conradi, *The King's Speech*, p. 181.

p. 118 '*The King … smash the radio*': Stephen Spender, *Journals, 1939–1983*, ed. John Goldsmith (New York: Random House, 1986), p. 24.

p. 119 '*admiration for the way … to do so*': 'Mass Observation Victory in Europe, June 1945', File Report 2263, p. 57.

p. 119 '*the centre of looks … of the room*': David Kynaston, *Austerity Britain 1945–51* (London: Bloomsbury, 2007), p. 11.

p. 120 '*like throwing biscuits … yup, yup*': Peter Hennessy, *The Prime Minister: The Office and Its Holders since 1945* (London: Allen Lane, 2000), p. 149.

p. 122 '*the dreams I forget … generosity, and love*': John Durham Peters, *Speaking into the Air: A History of the Idea of Communication* (Chicago, IL: University of Chicago Press, 1999), pp. 171, 21.

p. 124 '*The hearer listens … self-enhancement*': Malinowski, 'The problem of meaning in primitive languages', p. 314.

p. 124 '*ceremony of … the air*': Cyril Connolly, *Enemies of Promise* (London: Penguin, 1961), p. 119.

5. Stage Fright

p. 125 '*Like the ones … I met*': John Coldstream, *Dirk Bogarde: The Authorised Biography* (London: Weidenfeld & Nicolson, 2004), p. 65.

pp. 125–6 *'the wrong profession ... or bar'*: Dirk Bogarde, *Snakes and Ladders* (London: Phoenix, 2006), p. 94.

p. 126 *'You can't be ... poison of terror'*: Sheridan Morley, *Dirk Bogarde: Rank Outsider* (London: Bloomsbury, 1996), p. 68.

p. 127 *As a perennial wallflower* ...: Anna Massey, *Telling Some Tales* (London: Hutchinson, 2006), p. 53.

p. 127 *Laurence Olivier had a first-time attack* ...: Laurence Olivier, *Confessions of an Actor: An Autobiography* (New York: Simon & Schuster, 1985), p. 218.

p. 128 *'a great believer ... remote devotion'*: John Coldstream, 'Introduction', in Coldstream (ed.), *Ever, Dirk: The Bogarde Letters* (London: Weidenfeld & Nicolson, 2008), p. 8.

p. 128 *Over the previous century and a half* ...: see Nicholas Ridout, *Stage Fright, Animals, and Other Theatrical Problems* (Cambridge: Cambridge University Press, 2006), pp. 48–50.

p. 129 *'The audience intimidates ... strange faces'*: Polly Morland, *The Society for Timid Souls: Or, How to Be Brave* (London: Profile, 2013), p. 131.

p. 130 *'blasé attitude ... psychic state'*: Georg Simmel, 'The metropolis and mental life', in Richard Sennett (ed.), *Classic Essays on the Culture of Cities* (Englewood Cliffs, NJ; Prentice-Hall, 1969), pp. 51, 53.

p. 130 *Sigmund Freud identified a common embarrassment* ...: Sigmund Freud, *The Interpretation of Dreams*, trans. James Strachey (London: Penguin, 1976), pp. 340–41.

p. 130 *'it is a big deal ... impeccable'*: Edward Shorter, *A Historical Dictionary of Psychiatry* (Oxford: Oxford University Press, 2005), p. 30.

p. 131 *'You're going to die'*: Edward Shorter, *How Everyone Became Depressed: The Rise and Fall of the Nervous Breakdown* (Oxford: Oxford University Press, 2013), p. 68.

p. 131 *'like the vertigo ... before a thousand'*: Josiah Morse, *The Psychology and Neurology of Fear* (Worcester, MA: Clark University Press, 1907), pp. 91, 85, 92.

p. 131 *'like a culprit ... bacillus'*: Eugene Gruenberg, 'Stage-fright', *The Musical Quarterly* 5, 2 (1919), 226, 221.

p. 132 *Slated to perform in the end-of-term concert* ...: Janet Morgan, *Agatha Christie: A Biography* (London: Collins, 1984), p. 27.

p. 132 *'you had better ... talk now'*: Morgan, *Agatha Christie*, p. 42.

p. 132 *'the flustered ... set of rhythms'*: Goffman, *Interaction Ritual*, p. 103.

p. 133 *'like a fox ... following me everywhere'*: Agatha Christie, *An Autobiography* (London: HarperCollins, 2011), p. 353.

p. 133 *Her biographer Laura Thompson ...*: Laura Thompson, *Agatha Christie: An English Mystery* (London: Headline, 2007), p. 364.

p. 133 *'an inbuilt armour ... spent arrow'*: Max Mallowan, *Mallowan's Memoirs* (London: Collins, 1977), p. 195.

p. 133 *'completely imbecile with shyness'*: Agatha Christie, *Come, Tell Me How You Live: An Archaeological Memoir* (London: HarperCollins, 1999), p. 33.

p. 134 *'If you are doubly ... greased lightning'*: Agatha Christie, 'Hercule Poirot, fiction's greatest detective', *Daily Mail*, 15 January 1938.

p. 134 *'an egocentric creep'*: John Gross (ed.), *The New Oxford Book of Literary Anecdotes* (Oxford: Oxford University Press, 2006), p. 267.

p. 134 *'shy fits'*: Agatha Christie, 'Introduction', in Peter Saunders, *The Mousetrap Man* (London: Collins, 1972), p. 9.

p. 134 *'See you ... on Sunday'*: Morgan, *Agatha Christie*, p. 310.

p. 134 *'miserable, horrible ... coming downstairs!'*: Christie, *An Autobiography*, p. 517.

p. 136 *'a comfortably upholstered ... Roman Colosseum'*: Kevin Bazzana, *Wondrous Strange: The Life and Art of Glenn Gould* (New York: Oxford University Press, 2004), p. 179.

p. 136 *'great despair ... commensurate ecstasies'*: Lynne Walker, 'My life fell apart ...', *Independent on Sunday*, 30 May 2010.

p. 137 *'instrumentalists' hand problems ... piranha-filled waters'*: Alfred Hickling, 'Pain stopped play', *Guardian*, 9 March 2007.

p. 137 *'shambling shell ... and mild'*: Brian Masters, *Getting Personal: A Biographer's Memoir* (London: Constable, 2002), pp. 240, 245.

p. 137 *'as dormant ... Tristan da Cunha's volcano'*: Glenn Gould, 'The prospects of recording', in Tim Page (ed.), *The Glenn Gould Reader* (New York: Knopf, 1984), p. 332.

p. 138 *'charity of the machine ... second nature'*: Glenn Gould, 'Rubinstein', in Page (ed.), *Glenn Gould Reader*, pp. 289–90.

p. 138 *'It's always occurred to me ... being heard'*: Bazzana, *Wondrous Strange*, p. 284.

p. 138 *'Ibsenesque gloom'*: Geoffrey Payzant, *Glenn Gould: Music and Mind* (Toronto: Key Porter, 1992), p. 55.

p. 141 *The writer and musician Brian Cullman ...*: Brian Cullman, 'Nick Drake', in Jason Creed (ed.), *The Pink Moon Files* (London: Omnibus Press, 2011), pp. 48–9.

p. 141 *'defended'*: *Nick Drake: Remembered for a While* (London: John Murray, 2014), p. 368.

p. 141 *'Uh, hello?'*: Joe Boyd, *White Bicycles: Making Music in the 1960s* (London: Serpent's Tail, 2006), p. 191.

p. 143 *'there is no need ... your heart'*: 'Georges Moustaki', *Daily Telegraph*, 26 May 2013.

p. 145 *According to David Sandison ...*: Patrick Humphries, *Nick Drake: The Biography* (London: Bloomsbury, 1998), p. 129.

p. 145 *'a skin too few ... your performance'*: Peter Paphides, 'Stranger to the world', *Observer*, 25 April 2004.

p. 145 *'There you are'*: *Nick Drake: Remembered for a While*, p. 163.

p. 146 *his father's diary recorded ...*: *Nick Drake: Remembered for a While*, p. 353.

p. 146 *'the idea of ordering ... prostrated him'*: Morse, *Psychology and Neurology of Fear*, p. 89.

p. 146 *'how to seem off-hand enough'*: Taylor, *A Game of Hide and Seek*, p. 32.

p. 147 *'It wasn't ... productive afternoon'*: Rob Young, *Electric Eden: Unearthing Britain's Visionary Music* (London: Faber, 2010), p. 41.

p. 148 *'I am quite sure ... beautiful voice'*: Trevor Beeson, *In Tuneful Accord: The Church Musicians* (Norwich: SCM Press, 2009), p. 107.

p. 149 *'just edged its way ... into oblivion'*: Claire Walker, 'Return of the flower child', *The Scotsman*, 19 July 2000.

p. 151 *'in a coma for 30 years'*: Peter Ross, 'Vashti Bunyan', *Sunday Herald*, 16 October 2005.

p. 152 *'providential instrument ... taciturnitas'*: Carla Casagrande, 'The protected woman', in Christiane Klapisch-Zuber (ed.), *A History of Women in the West: Silences of the Middle Ages* (Cambridge, MA: Harvard University Press, 1992), pp. 88, 100.

p. 153 *'as a domestic skill ... laying a table'*: Charlotte Greig, 'Molly Drake: how the wild wind blows', *New Welsh Review* 103 (Spring 2014), 42.

p. 154 *'a complete deprivation ... the performance'*: Donald Kaplan, 'Stage fright', in *Clinical and Social Realities*, ed. Louise J. Kaplan (Northvale, NJ: J. Aronson, 1995), p. 132.

p. 155 *'where the waxen mask ... freedom'*: Terry Pinkard, 'Introduction', in Heinrich Heine, *On the History of Religion and Philosophy in Germany and Other Writings*, ed. Terry Pinkard, trans. Howard Pollack-Milgate (Cambridge: Cambridge University Press, 2007), p. viii.

6. Shy Art

p. 157 *'like Jacques Tati ... de Gaulle'*: Shelley Rohde, *A Private View of L. S. Lowry* (London: Collins, 1979), p. 252.

p. 157 *'All those people ... everyone else'*: Alan Woods, 'Community, crowds, cripples', *Cambridge Quarterly* 10, 1 (1981), 7.

p. 158 *Once Alick Leggat, treasurer ...*: Allen Andrews, *The Life of L. S. Lowry* (London: Jupiter, 1977), p. 108.

p. 159 *'Had I not been lonely ... have happened'*: L. S. Lowry, *1887–1976* (London: Royal Academy of Arts, 1976), p. 36.

p. 160 *'some Asperger ... back of a cave'*: Rhys Blakely, 'How we're failing children with autism', *The Times*, 12 April 2014.

p. 162 *'To say the truth ... that haunted me'*: Michael Howard, *Lowry: A Visionary Artist* (Salford: Lowry Press, 1999), p. 123.

p. 162 *'You like that picture ... I am pleased'*: Andrews, *Life of L. S. Lowry*, p. 23.

p. 163 *'never draws a straight line without smudging it'*: Lorna Wing, 'Syndromes of autism and atypical development', in Donald J. Cohen and Fred R. Volkmar (eds), *Handbook of Autism and Pervasive Developmental Disorders* (London: John Wiley, 1997), p. 160.

p. 164 *'speako'*: Clara Claiborne Park, *Exiting Nirvana: A Daughter's Life with Autism* (London: Aurum Press, 2001), p. 129. See also p. 126.

p. 164 *'fortunate enough to lead ... uneventful life'*: Édouard Roditi, *Dialogues on Art* (Santa Barbara, CA: Ross-Erikson, 1980), p. 106.

p. 164 *'the same kind of ... shyness and asceticism'*: Roditi, *Dialogues on Art*, p. 105.

p. 165 *'voice of a man ... to himself'*: Joseph Brodsky, 'In the shadow of Dante', in *Less Than One: Selected Essays* (London: Penguin, 2011), p. 101.

p. 166 *'I have nothing in common ... a single object'*: Cesare Pavese, *Dialogues with Leucò*, trans. William Arrowsmith and D. S. Carne Ross (London: Peter Owen, 1965), p. vii.

p. 166 *'It is always ... uncontrollable shyness'*: Giuseppe Tomasi di Lampedusa, *Letters from London and Europe (1925–30)*, eds Gioacchino Lanza Tomasi and Salvatore Silvano Nigro, trans. J. G. Nichols (London: Alma Books, 2010), p. 63.

p. 166 *'I have never seriously ... important role'*: Philip Roth, 'Conversation in Turin with Primo Levi', in *Shop Talk: A Writer and His Colleagues and Their Work* (London: Vintage, 2002), p. 6.

p. 167 *'gains his ends ... great artists'*: Alex Danchev, *Paul Cézanne: A Life* (London: Profile, 2012), p. 225.

p. 167 *He rarely allowed buyers of his paintings ...*: Janet Abramowicz, *Giorgio Morandi: The Art of Silence* (New Haven, CT: Yale University Press, 2004), p. 216.

Notes

p. 168 '*When he walks … the first time*': Karen Wilkin, *Giorgio Morandi: Works, Writings, Interviews* (Barcelona: Ediciones Poligrafa, 2007), p. 39.

p. 168 '*can truly be understood … street from street*': Wilkin, *Giorgio Morandi*, p. 128.

p. 169 '*Always walk with others … flesh of others*': A. Wainwright, *Fellwanderer: The Story behind the Guidebooks* (Kendal: Westmorland Gazette, 1966), no pagination.

pp. 169–70 '*Dear Mr Owen … say hello*': Hunter Davies, *Wainwright: The Biography* (London: Orion, 2002), pp. 125, 111.

p. 170 *After they moved to Kendal …*; Hunter Davies, 'The fan', *New Statesman*, 13 March 2006, 59.

p. 171 '*building up mountains … sheets of paper*': Richard Kelly, 'The guide who shuns his followers', *Guardian*, 18 December 1982.

p. 171 '*a tough and rubbery … pull of gravity*': A. Wainwright, *The Western Fells* (Kendal: Westmorland Gazette, 1966), Yewbarrow 7.

p. 172 '*slovenly layabouts, of both sexes*': A. Wainwright, *The Southern Fells* (Kendal: Westmorland Gazette, 1960), 'Some personal notes in conclusion'.

p. 172 '*a common characteristic of the inefficient*': Wainwright, *Fellwanderer*.

p. 172 '*after many years … their shrines*': A. Wainwright, *The Eastern Fells* (Kendal: Westmorland Gazette, 1955), 'Introduction'.

p. 173 '*Why does a man … of the peaks*': Wainwright, *The Southern Fells*, Scafell Pike 24.

p. 173 '*amiable giants*': Wainwright, *Fellwanderer*.

p. 174 '*preparing a book … no public*': A. Wainwright, *The Northern Fells* (Kendal: Westmorland Gazette, 1962), 'Some personal notes in conclusion'.

p. 174 '*a special treat for readers*': A. Wainwright, *The Central Fells* (Kendal: Westmorland Gazette, 1958), Raven Crag 4.

p. 174 '*in an uncharacteristic … since regretted*': A. Wainwright, *The Western Fells*, Lank Rigg 7.

p. 175 '*Yes I am antisocial … rather be alone*': *Desert Island Discs*, BBC Radio 4, 26 March 1989.

p. 176 '*in its origin … absent person*': Sigmund Freud, 'Civilization and its discontents', in *Civilization, Society and Religion*, trans. James Strachey, ed. Albert Dickson (London: Penguin, 1985), p. 279.

p. 176 '*make another blissfully happy … to despair*': Sigmund Freud, *Introductory Lectures on Psychoanalysis*, trans. James Strachey, eds James Strachey and Angela Richards (London: Penguin, 1991), p. 41.

p. 177 '*The shy individual ... castration fear*': Hilde Lewinsky, 'The nature of shyness', *British Journal of Psychology* 32, 2 (1941), 112.

p. 177 '*a clever, uncertain man ... the content*': Janet Frame, *The Envoy from Mirror City: Autobiography* 3 (London: Flamingo, 1993), p. 127.

p. 179 '*primitive shyness ,,, the named*': Frame, *Envoy from Mirror City*, p. 173.

p. 179 '*In conversation I am ... will visit*': Janet Frame, 'A statement', in Denis Harold and Pamela Gordon (eds), *Janet Frame: In Her Own Words* (Rosedale, New Zealand: Penguin, 2011), p. 50.

p. 180 '*It's not brilliant ... will do*': Frame, *Envoy from Mirror City*, p. 133.

p. 180 '*watchful, over-anxious ... self-revelation*': Anthony Storr, *Solitude* (London: HarperCollins, 1997), p. 115.

p. 181 '*the evanescent nature ... art and science*': Robert Hugh Cawley, 'Janet Frame's contribution to the education of a psychiatrist', in Elizabeth Alley (ed.), *The Inward Sun: Celebrating the Life and Work of Janet Frame* (Sydney: Allen & Unwin 1994), p. 11.

p. 182 '*a shortish woman ... quite disconcerting*': Geoffrey Moorhouse, 'Cold comfort', *Guardian*, 5 July 2008.

p. 182 '*scuttle to the sheltering foliage of incoherence*': Janet Frame, *Towards Another Summer* (London: Virago, 2009), p. 88.

p. 182 '*from an uncomplicated store ... signals to herself*': Frame, *Towards Another Summer*, pp. 14, 41.

p. 182 '*I have so little confidence ... my typewriter*': Michael King, *Wrestling with the Angel: A Life of Janet Frame* (London: Picador, 2001), p. 438.

p. 183 '*typing for dear life*': *Wrestling with the Angel* (dir. Peter Bell, 2004), available at http://www.nzonscreen.com/title/wrestling-with-the-angel-2004 (accessed 10 June 2014).

p. 183 '*my typewriter is wearing ... my table*': King, *Wrestling with the Angel*, p. 248.

p. 183 '*Yes. I see what you mean ... this light*': Frame, *Towards Another Summer*, pp. 119–21.

p. 184 '*What is the use ... its clear stream*': Janet Frame, *Scented Gardens for the Blind* (London: The Women's Press, 1982), pp. 12, 87.

pp. 184–5 '*Nothing must be allowed ... approaching storms*': Frame, *Scented Gardens*, pp. 106, 180–81.

p. 185 '*penis-motormowers*': King, *Wrestling with the Angel*, p. 367.

p. 185 '*the star witness ... resting her voice*': Douglas Wright, *Ghost Dance* (Auckland, New Zealand: Penguin, 2004), pp. 140–41.

p. 188 '*If my stories … anxious and lonely*': Tuula Karjalainen, *Tove Jansson: Work and Love*, trans. David McDuff (London: Particular Books, 2014), pp. 125–6.

p. 189 '*a symbol of constructive … out of compulsion*': Boel Westin, *Tove Jansson: Life, Art, Words: The Authorised Biography*, trans. Silvester Mazzarella (London: Sort Of Books, 2014), p. 431.

p. 189 '*I could vomit over Moomintroll*': Westin, *Tove Jansson*, p. 283.

p. 189 '*any disposition to encourage … its troubles*': Tove Jansson, 'Travelling Light', in Tove Jansson, *A Winter Book: Selected Stories*, trans. Silvester Mazzarella, David McDuff and Kingsley Hart (London: Sort Of Books, 2006), p. 185.

p. 190 '*with her whole … more than silence*': Tove Jansson, 'The Listener', in *The Listener*, trans. Thomas Teal (London: Sort Of Books, 2014), pp. 13–14.

p. 190 '*wants something … Thanks in advance*': Westin, *Tove Jansson*, pp. 495, 306.

p. 190 '*My cat's died … to understand*': Tove Jansson, 'Messages', in *A Winter Book*, pp. 164, 167–8.

p. 190 *She proposed an authors' law …*: Karjalainen, *Tove Jansson*, p. 270.

p. 190 '*I do hate these children … rubber band*': Adrian Mitchell, 'Valley of the trolls', *Sunday Times*, 6 December 1992.

p. 191 '*with worried greetings*': Westin, *Tove Jansson*, p. 496.

p. 191 '*getting rid of the days*': Frank Kermode, 'What Lowry did', *The Listener*, 27 September 1979, 418.

7. The War against Shyness

p. 194 '*often nervous and speechless … joined the club*': Arthur Hopcraft, *The Football Man: People and Passions in Soccer* (London: Collins 1968), p. 127. See also pp. 86, 12.

p. 195 '*His presence seemed … communicate with him*': Gordon Burn, *Best and Edwards: Football, Fame and Oblivion* (London: Faber, 2006), p. 223.

p. 195 *The historian Deborah Cohen …*: Deborah Cohen, *Family Secrets: Living with Shame from the Victorians to the Present Day* (London: Viking, 2013), p. xviii.

p. 196 '*shyness and stranger-feeling*': Tom Harrisson and Charles Madge, *Britain by Mass-Observation* (London: The Cresset Library, 1986), p. 183.

p. 196 '*developed a special secondary ... dance-hall*': Tom Harrisson, 'Whistle while you work', in John Lehmann (ed.), *New Writing, New Series I, Autumn 1938* (London: The Hogarth Press, 1938), p. 51.

pp. 196–7 '*What are the main things ... wizard*': Mass-Observation, 'Awkward Moments', File Report 3002, May 1948.

p. 197 '*enjoys the darkness ... for coldness*': B. Seebohm Rowntree and G. R. Lavers, *English Life and Leisure: A Social Study* (London: Longmans, 1951), pp. 119, 74, 80.

p. 197 '*common ... pushing yourself forward*': Alan Bennett, 'Written on the body', in *Untold Stories* (London: Faber/Profile, 2005), p. 148.

p. 197 '*theatres of humiliation ... clothes off*': Alan Bennett, 'Dinner at noon', in *Writing Home* (London: Faber, 1994), p. 32. See also p. 34.

p. 198 '*lapsed into ... silent irritability*': Erving Goffman, *The Presentation of Self in Everyday Life* (London: Penguin, 1971), p. 133. See also p. 120.

p. 198 '*most English people ... exceptionally shy*': Geoffrey Gorer, *Exploring English Character* (New York: Criterion Books, 1955), pp. 18, 77.

p. 199 '*mod shop for the extrovert male*': Duncan Hamilton, *Immortal: The Approved Biography of George Best* (London: Century, 2013), p. 115. See also pp. 58, 118, 11.

p. 199 '*publicity has become ... vice anglais*': Jonathan Aitken, *The Young Meteors* (London: Secker and Warburg, 1967), p. 299.

p. 200 '*I've never really got over my shyness*': George Best, *Blessed: The Autobiography* (London: Ebury Press, 2002), p. 54.

p. 200 '*Class isn't what ... is embarrassment*': Bennett, 'Dinner at noon', pp. 46, 42.

p. 201 '*I clung far too long ... a bore*': Alan Bennett, 'What I didn't do in 2007', *London Review of Books*, 3 January 2008, 4.

p. 201 '*horseshit from start ... fucking minds*': Jules Evans, 'Albert Ellis', *Prospect*, August 2007, 56.

p. 202 '*nobody vomited and ran away*': Dan Hurley, 'From therapy's Lenny Bruce: Get over it! Stop whining!', *New York Times*, 4 May 2004.

p. 202 *In 1939, aged five, he caught double pneumonia...*: Christina Maslach, 'Emperor of the edge', *Psychology Today* 33, 5 (2000), 35.

p. 202 *Zimbardo had a younger brother ...*: Philip G. Zimbardo, *Shyness: What It Is, What To Do About It* (Reading, MA: Addison-Wesley, 1977), pp. 10–11.

p. 203 *Eighty per cent of those interviewed ...*: Zimbardo, *Shyness*, pp. 13–14.

p. 204 *He was saddened by the Saturday shopping-mall children* ...: Zimbardo, *Shyness*, p. 50.

p. 204 *In his much-cited 1965 article* ...: Michael Argyle and Janet Dean, 'Eye-contact, distance and affiliation', *Sociometry* 28, 3 (1965): 289–304.

p. 205 *In another study Argyle and his team* ...: Michael Argyle, Florisse Alkema and Robin Gilmour, 'The communication of friendly and hostile attitudes by verbal and non-verbal signals', *European Journal of Social Psychology* 1, 3 (1971): 385–402.

p. 205 *In a field study of couples* ...: Sidney M. Jourard, 'An exploratory study of body accessibility', *British Journal of Social and Clinical Psychology* 5, 3 (1966), 221–2.

p. 206 *'contactless societies ... soothing caress'*: Sidney Jourard, 'Out of touch: the body taboo', *New Society*, 6 July 1967, 660.

p. 206 *'non-touching culture'*: 'Touch of reserve over tea', *Daily Mirror*, 2 September 1966.

p. 207 *'very low level of rewardingness to others'*: Michael Argyle, Peter Trower and Bridget Bryant, 'Explorations in the treatment of personality disorders and neuroses by social skills training', *British Journal of Medical Psychology* 47, 1 (1974), 71.

p. 207 *patients were given a voice key* ...: Peter Trower, Bridget Bryant and Michael Argyle, *Social Skills and Mental Health* (London: Methuen, 1978), p. 218.

p. 208 *'The happy people are a lot ... nearer the truth'*: Julian Champkin, 'The secret of happiness', *Daily Mail*, 7 June 1993.

p. 208 *'the amazingly inept ... much discussion'*: Michael Argyle, 'Why I study ... social skills', *The Psychologist* 12, 3 (1999), 143.

p. 210 *'he had a shield round him'*: Tony Fletcher, *A Light That Never Goes Out: The Enduring Saga of The Smiths* (London: Heinemann, 2012), p. 77.

p. 210 *'back-bedroom casualty'*: Fletcher, *A Light That Never Goes Out*, p. 154.

p. 210 *'the adolescent homelessness of self'*: Janet Frame, *To the Is-Land* (London: Flamingo, 1993), p. 136.

p. 211 *'those tiny crackles ... that record'*: Simon Goddard, *Mozipedia: The Encyclopedia of Morrissey and the Smiths* (London: Ebury Press, 2012), p. 512.

p. 211 *'Go and see them first ... stupid sluts'*: Pat Long, *History of the NME: High Times and Low Lives at the World's Most Famous Music Magazine* (London: Portico Books, 2012), p. 160.

p. 211 '*If these rock classics … your intelligence*': Johnny Rogan, *Morrissey and Marr: The Severed Alliance* (London; Omnibus Press, 1993), p. 84.

pp. 211–12 *The most intense crisis of his adolescence …*: Simon Goddard, *The Smiths: Songs That Saved Your Life* (London: Reynolds & Hearn, 2002), p. 201

p. 212 '*You started counting the lampposts*': Fletcher, *A Light that Never Goes Out*, p. 230.

p. 213 '*vigorous virtues … softer virtues*': Shirley Robin Letwin, *The Anatomy of Thatcherism* (London: Fontana, 1992), pp. 33, 39–40.

p. 213 '*All self-communings … drowned out by noise*': C. G. Jung, *Psychological Types* (London: Routledge & Kegan Paul, 1971), p. 550.

p. 214 '*Mr Erm*': 'Obituary of Oliver Knox', *Daily Telegraph*, 19 July 2002.

p. 214 '*the golden age of dole culture*': Miranda Sawyer, 'An absurdist Englishman', *Observer*, 18 December 1994.

p. 214 '*attracted that kind of energy … fragile music*': Martin Aston, *Facing the Other Way: The Story of 4AD* (London: The Friday Project, 2013), p. 144.

p. 215 *When the Smiths were in the recording studio …*: Fletcher, *A Light That Never Goes Out*, p. 350.

p. 216 '*Morrissey, the lead singer … romantic failure*': Mary Harron, 'The Smiths', *Guardian*, 14 February 1984.

p. 216 '*the huddled shyness of my life*': Lynn Barber, 'The man with the thorn in his side', *Observer*, 15 September 2002.

p. 217 '*Sitting on an Intercity … didn't speak*': Tom Gallagher, Michael Campbell and Murdo Gillies (eds), *The Smiths: All Men Have Secrets* (London: Virgin, 1995), p. 102.

p. 218 '*intrusive and obsessive thoughts … unsettling shyness*': Dorothy Tennov, *Love and Limerence: The Experience of Being in Love* (New York: Stein and Day, 1979), pp. 16, 24.

p. 218 *what Diana Athill calls the quickest …*: Diana Athill, *Stet: An Editor's Life* (London: Granta, 2011), p. 85.

pp. 219–20 '*among the sane … embarrassment unthinkable*': Christopher Ricks, *Keats and Embarrassment* (Oxford: Clarendon Press, 1974), p. 38.

p. 220 '*a human victory … contagious embarrassment*': Ricks, *Keats and Embarrassment*, pp. 77, 12, 85, 83.

p. 220 '*launch my diary to music*': *The Importance of Being Morrissey*, Channel 4, 8 June 2003.

p. 221 '*The suggestion … obsession with death*': Stuart Maconie, 'Morrissey: Hello, cruel world', *Q*, April 1994; Len Brown, 'Stop me if you've heard this one before', *NME*, 20 February 1988.

p. 222 '*the slimy, unstoppable urges*': Tony Parsons, *Dispatches from the Front Line of Popular Culture* (London: Virgin, 1994), p. 93.

p. 222 '*communication with people ... phoning anybody up*': *The Importance of Being Morrissey*.

p. 222 '*going to bed is the highlight ... brother of death*': *Desert Island Discs*, BBC Radio 4, 4 December 2009.

p. 222 '*so today ... explain myself better*': Leo McKinstry, *Jack & Bobby: A Story of Brothers in Conflict* (London: CollinsWillow, 2002), p. 21.

8. The New Ice Age

p. 224 '*parasite singles*': David Pilling, *Bending Adversity: Japan and the Art of Survival* (London: Penguin, 2014), p. 191.

pp. 226–7 *Saitō claimed that hikikomori ...*: Saitō Tamaki, 'Preface to the English edition', in Saitō Tamaki, *Hikikomori: Adolescence without End*, trans. Jeffrey Angles (Minneapolis, MN: University of Minnesota Press, 2013), pp. 5–6.

p. 227 '*cynical shyness*': Bernardo Carducci, 'Shyness: the new solution', *Psychology Today*, January 2000, 40.

p. 227 *Time magazine reported ...*: Alice Park, 'When shyness turns deadly', *Time*, 17 August 2007.

p. 228 *In a review of the Maudsley's phobic caseload ...*: Isaac Marks, *Fears and Phobias* (London: Heinemann Medical, 1969), p. 113.

p. 228 *Agoraphobia was suffered mostly by women ...*: Isaac M. Marks, 'The classification of phobic disorders', *British Journal of Psychiatry* 116 (1970), 383.

p. 229 '*You know what it's like ... allergic to people*': Christopher Lane, *Shyness: How Normal Behavior Became a Sickness* (New Haven, CT: Yale University Press, 2007), p. 124.

p. 229 '*an ecological niche*': Ian Hacking, *Mad Travelers: Reflections on the Reality of Transient Mental Illnesses* (Cambridge, MA: Harvard University Press, 2002), p. 81.

p. 230 *The fears that Marks's 1960s' social phobics had ...*: Marks, *Fears and Phobias*, p. 153.

p. 230 '*What is become of all ... Paralytic complaints*': Letter dated 8 February 1807, in Deirdre Le Faye (ed.), *Jane Austen's Letters* (Oxford: Oxford University Press, 2014), p. 124.

pp. 230–1 '*a new ice age ... social glue*': Linda Grant, 'Silence of the sheepish', *Guardian*, 22 July 1997.

p. 231 '*sociable robots*': Sherry Turkle, *Alone Together: Why We Expect More From Technology and Less from Each Other* (New York: Basic Books, 2011), p. 1. See also pp. 8–9.

p. 233 '*normative shyness ... selective mutism*': American Psychiatric Association, *Diagnostic and Statistical Manual of Mental Disorders: DSM-5* (Washington, DC: American Psychiatric Association, 2013), pp. 206, 203, 207.

pp. 234–5 '*even in stiff England ... in everyone*': Oliver Sacks, *On the Move: A Life* (London: Picador, 2015), p. 73.

p. 235 '*forbidden to exist*': John Heilpern, 'A fish out of water', *Independent*, 17 February 1991.

p. 236 '*publish ... punish*': Sacks, *On the Move*, p. 155.

p. 236 '*sorry to be as agonizingly shy ... at 20*': Oliver Sacks, 'The joy of old age', *New York Times*, 6 July 2013.

p. 237 '*aggressive, shy ... solitary places*': Pamela Bright, *The Day's End* (London: MacGibbon and Kee, 1959), pp. 163, 182.

pp. 238–9 '*that illusion of a world ... undiscovered countries*': Virginia Woolf, 'On being ill', in *Collected Essays: Volume Four* (London: The Hogarth Press, 1967), 196, 193.

p. 239 '*who suffered ... hid the truth*': Daphne du Maurier, *Rebecca* (London: Pan, 1975), p. 288.

p. 240 '*redundant embroidery*': Richard Mabey, 'Life on Earth', in *In a Green Shade: Essays on Landscape* (London: Allen & Unwin, 1985), p. 128.

p. 241 '*the first few million years ... the worst*': Elaine Morgan, *The Scars of Evolution* (London: Souvenir Press, 1990), p. 27.

p. 241 *crown shyness*: M. R. Jacobs, *Growth Habits of the Eucalypts* (Canberra: Forestry and Timber Bureau, 1955), p. 128.

p. 242 *But for Richard Mabey crown shyness ...*: Richard Mabey, *Fencing Paradise: Reflections on the Myths of Eden* (London: Eden Projects Books, 2005), p. 194.

ACKNOWLEDGEMENTS

I am grateful to all the people who helped me while writing this book by reading material, making suggestions or talking to me about it: Jo Croft, Alice Ferrebe, Jim Friel, Elspeth Graham, Lynsey Hanley, Michael Moran, Wynn Moran, Jamie O'Brien, Joanna Price, Gerry Smyth, Sami Suodenjoki, Karolina Sutton, Lucinda Thompson and Kate Walchester. I also thank the audiences at Liverpool Central Library and the Warrington Literary and Philosophical Society with whom I shared my ideas.

Daniel Crewe commissioned this book and was a great support in its early stages; Cecily Gayford saw it through to completion with her kind words and meticulous editing. I also thank Matthew Taylor for his careful copy-editing and Penny Daniel, Andrew Franklin and Anna-Marie Fitzgerald at Profile for all their help.

The Mass Observation material I have quoted is copyright of the Trustees of the Mass Observation Archive and is reproduced with their permission.

INDEX

Index

Index